REMEMBER MY SACRIFICE

REMEMBER MY SACRIFICE

The Autobiography of Clinton Clark, Tenant
Farm Organizer and Early Civil Rights Activist

EDITED BY ELIZABETH DAVEY AND RODNEY CLARK

 Louisiana State University Press   Baton Rouge

Published by Louisiana State University Press
Manufactured in the United States of America
First printing

The manuscript of Clinton Clark's autobiography is reproduced with the permission of Rodney Clark and the Moorland-Spingarn Research Center at Howard University.

DESIGNER: Amanda McDonald Scallan
TYPEFACE: Caslon Book BE
TYPESETTER: Newgen
PRINTER AND BINDER: Edwards Brothers, Inc.

Library of Congress Cataloging-in-Publication Data
Clark, Clinton, 1903–
    Remember my sacrifice : the autobiography of Clinton Clark, tenant farm organizer and early civil rights activist / edited by Elizabeth Davey and Rodney Clark.
        p. cm.
    Includes bibliographical references and index.
    ISBN 978-0-8071-3277-7 (cloth : alk. paper)
    1. Clark, Clinton, 1903–   2. African American labor leaders–United States–Biography.   3. Labor unions–Organizing–United States–History.   I. Davey, Elizabeth, 1964–   II. Clark, Rodney, 1945–   III. Title.
    HD8073.C54A3 2007
    331.88092–dc22
    [B]

                                                                                    2007006797

Contents

Illustrations

Acknowledgments

Over five years have passed since we first met and began working on this book. One of us knew Clinton Clark as an older uncle and through family stories of his leadership and imprisonment in the freedom movement, and one of us knew Clinton Clark through the typed story of his travels around the country looking for work and organizing for the Louisiana Farmers' Union. During these years, many people have helped us fill in more details of Clinton Clark's life and have given us advice on how to present his story.

This book owes a particular debt to libraries and archivists who preserve materials from African American, civil rights, and labor history. On slim budgets, these centers and their staffs protect and make available historical materials of known and not yet fully known importance.

The Moorland-Spingarn Research Center at Howard University holds Clinton Clark's manuscript and most of the surviving letters in the Sterling A. Brown Papers. Joellen P. ElBashir, Curator of the Manuscripts Division, did the initial work organizing the collection and first identified Clark's manuscript. She and her staff have been extremely helpful over ten years of visits and inquiries. We also thank John Dennis, Sterling A. Brown's son, for his support of this project.

We owe a special thanks to Veronica O. Carey, Ruby O. Hunter, Florence C. Smith, Helen C. Kamanda-Kosseh, John Clark, Richard "Hock" Sterling, Ben Charles "Scott" Sterling Jr., Peg McIntire, and her son Jo McIntire for sharing their memories of Clinton Clark and the Louisiana Farmers' Union.

This book has been made possible through a Louisiana Publishing Initiative Grant from the Louisiana Endowment for the Humanities, a state affiliate of the National Endowment for the Humanities. Of course, opinions expressed in this book do not necessarily represent the views of the Louisiana Endowment for the Humanities or the National Endowment for the Humanities.

Historian Greta de Jong's *A Different Day: African American Struggles for Justice in Rural Louisiana, 1900–1970* should be read as a companion piece to this book. She tracks the interaction of the Louisiana Farmers' Union with large federal bureaucracies with imagination and thoroughness. She left a clear trail for researchers interested in the LFU and thoughtfully donated copies of FBI files and other research materials to the Amistad Research Center. She gave us important direct assistance. It was Greta who thought to look up Peg McIntire in online white pages; she also obtained Clark's FBI file for us.

We also owe tremendous thanks to Darby Penney, who as Director of Historical Projects, New York State Office of Mental Health, assisted us in obtaining a copy of Clinton Clark's medical file from Manhattan State Hospital.

Many archivists and librarians helped as we searched for details of Clark's work and family. Outside of New Orleans, we thank Louis Jones and the Archives of Labor and Urban Affairs, Wayne State University; James Dankey and the Wisconsin Historical Society; Gail Malmgreen and the Tamiment Library/ Robert F. Wagner Labor Archives, New York University. In New Orleans, we relied on the Amistad Research Center and, at Howard-Tilton Library at Tulane University, the Louisiana Collection and especially the librarians of the Microfilm Room and the Interlibrary Loan office, who gave five years of assistance. At the Louisiana Division of the New Orleans Public Library we pieced together an account of Clark's family in the early twentieth century. It was our regular meeting place, and, we should note, for several months after Katrina, the only research library open in New Orleans.

The guidance of John Edgar Tidwell of the Department of English, University of Kansas, and the anonymous reviewers who read the manuscript for Louisiana State University Press helped us make important decisions about the manuscript and how we presented it. The publication of this book also owes a great deal to Liz's teachers and colleagues in the Department of English at Cornell University between 1988 and 1996.

We are grateful to the team at LSU Press for carrying this book through the last steps of publication. In particular, Rand Dotson's enthusiastic and immediate interest in the manuscript in the summer of 2005 gave us the impetus to finish revisions and put the complete manuscript in the mail by mid-August. Within a few days Rand wrote that he had received the manuscript and had sent it to a reviewer. The following Monday Hurricane Katrina flooded our homes in New Orleans. Without Rand's encouragement, the manuscript would have been left unfinished as we each struggled with returning and rebuilding.

In the aftermath of Hurricane Katrina, we each have a larger circle of family, friends, colleagues, and neighbors who have given support and assistance. Thanks to you all for your encouragement, willingness to listen, and also for sharing a place to stay, meals, clothes, new furnishings, advice, and help with the hard work of cleaning up and rebuilding.

Abbreviations Used in Notes

CJP   Clyde Johnson Papers, *The Green Rising, 1910–1977: A Supplement to the Southern Tenant Farmers' Union Papers.* Glenn Rock, N.J.: Microfilming Corporation of America, 1978.

FBI-CC   "Clinton Clark," Federal Bureau of Investigation, file 100-7431-24.

FBI-LFU   Louisiana Farmers' Union, Federal Bureau of Investigation, file 100-45768. Copy held in box 1, Greta de Jong Collection, Amistad Research Center, Tulane University, New Orleans.

FBI-RHP   "Richard Harold Preece," Federal Bureau of Investigation, file 100-HQ-17319.

HLP   Harold N. Lee Papers, Manuscripts Division, Howard-Tilton Library, Tulane University, New Orleans.

LFU-VF   Louisiana Farmers' Union and *Louisiana Farmers' Union News,* vertical files, Tamiment Library/Robert F. Wagner Labor Archives, Elmer Holmes Bobst Library, New York University, New York.

MHS   Medical records of Clinton Clark, Manhattan State Hospital, New York.

MSRK   Mark Solomon and Robert Kaufman Research Files on African Americans and Communism, 1919–93, Tamiment Library/Robert F. Wagner Labor Archives, Elmer Holmes Bobst Library, New York University, New York.

NNC   National Negro Congress Records, 1933–47, Schomburg Center for Research in Black Culture, New York Public Library, New York.

NYHTC   Papers of the New York Hotel and Motel Trades Council, Tamiment Library/Robert F. Wagner Labor Archives, Elmer Holmes Bobst Library, New York University, New York.

SAB   Sterling A. Brown Papers, Moorland-Spingarn Research Center, Howard University, Washington, D.C.

WSU   SEIU Executive Office Microfilm Collection, box 36, Archives of Labor and Urban Affairs, Wayne State University, Detroit.

Introduction

This book brings into print for the first time the autobiography of Clinton Clark, the state organizer of the Louisiana Farmers' Union in the 1930s. An African American, Clark was born in rural Louisiana, schooled to age fifteen, and then self-educated. He wrote the story of his life in 1942, while he was recovering in New Orleans after a three-month imprisonment and a remarkable decade of hard work. In 1932, while living in California, he had become involved in organizing through an Unemployed Relief Council, a group that brought together unemployed workers and neighbors to lobby for food relief and work. Clark soon proved to be an excellent organizer and speaker. He was determined to bring the ideas and strategies he had learned to black people in the South. Once back in Louisiana, Clark began organizing plantation workers, starting with an action for higher wages on a plantation where he was working with members of his family. In 1937 Clark became the rural organizer for the Louisiana Farmers' Union. He helped tenant farmers receive the payments they were due under the Agricultural Adjustment Act (AAA), a New Deal program that compensated farmers for taking land out of production (thus reducing the total crop and helping to raise prices), and he helped sugar workers win higher wages. He set up cooperative buying programs to give sharecroppers independence from the high prices of plantation stores. Much of this autobiography describes his efforts to organize and assist poor rural farmers and farm workers in Louisiana and Mississippi.

Clark is almost completely unknown and unremembered today, with his name only appearing briefly in histories of civil rights organizing in Louisiana. Much of his work was conducted almost in secret during the 1930s. He worked locally, in small towns and on plantations. He spoke at night in sharecroppers' shacks and in black churches, sometimes walking all day to reach the next meeting. To protect himself, he concealed his identity from white people, and he often hid in fields, swamps, and woods. His ability to elude police and lynchers earned him the name "the Black Ghost of Louisiana" among Farmers' Union members. However, in July 1940, he was detained by police in Natchitoches, Louisiana, on the morning of a mass meeting he had organized. He was held for three weeks without being charged and was threatened with lynching. The case attracted the attention of New Orleans and national civil liberties groups, and it made him a national figure in the struggle for civil rights after years of invisibility. His release was front-page news in the *Louisiana Weekly,* the state's African American newspaper. He traveled to rallies and meetings in Chicago and Washington, D.C., and had his picture published prominently in the *Chicago Defender,* an African American newspaper that had national distribution. He became a key figure in the rural organizing efforts of the Southern Negro Youth Congress (SNYC), an organization of black students and young adults that anticipated the work of the civil rights organizations of the 1950s and 1960s. During these years—the end of the Great Depression and the first years of World War II—his work and leadership gave many hope that southern blacks were about to throw off the segregation and economic exploitation that had kept them in slavelike conditions long after the Emancipation Proclamation.

One man who looked with hope to Clark was Sterling A. Brown, an African American poet, Howard University professor, and perceptive observer of racial politics and African American life in the United States. In the 1930s Brown had published poems, studies of American literature, and monthly book reviews, many focusing on the particularities of life and culture within the South's many different black communities. He had also watched the South carefully during the New Deal from his position as Editor of Negro Affairs for the Federal Writers' Project. He reviewed copy from writers across the South about their states, often correcting or questioning their representations of black communities. Brown traveled often in the South and planned to write his own documentary book about the South during the late 1930s and 1940s. To be titled "A Negro Looks at the South," it was to present an African American perspective on the people and places that had been recorded by white documentary photographers such as Walker Evans and Dorothea Lange, a perspective informed by his travels through the segregated South and by a tremendous network of contacts that included faculty at black colleges and leaders of political and civil rights organizations.

Brown planned to dedicate an entire chapter of his book to Clinton Clark. Though the book was never published, Brown later wrote about Clark in a major essay that assessed the state of civil rights in America during World War II. In this essay, Clinton Clark is Brown's key figure of the growing resistance: "I found a large degree of militancy in Negroes who were Southern born and bred, some of

whom have never been out of the South. I talked with sharecroppers, union organizers, preachers, schoolteachers, newspapermen and bankers who spoke with
bitter desperation and daring. Clinton Clark, certainly among the sturdiest fighters,
was born in one of the back country parishes of Louisiana; when he was arrested
for organizing in a parish nearby, the planters refused to believe him a native of
the section. The protest I heard ranged from the quietly spoken aside, through
twisted humor and sarcasm, to stridency." [1]

Later Brown describes how Clark and others would continue their activism, in
spite of the violence that threatened: "They had been hurt, no doubt of that. But
it is unlikely that they, or many other Negroes, merely because of the violence,
will become reconciled to what caused it. Many Negroes are still going to protest rough language to their wives, as Roland Hayes did; or unfair travel accom-
modations, as Hugh Gloster did; or exploitation in the cane and cotton fields, as
Clinton Clark did. 'Get out and stay out of this parish,' the jailer in Natchitoches
told Clark. 'I'll be back,' said Clark, 'I'll have a stronger organization behind me
the next time.'" [2] At both moments in his essay, Brown moves from describing
Clark to describing a larger, growing protest among black people in the South. His
southern travels had enraged Brown, but he had also witnessed a growing opposi-
tion. Clinton Clark was his example of hope and resistance.

Brown and Clark may have met in Louisiana as Brown traveled in the early
1940s. Brown would later refer to a "six months' stay in the deep south of wartime" and describe a conversation on a bus near Baton Rouge and a stay in
Natchitoches—cities not too far from Clark's organizing.[3] Brown writes: "On trips
through the South, I have talked with several who had been hurt . . . With Clinton
Clark, who had been beaten, arrested, jailed and threatened with the rope time
and time again for organizing the cane-cutters and cotton hands of Louisiana into
a union." [4] Brown visited Southern University in Baton Rouge in October 1942,
traveling through New Orleans, where Clark was living.[5] During this visit, they
may have met, and Clark may have told Brown that he was writing his life story.
Within months, Clark began sending Brown sections of his manuscript.

It is this manuscript, sent by Clark to Brown toward the end of 1942, that this
book brings to print. In Clark's own words, his mostly self-taught sentences, spelling, and structure, it tells a much fuller story of a person celebrated but only briefly
mentioned in accounts of the struggle for civil rights in the first half of the twentieth
century. Today, Clark's voice speaks to us directly from the swamps and sugarcane

and cotton plantations of Louisiana, out of the dislocations and deprivations of the Great Depression, out of the moment when southern agriculture began to turn from mules and plows to tractors, casting people off of the land and into the cities. It brings into print the personal account of a Louisiana labor organizer whose work prefigures the southern civil rights movement that would follow the war.

The introduction and afterword are meant to help readers place Clark's story within histories of twentieth-century civil rights and labor organizing. This introduction provides additional background on Clark's family and home community of Pointe Coupee Parish, Louisiana, and the organizations within which he worked in the 1930s. It closes by considering Clark's autobiography as a work of literature and outlining the traditions of African American writing and the experiences that may have shaped how he wrote his own story. The afterword describes his life after 1942, following him north to New York and into the changing politics of the 1940s and later back to Louisiana and his death in New Orleans in 1974. Providing autobiography and biography, this book forms an account of Clark's remarkable life, which began in 1903 and stretched throughout most of the twentieth century. It gives new insight into the place of the Great Depression and its labor and civil rights activism in the long arc of the African American struggle for freedom and equality.

Circling Out from Pointe Coupee Parish

Clark was born in Fordoche, Louisiana, an isolated corner of an isolated parish. Pointe Coupee Parish lies in a region of Louisiana just northwest of Baton Rouge and, more significantly, between the Mississippi and the Atchafalaya Rivers. The Atchafalaya breaks off from the Mississippi at the northern tip of the parish; Pointe Coupee is the triangle of land between them. It lies in a kind of valley in the already low land of Louisiana, a low flat valley edged by the high ground of natural levees, the built-up banks of rivers and bayous.[6] In the nineteenth century, Pointe Coupee was dominated by cotton and sugar plantations, and the parish had one of Louisiana's highest concentrations of slaves, over 70 percent of the population. At the beginning of the twentieth century, the time of Clinton Clark's birth, Pointe Coupee Parish was still a place of cotton and sugar plantations. During his childhood the parish remained predominantly black, though the black population declined in the 1910s and 1920s as many families, including the Clarks, sought better opportunities elsewhere.[7]

Clark's account of his childhood and youth is brief, written almost as if he were racing to get to the story of his more recent organizing work. In writing about his childhood, Clark gives some sense of this community and place, but much of his description focuses on moments that prefigure and form the foundation of his later leadership. He emphasizes moments when he is singled out for praise, moments speaking publicly, and his experiences working as child and teenager. He does not describe his family and community in much detail. Within his narrative there are single sentences or remarks that point toward a traumatic personal loss or experience, but these pass unexplained by Clark. In addition to these underdescribed events, the census records, which give the barest outline of his family's membership and location every ten years, suggest upheavals and losses that Clark does not mention in his narrative.

His parents were Arthur and Bridget Lewis Clark. The 1900 census places them together as husband and wife, farming in Pointe Coupee Parish and living with five children: Houston, Orelia, Walter, Arthur, and Roger. Clinton and his sister Caroline (called Carolina or Elmonia in some records) would be born in 1903 and 1907, respectively. The census identifies Arthur Clark as a farmer and his wife and oldest son as farm laborers. Arthur was born in 1869, the second son of John and Cydalise Clark. Although Clinton writes that his father was born in Ville Platte, Louisiana, Arthur was probably born and raised in the Lafayette area. Arthur's death certificate identifies his birthplace as Broussard, Louisiana, just southeast of Lafayette, and the 1880 census indeed places the child Arthur and his family in Lafayette. By the 1900 census, Arthur's parents and younger siblings had moved north to St. Landry Parish, which lies just west of Pointe Coupee Parish, across the Atchafalaya River. Bridget Lewis was born in 1870; there is little information on her childhood and family beyond Clinton Clark's statement that his mother was born in Ville Platte.

Clark writes that both of his parents were "a French decent." This probably means that they spoke Creole, a version of French first spoken on Mississippi River plantations which became a regional language on the Gulf Coast.[8] Creole is one of a number of kinds of French that coexisted in Louisiana during Clark's parents' time. Today, linguists categorize the variations as Standard French, spoken by people who maintained a connection with France; Plantation Society French;

Cajun, a French that goes back to the Acadians cast out of Nova Scotia in the 1700s; and Creole.[9] Even though Clark and census records describe the language spoken by his grandmother, father, and mother as French, they probably spoke Creole. Members of the Clark family today describe older relatives as speaking Creole or being "so creolish," and the areas in which the family lived–Lafayette, Ville Platte, and Pointe Coupee–were areas with strong or predominant contingents of Creole speakers.[10] Linguist Thomas Klingler observes that speakers of Creole and Cajun may sometimes name their language as "French," including in response to census questions.[11] He also notes that "Creole is often referred to as 'broken French' or 'broken down French,'" which is similar to Clark's description of his grandmother: "She would talk real bad broken language."[12]

Clark was born just as his family and other African Americans in his area shifted from Creole to English. The 1910 census records Clark's mother and oldest brother Houston as French speakers, while marking all the younger children, including Clinton, as English speakers. English was more present in the black community than among whites in Pointe Coupee at the turn of the century, as trade in slaves had brought English-speaking slaves from other parts of the South to Louisiana plantations in the nineteenth century.[13] Clark's mother mainly spoke Creole, but his parents were probably bilingual, having told a census taker in 1900 that they both could speak English.[14] Generally, the shift to English happened as blacks began to circle out from plantations in search of work and found that speaking English increased their job opportunities.[15] English had also become the language spoken in schools, and it was probably a conscious decision of Clark's parents to raise the younger children speaking English. Clark's grandniece Veronica Carey remembers that Clark's parents' generation spoke French among themselves but not around their children. She describes it as an issue of education and aspiration. Both Clinton and Caroline knew some Creole, but the elders wanted them to be more educated and well-read, which meant speaking English. We see both of these pulls toward English at work in Clark's life, as his search for opportunities to work and learn pulled him away from a Creole-speaking community and into English-speaking America. He understood Creole and sometimes used Creole phrases, but he didn't converse in Creole, even with his brother Roger and sister Caroline, who were bilingual.

Around the time that Clark reached school age, his family suffered the first in a series of losses and displacements. Clark marks this in the opening sentences of his autobiography, when he writes, "It was only at the age of nine that I first became conscious of the world. And the experience which initiate me into it was— tragedy." Clark never describes the tragedy, only writing about the outcome, that his mother was now raising the family alone. Clark borrowed the idea of coming into consciousness through a family tragedy, and even almost the exact words, from another autobiography, Angelo Herndon's *Let Me Live,* but there were several tragedies experienced by the Clark family during these years.

The tragedy may have been the loss of Clark's father or perhaps the loss of a stepfather. Clark's parents separated around the time of the birth of their youngest child, Caroline, in 1907. Clark's mother may have remarried shortly after. By the 1910 census, Bridget Clark and her children were living with Jerry Dollis, who the census taker recorded as Bridget's husband of three years. Dollis does not appear in any more family records. He is not mentioned by Clinton Clark in his story. Dollis's death or departure is possibly the tragedy that left his mother alone when Clinton was nine. The family suffered another loss during Clark's youngest years; his older brother Arthur disappears from the census records, suggesting that he died sometime between 1900 and 1910.

The tragedy of Clark's childhood may also have been related to the 1912 flood, which occurred when Clark was nine. The entire basin of the Atchafalaya River flooded, beginning with Pointe Coupee Parish. The region was naturally subject to flooding, but the construction of levees along the Mississippi in the late nineteenth and early twentieth centuries had made it vulnerable to catastrophic floods. In 1912 floodwaters broke through the levee at the town of Torras, about thirty miles north of Fordoche at the northern tip of Pointe Coupee. A total of 3,000 square miles of land flooded in Louisiana, affecting 350,000 people, 70,000 of whom would need government assistance to recover.[16] Clark's family was among them. Again, his description is limited to a few sentences, raising more questions about his experience than they answer. "In 1912. it was a flood in our section of the state," he writes. "The water taking everything we had and drowned out our crop. All the poor farmers was on charity. We would almost starve. Because it was so little relief that was giving to the poor Negroes."

J. P. Kemper, an engineer and author involved in the flood control politics of the time, later tried to convey the magnitude of the destruction and human suffering caused by the 1912 flood, an event that largely affected poor black sharecroppers and was later overshadowed in history by the flood of 1927. In his book

Rebellious River, he describes the flood of Clark's childhood as "the most devastating flood the Atchafalaya Basin ever experienced, not excepting that of 1927." Kemper compared the aftermath of the flood to images from the world wars:

> A flood such as this is a depressing sight, or at least was before we became hardened by world wars. Its destructiveness is hard to realize for one who has not seen it . . .
>
> Only narrow fringes along the Mississippi River above Donaldsonville, along the west side of Bayou Lafourche and the east side of Bayou Teche remained out of the water. Livestock huddled onto knolls, to stand there in the water until the end came. It was the same with the deer. Piles of bones were found on the little mounds after the water went down. The hogs and birds sought the levees, the former to be shot for rooting, and thus menacing the levee, and the latter to die of starvation. Day by day they grew weaker until, finally, they could not fly. The chickens were all lost. Only the ducks and geese survived. They were in paradise. Besides minnows, they got every kind of seed and flotsam brought down by the angry waters.
>
> Some people refused to be rescued. They elected to stay to protect their belongings. They could only watch their animals die and see their improvements swept away.[17]

After the flood the Clarks returned to farming in Fordoche for one more season, then lived off the wage labor of every single member of the family. "My brothers was working at a stave mill," Clark writes of his early teen years, "and my sisters work in the field." Clark had just two sisters; the younger, Caroline, would have only been eleven years old at this time. The flood ruined the economy of the parish, causing many foreclosures and business failures, including banks. The economy of the parish would remain depressed until the 1940s.[18]

In 1916, when Clinton Clark was thirteen years old, his older brother Walter died in a shooting following a baseball game. His murder is not mentioned in Clark's autobiography, but it is remembered by family members today. Walter, who was sixteen years old, had pitched a great game. Afterward, a man on the losing team went home to get a shotgun and returned to kill him. On his death certificate the words "Shot to death by another in cold blood" have been crossed out and "homicide by firearm" written beneath.

When the stave mill where Clark's brothers worked closed, the family made one last attempt to earn a living sharecropping. Clark's uncle persuaded Bridget Clark to move to a plantation in Cheneyville, about fifty miles to the northwest. The 1920 census confirms Clark's account, as it locates Bridget Clark in Cheneyville, living with James Lewis, who may have been the uncle Clinton describes in the story; her nephew Wilson Lewis; her children Houston, Roger, Clinton, and Caroline; granddaughter Beatrice; and a boarder. After farming one crop, they were in debt to the plantation owner and realized the futility of sharecropping. They wouldn't be able to earn a living farming themselves. They moved back to Fordoche. By this time Bridget Clark's children were almost grown. Clinton was seventeen. He followed his brothers from job to job, working on higher-paying "public jobs" whenever they could. As an absolute last resort he would work on sugarcane plantations, going south to White Castle, along the Mississippi in Iberville Parish just south of Baton Rouge.

From the very first paragraph, much of Clark's account of his childhood describes work. His later work as a labor organizer shapes his description of his childhood community and experiences. He usually describes the wage paid on a job, and he emphasizes moments when workers stuck together and demanded better conditions, beginning with the protection that his brother Roger gave him when he first started working in lumber mills. When Clark is assigned a job that is too strenuous and dangerous for him, his brother and the other workers together ask that he be moved to a safer job. Sometimes his demands for fairer wages or safer conditions win improvements for everyone; sometimes he is punished and has to quit. During his childhood and young adult years, he is constantly traveling. His ongoing search for better opportunities takes him first to towns throughout Louisiana, and then to Arkansas and Texas. The laying of pipelines by Standard Oil in the 1920s opened relatively lucrative but short-term jobs to black workers. Clark tries to take advantage of these jobs, but is often forced back to what he calls—with good reason—the "slave plantations."

Toward the end of his description of his childhood and youth, Clark tells an important story of literally fighting back when forced by the local sheriff to work on flood control. As the Atchafalaya rose and threatened flooding one spring, Clark led a group of black workers from his town who refused to work on the levees without pay. They physically fought against a sheriff, then ran to escape. Clark identifies the year of this flood and fight as 1922. Historical accounts agree that during the flood of 1922 there was a tremendous effort to patrol and sandbag the river levees in Louisiana and Mississippi, which may have included forced labor. Clark's description of the incident and the flood that followed, however, bear a great resemblance to the flood of 1927.[19] In his book *Rising Tide: The Great Mississippi Flood of 1927 and How It Changed America,* John Barry describes the forced conscription of black men to sandbag the levees during the 1927 flood. At least three times during the 1927 flood, black men who resisted working unpaid on the levees were killed.[20] In his autobiography, Clark describes anxiously waiting after the flood for his mother and sister in Baton Rouge and finally finding them on a bus full of refugees. The 1922 flood broke the levee near Ferriday, Louisiana, about seventy miles north of St. Landry Parish, where the Clarks sometimes lived; the crevasse displaced 20,000 people.[21] The flood of 1927 inundated both sides of the Atchafalaya, covering Clark's home region. It split the levee at Melville on the west side of the Atchafalaya on May 17, 1927, and at McCrea in Pointe Coupee Parish on the east bank of the Atchafalaya on May 24. In the days before the McCrea breach, just north of Clark's hometown of Fordoche, thousands of men worked to reinforce the levee. The subsequent flood was over thirty feet deep in places. Clark and his family were most likely among the 150,000 refugees displaced by this breach.[22]

Clark's account of his childhood has many absences and unexplained moments, yet the slim chapter tells the important story of a family that watched out for each other and stuck together through terrible tragedies. They continually moved through their region, circling away from home in the search for work, then returning to Fordoche, and later to homes in the nearby towns of Palmetto and Melville. Throughout his life Clark would return again and again to his family in Pointe Coupee and St. Landry parishes. There he would return after learning to organize with others to win better wages and benefits. His family, in turn, traveled out from this region to check on him, support him through his dangerous organizing work, and sometimes rescue him. Two family stories give a sense of their connection to him and the risks they all took. Once, Caroline went to check on Clinton when he was organizing in Mississippi, and after asking around was told that he was living in the woods outside of town. She walked through the woods shouting "Clinton, Clinton!" When he came to her, he asked, "Girl, how you found me?"[23] On another occasion, when Clark was held in prison in Vidalia, the sheriff got word to the family. Clark's brother Roger and Ed Henry drove to the back of the jail, where Clark was released on the condition that they take him out of the parish. In Clinton Clark's difficult later years, Caroline would twice bring him back to Louisiana from New York.

A Life in Organizations

On a handwritten draft, Sterling Brown titled an essay about Clark "Saga of an Organizer." Although Clark's autobiography covers his life from childhood through 1942, it is centered on the Great Depression. His story tells one person's long journey helping the country's most impoverished people better their circumstances during the 1930s and early 1940s. As Clark describes, in the early twentieth century black people in the rural South struggled to earn a living in conditions that were not much less oppressive than slavery. Many were sharecroppers, farming someone else's land in exchange for a share of the crop. Others rented land as tenant farmers or worked in the fields for wages. They had no control over their wages or the price they were paid for their crops, and high prices for credit and goods in plantation stores held them in debt. In Clark's story, we see flooding and very bad prices for their crops drive his family from sharecropping to wage work. After the stock market crash of 1929, prices for farm crops would drop further, making it almost impossible to earn a living in rural areas. In the first years of the Depression, employers laid off workers, cut wages, and cut hours, sometimes operating only a few days of the week. All of these impacts were magnified in black communities. A 1933 study of unemployment in Atlanta, for example, found 25 to 30 percent unemployment citywide, but 70 to 75 percent for blacks. To worsen the situation, there was almost no relief or assistance—just charity and a few city relief programs. Many people went hungry, many were evicted, and many traveled, like Clark, looking for work.[24]

Clinton Clark's story gives us an important perspective on how people fought back. By the end of the Depression, thousands of workers had joined unions and worked together for better wages and benefits and to challenge racial discrimination in the workplace. New government programs provided assistance, work, and protections for workers—many of which continue to protect us today. Clark's story helps us understand the complicated and changing politics and organizations of the 1930s. Like Clark, many people, and especially many African Americans, first found a way of responding to unemployment and hunger through their involvement in the Unemployed Councils, which were neighborhood groups organized by the Communist Party to help poor people get relief during the bleakest years of the early Depression. Like Clark, many people continued organizing through the decade and helped create a powerful labor movement by its end. Like other members of labor and left organizations in the 1930s, Clark's life and the lives of his colleagues were dramatically changed by World War II and the anticommunism that followed. Clark's story of working and learning through a series of organizations can help us better understand how the decade's organizing unfolded, and better understand the relationships among Communist organizations, labor unions, and civil rights organizations in the 1930s and early 1940s. It gives us a glimpse of civil rights organizing in the South just before the *Brown v. Board of Education* decision and the Montgomery bus boycott. This book tells one remarkable person's story, and through his story of a life lived organizing and in organizations, it tells a larger story of the Great Depression.

Like many others at the beginning of the 1930s, unable to find a job in his home state, Clark hopped a train and headed to California to look for work. There, in Sacramento in 1932, Clark first found political expression for his intelligence and outrage in an Unemployed Benefits Council. These councils organized hungry, homeless, and unemployed people to go together with their demands to relief offices and city halls. Clark's group pressed a relief agent into giving them "flour. meat. irish potatoes sugar. lard," and after enduring a beating by police in the agent's office, they won regular relief for themselves and the people they later brought to the office. Clark's experience in the Unemployed Council was shared by people in cities across the country. In other cities, members of Unemployed Councils were known for carrying the belongings of evicted tenants back into their homes. In some cases they protested unequal distribution of relief to blacks. The key tactics of these councils, as described by historian Robert Fisher, sound a lot like those of Clark's Sacramento group: they brought people together to demand food aid from local officials, they organized themselves to fight evictions, they were unquestionably and actively interracial, and they educated and politicized people who had not previously had any access to education and politics. They were relatively successful at organizing across racial lines.[25] African Americans were involved in Unemployed Councils in Harlem, Birmingham, Chicago, Chattanooga, Atlanta, and Greenville, South Carolina, suggesting that many black people shared Clark's experience of awakening to his rights and abilities through involvement in the Unemployed Council. Robin D. G. Kelley describes the councils (which he also refers to as "neighborhood relief committees") as an entryway into Communist Party organizing for many people in Birmingham, including black women, while another historian characterizes them as a training ground for the labor movement that would grow later in the decade.[26] It was a moment in U.S. history when the Communist Party played a key role in helping Americans across the country meet their basic needs, including the need to understand the politics and economy of the nation and larger world.

In his work with the Unemployed Council in Sacramento, Clark recognized a strategy needed by black people in the South. After a year in California he took the remarkable step of traveling back to Louisiana to organize on his own, with apparently nothing but the address of the Unemployed Council's national office connecting him to a larger organization. Clark returned to the region of his childhood, the Louisiana parishes bordering the Mississippi and Atchafalaya rivers. In these years, a lot of what he did was share the news of what he had experienced in California and the organizing that was happening elsewhere. He spoke frequently about the Scottsboro trials and convictions, the case in Alabama of nine young black men who had hopped a train—much like Clark had—and had been charged with rape when they were caught on board, several cars away from two white women. He estimates that he gave two thousand people the address of the Unemployed Council office.

Around this time, the organizing of tenant farmers and sharecroppers was just beginning in other southern states but not in Louisiana. In Arkansas, the Southern Tenant Farmers' Union (STFU) was founded in 1934 by Socialists and would grow to a reported membership of 25,000 by 1936.[27] More social movement than labor union, the STFU sought a more sustaining relationship between people and land in the South. While it challenged evictions and organized at least one strike, its activities were aimed at raising the nation's awareness of the problems faced by sharecroppers and tenant farmers. It was insistently interracial and directed considerable national media attention to the conditions experienced by southern sharecroppers and farm laborers under New Deal agricultural policies.[28] In Alabama, Communist-led organizing of black sharecroppers and agricultural workers began around 1931, with almost immediate violent reprisals. In July 1931, a sheriff and vigilantes attacked a meeting in Camp Hill, wounding Ralph Gray, a local leader who was standing guard outside the meeting. Gray died later that night; it is not clear whether he died from his wounds or was murdered as he lay injured in his home. These Alabama groups would soon form themselves into the Share Croppers' Union (SCU). Clyde Johnson organized for the SCU in Alabama beginning in early 1935. In extremely violent and dangerous circumstances–a number of organizers were arrested, then released by police to armed vigilantes and beaten; several were killed–he organized strikes of cotton choppers (spring) and cotton pickers (fall) in 1935. The cotton choppers demanded a wage of one dollar a day, and the cotton pickers sought to earn one dollar for every one hundred pounds picked, with a dollar a day minimum. Both strikes sought other improvements in working and living conditions, including an end to racial discrimination in the fields. Both strikes had major successes and devastating losses. In some areas strikers won wage increases, while in others they suffered terrible violence and returned to work in the same conditions.[29]

In Louisiana, Clark read about these strikes and used their successes to inspire plantation workers to act together for higher wages and a ten-hour day. Clark's work would connect with the larger movement to organize rural agricultural laborers when the Louisiana Farmers' Union was formed in 1937. In 1936, Clyde Johnson moved the SCU office from Alabama to New Orleans, in hopes that they could have an open office, and eventually he affiliated the union with the National Farmers' Union (which was also called the Farmers' Educational and Cooperative Union of America). Johnson would later recall that he needed to be in a place where he could write down addresses, where he did not have be underground.[30] But in his autobiography, Clark attributes Johnson's move to his own success organizing in Louisiana: "In less then three month we had organize more then one thusand sharescropper into the unemployed council, We was organizeing so fast until an state organizer was forced to come in and organize a state office, and in a little while, When the organizer came we receive a state charter from the Farmer Education and Cooperative Union of America, the state organizer was a very good organizer he was a young man his name was Claud Johnson, He would organize the white, While I would organize the Negroes." Johnson was soon joined by Gordon McIntire, who came from Commonwealth College in Arkansas and became secretary–the director–of a new organization, the Louisiana Farmers' Union.[31]

The Louisiana Farmers' Union (LFU), which existed between 1937 and 1942, was tireless in its efforts to organize sharecroppers, small farmers, and farm laborers in Louisiana. McIntire, who was later joined by (and still later married)

Margery "Peggy" Dallet, provided support and news on farm policy to local unions of farmers throughout the state. The union was formally launched by a state convention held in the Congress of Industrial Organizations (CIO) union hall in New Orleans in November 1937. A white citrus grower, Charles Gille of Boothville–a town on the slim edge of the Mississippi *downriver* from New Orleans–was elected president, and J. B. Richard, an African American farmer from St. Landry Parish, was elected vice president. Twenty-eight of the thirty-three locals sent representatives, and the union reported over one thousand dues-paying members.[32] The union was interracial but served a diverse collection of locals that were mostly segregated by the existing racial lines of the times–locals of independent citrus and lily farmers south of New Orleans, locals of sugarcane and cotton laborers in the plantation areas of the state, and locals of dairy farmers in the north near Shreveport. Though the newsletter provided locals with regular updates on national and state farm policy, the LFU was specifically geared to the needs of particular locals and farmers. Once they produced three parallel issues of their newsletter: a sugarcane edition, a dairy and vegetable edition, and an edition for the locals in cotton areas.[33] Sixty-five years later, Peggy Dallet McIntire would remember the union's work as mostly tackling projects very specific to local needs–such as establishing a successful lily bulb co-op or fighting for a statewide farmers' market reform–which were carried out with a worldwide consciousness.[34]

Working with the LFU and Gordon McIntire taught Clark new strategies for winning benefits for sharecroppers and laborers. Much of their work aimed to connect small farmers and farm workers with the programs and benefits implemented by President Franklin Delano Roosevelt to bring the country out of the Depression, and to make these agencies and their officials accountable to even the poorest tenant farmers. The Agricultural Adjustment Act was enacted to raise farm prices by making payments to those farmers who agreed to reduce the size of their crops, but often this resulted in evictions, and the payments went to the landowners, rather than to the tenant farmers and sharecroppers who lost their livelihoods. Actually, it was a double hit for tenant farmers, as there was less land to be farmed, while with the extra cash, landowners could buy tractors or hire day labor as needed. "Some evictions occurred as soon as the program began in 1933," writes historian Jack Temple Kirby, who describes "a massive expulsion of tenants" from cotton plantations in 1933 and 1934.[35]

Clark helped scores of sharecroppers write to the government for the checks owed them when their landlords took their land out of production. Clark describes helping over one hundred sharecroppers on a plantation write for AAA payments. "When every sharecropper receive his check it was a great shock all over the plantation." The sharecroppers tried to hand him money to thank him, while "the rideing boss began to get busy looking for the fellow who was doing all that writting to the government." Clark also helped create new opportunities for evicted tenant farmers. With McIntire's guidance, he organized LFU members in Natchitoches to meet with the local Farm Security Administration (FSA) official about a large plantation that was up for sale. The FSA bought the plantation and resettled forty-seven families on it. Clark writes, "There was a oppertunity for the sharecropper that they had never had before in life."

Another bill that was particularly important in Louisiana was the Sugar Act of 1937. The LFU constantly lobbied, complained, and prodded for enforcement of the Sugar Act, which had established minimum wages for sugar plantation workers. Planters who violated the act could have their AAA payments withheld. In 1938, Peggy McIntire represented the LFU at Sugar Program hearings, asking for better wages and fairer wages for women, and that all payments be made in cash rather than in credit at the plantation commissary or in room and board (which when provided was almost always inadequate and unlivable). She remembers traveling to plantations to teach workers how to fill the daily cards recording their hours and wages. The union helped workers file claims for back wages and accompanied members to the hearings on their back-wage claims.[36] In 1939, Gordon McIntire drove Clark to Lecompte, Louisiana, to assemble black sugarcane laborers to testify at a hearing in Baton Rouge. Clark got over two hundred people to attend a meeting and fill out their cards about the hours they had worked and the wages they had received. They elected delegates and chipped in money to pay expenses to the Baton Rouge hearing. When they arrived, they weren't allowed admission. Clark remembers: "But McIntire protest that they let the Negro come in and testify. So they did let us in to testify." After the claims for back wages were successfully filed, planters in Rapides Parish struck back by terrorizing Clark.[37]

The LFU was a strong promoter of forming cooperatives to give union members a way to buy salt, sugar, and flour from outside the plantation commissaries (which Clark and LFU newsletters frequently call "the robbeserry"). McIntire drove up from New Orleans to help Clark set up a co-op in Natchitoches. McIntire made the arrangements with the wholesale companies, and from then on the buying club made purchases every two weeks. Although McIntire had expected orders of around fifteen to twenty dollars, the first order from Clark's locals in Natchitoches was over $200.[38] They purchased tons of fertilizer together from a company in Shreveport. Peg McIntire remembers helping to pack supplies for the buying clubs into her husband's car—"and he would come home with bullet holes." In southern Louisiana, the LFU set up several cooperative marketing endeavors. They received a federal loan to build a citrus grading and packing shed in Booth-ville which enabled farmers to get a better price for their fruit. They set up a Cre-ole Easter lily marketing cooperative to ship Easter lily bulbs to Michigan and had at least three successful years of sales.

Though focused on local projects for practical reasons, Gordon McIntire envisioned a union that would ultimately transform the social and economic landscape of the South. In a fundraising letter for the Southern Organizing Committee of the National Farmers' Union, he outlined plans to extend the union to Georgia, Mississippi, Tennessee, and the Carolinas:

> The National Union is actively interested in the Southern Union's efforts to bring justice and democracy in landlord-tenant relationships. The Union advocates the Sharecrop Contract for this purpose. It stands for abolition of the sharecropping system. The Farmer's Union is working with other groups for the extension of the democratic rights of the common people, that is, for the abolition of the Poll Tax, for the right of all people to vote and hold public office, and for repeal of all laws restricting the rights of the people and the unions. The Farmers Union is organizing the first bona fide democratic cooperative movement in the South. Buying clubs are functioning and plans for cooperative cotton gins and grist mills are under way . . . With this aid the Southern Organizing Committee is confident it can successfully organize the most under-privileged people of America to bring more democracy, more security and happiness to a NEW SOUTH.[39]

Until 1940, references to Clark in the surviving written record of the LFU are few and sometimes secretive. The first mention may be a description in the July 1936 *Southern Farm Leader:* "There is a good Negro brother in Pointe Coupee Parish, Louisiana, who recently organized another Farmers' Union Local of 49 members. He has been doing very fine work in the fight for schools and now has presented us with almost a hundred names of sharecroppers and tenants who did not get their benefit payments under the AAA. I mention these brothers because of the fine work they are doing, although we are not forgetting the many good organizers working hard in the field right now too." [40] A few years later, Clark's identity was given as "C.C." to protect his safety when the union newsletter printed his report on organizing in the Red River Valley in 1938. He described the low wages, the extremely poor clothing of the Negro sharecroppers, and the fact that most had no domestic livestock or gardens. He reports "four locals with about 200 members" actively engaged in recruiting new members, setting up a union store, and filing applications for resettlement and farm security loans. [41] In May 1940 the Natchitoches Parish locals held "a jumbo weekend of Union meetings," with seven meetings held in different locations, featuring as speakers Clinton Clark, Peggy Dallet McIntire, and Harry Koger, who was from Texas and with the United Cannery, Agricultural, Packing and Allied Workers of America (UCAPAWA). Peggy McIntire summarized the locals' achievements under Clark's leadership: "The Union is making real headway in replacing robbissaries with co-op buying clubs, and in bringing Parish agencies to respect the needs and demands of our members." [42]

During the same years that the LFU formed and grew in the rural parishes, the Congress of Industrial Organizations had come to New Orleans and was organizing dockworkers and truckers. Though known today as the half after the hyphen of AFL-CIO, the CIO in the late 1930s was a network of progressive, integrated unions that were challenging the conservative, segregated unions of the American Federation of Labor (AFL) in many industries—and, in many cases, winning. There is evidence that Clark worked with the CIO organizers. He traveled to New Orleans in 1940 to seek the endorsement of the CIO for a mass meeting in Natchitoches. When New Orleans CIO leaders Willie Dorsey and Ernest Wright traveled to Natchitoches, their presence provoked local authorities. The police pursued Clark and the CIO delegation, arrested them, and shut down the meeting. In many ways the CIO was the urban counterpart to the LFU. Organizers who were white, leftist, antiracist, often not southern, and often Communist struck alliances with local African Americans, and together they mounted a powerful challenge to segregated unions and local employers. [43]

Dorsey and Wright, both black and from Louisiana, earned prominent leadership positions in New Orleans CIO unions through difficult and unsuccessful union-organizing campaigns. In many ways Dorsey was Clark's New Orleans counterpart, a black Louisianan whose partnership with outside organizers had grown a union in the late 1930s and early 1940s. Dorsey had been a dockworker when organizers for the International Longshoremen's and Warehousemen's Union (ILWU), a progressive and interracial CIO union from the West Coast, had come in 1937 to organize the first CIO union in New Orleans. He became, as labor historian Bruce Nelson describes, an "indigenous spokesman for the CIO."[44] While Clark was organizing rural sharecroppers and laborers, Dorsey and the CIO led a campaign to shift union representation of longshoremen on the New Orleans riverfront to an interracial CIO union. The campaign was subjected to aggressive reprisals from local police. At one point the police confiscated union records and ninety people were arrested at the CIO headquarters. After the ILWU lost the election to represent the longshoremen in 1938, Dorsey became president of the local and focused on organizing warehouse workers. Under Dorsey's leadership, the union added contracts with a number of warehouses and lost several strikes.[45]

Also organizing in New Orleans during these same years was the Southern Negro Youth Congress (SNYC), a civil rights organization that had a strong focus on working with labor unions to improve the economic opportunities of Negro youth in the South. Formed by black college students in 1937, the SNYC had helped organize unions in the south, as well as run voting rights campaigns similar to those of the civil rights movement of the 1950s and 1960s. Many of its members joined the later movement.[46] Clark attended the SNYC's annual All Southern Negro Conference when it was held in New Orleans in 1940. The meeting brought together presidents and faculty of black colleges with union officials and civic leaders to discuss an agenda of economic and political rights. The front page of the conference brochure sketches their mission: it reads "Cast Your Vote for Youth in 1940" and features a drawing of young people behind ballots that say "Better Schools," "Jobs," and "Citizenship Rights." That year there were five thousand SNYC members in New Orleans, with chapters in several different neighborhoods. An FBI report of the gathering states that Clark was elected to the SNYC's national council.[47]

Though the activities of the CIO and the SNYC in New Orleans were far removed from Clark's everyday work organizing in rural areas in the north and central parts of the state, those groups supported him at key moments—attending rural rallies, providing Clark a home base in New Orleans, and working for his release when he was imprisoned. Clark would later join the Transport Workers

Union, another CIO union, and work at a New Orleans trucking company when he was unable to return to rural organizing. Through these New Orleans labor actions, one can begin to see more of the larger labor movement of which Clinton was a part during these years. The CIO, as well as other unions and organizations like the SNYC, dramatically increased union membership across the country and changed the labor movement from organizations comprised of white, skilled workers, to organizations that were interracial and that sought to include every worker within an industry.

Clark's imprisonment in Natchitoches in 1940 would bring his work to the attention of national organizations. His experience inside the Natchitoches jail is one of the key events of his autobiography. He was picked up by police on July 27, 1940, on the morning of a huge parishwide rally. Peggy Dallet of the LFU would report that 800 Negro farmers came to town that day. Dorsey, Wright, and three others from New Orleans were also jailed. In New Orleans, Dallet called a meeting of the ILWU, the SNYC, and a lawyer; their first task was getting a lawyer to Natchitoches to find Clark and the others legal representation.[48] When the police released the New Orleans visitors three days later but continued to hold Clark, Dallet contacted federal officials, the black press, and local and national civil rights and labor organizations, asking for help to secure his release. Many sent telegrams or letters to protest Clark's imprisonment. In New Orleans, the Council of CIO Unions set up a "Clinton Clark Defense" fund and the Colored Gentlemen Boosters' Club held a mass meeting.[49] Dallet wrote a long letter to John P. Davis of the National Negro Congress (NNC) in Washington, D.C., who also received a letter from Raymond Tillman, a New Orleanian who was a field representative for the Southern Negro Youth Congress. Davis and Louis Burnham acted immediately, joining with the SNYC and the National Federation for Constitutional Liberties to meet with the head of the civil liberties unit of the Department of Justice about the case.[50]

Dallet would eventually credit Clark's release to the telegrams, phone calls, and letters sent to officials in Natchitoches, and the intervention of a representative of the Agricultural Adjustment Administration, who came to Natchitoches and met with planters.[51] This event made Clark a public figure, especially among civil rights organizations. After his release, he appeared on the cover of the *Louisiana Weekly*, the state's African American newspaper, jubilant and with arms raised in triumph, under the headline "CLINTON CLARK FREED!" When Dallet wanted to strike back against Natchitoches officials by suing them for violating Clark's civil rights, Davis of the NNC urged her to run a publicity campaign instead. "Statements should be issued," he wrote, "articles published, giving in detail a picture of the terror visited upon the Union and its organizer. Of this step we are sure." [52] Perhaps following this advice, Clark left Louisiana almost immediately for Chicago, where he spoke at the national meeting of the American Peace Mobilization. His picture appeared in the *Chicago Defender,* an African American paper with national circulation, under the headline "I May Be Lynched." From Chicago, Clark would travel with delegates from the meeting to Washington, D.C.; on his return to Louisiana, he stopped to meet with SNYC officials in Birmingham.

In his last two years organizing for the Louisiana Farmers' Union, Clark worked closely with the Southern Negro Youth Congress and its network of young African American leaders. The SNYC may have been an important source of support for him, as the leadership of the LFU in New Orleans first changed, then failed. Clark's experience and network jump-started the SNYC's rural program. Clark and the rural Louisiana committees had a strong presence in the few published issues of *Cavalcade,* the SNYC's newsletter. He was profiled in the newsletter, with a portrait. When the SNYC set up a rural committee, half of its initial rural councils were in Louisiana. [53] Clark always listed himself as an organizer for the LFU, but he affiliated with SNYC to more completely serve the rural communities where he worked. He organized Farmers' Union Junior Clubs–affiliated with the SNYC–for the youth and women. He wrote about his inclusive approach to labor organizing for SNYC readers: "But I say that some of the rural people are not going to take it lying down. Pointe Coupee Parish, Avolle, and St. Landry have organized six local clubs of women and young people. The fathers and husbands were already in the Farmers' Union, so the women and youth said, 'The men cannot solve our problem alone. We are going to show them that we feel our suffering too and are going to do something about it.'" [54]

Another article in *Cavalcade* reports the celebration of the fifth anniversary of the LFU, held in Torras, Louisiana, on May 25, 1941, with Clark as the master of ceremonies. Representatives of the American Peace Mobilization, the New Orleans CIO, the New Orleans Community Theater, and Ethel Goodman, chairman of the Rural Committee of the SNYC, attended. [55] In her remembrance of the SNYC published in *Freedomways* in 1964, Augusta Strong's description of the rural work of the SNYC seems to refer directly to Clinton Clark and Louisi-

"I May Be Lynched," *Chicago Defender,* September 14, 1940. This photograph
was used to identify Clark when he returned to Louisiana.
Courtesy *Chicago Defender*

ana: "The leadership of the national office gave special help in the formation of
rural youth councils; self-help projects of quilting and basketry, products sold outside the area, helped these groups establish educational and recreational programs
for the youth in their areas, and to raise money for civil rights activities . . . Rural
councils aided the formation of sharecroppers' and farmers' unions–and often em-

braced whole families, parents as well as young people."[56] These local organizations may have continued well into the 1940s, even as Clark left rural Louisiana and, eventually, the state. Strong notes that a group from Natchitoches–the area where Clark had organized for four years in the late 1930s–attended the 1946 SNYC Congress in Columbia, South Carolina. In working with SNYC on developing a rural program, he may have provided a direct link between the work of the LFU and the later civil rights movement of the 1950s and 1960s.

As his life in organizing took him from the Unemployed Councils to the Louisiana Farmers' Union to the Southern Negro Youth Congress, Clark had his own particular relationship to the Communist Party. Clark entered into his work as an organizer through a Communist organization. During that year in California, the party provided him with an opportunity to read, learn, and talk about issues that had not been available to him in Louisiana. He attended a workers' school run by the party. He spent days at the offices of the Unemployed Council reading and discussing Communist papers, and nights reading and discussing the papers with his sister. He learned to recognize himself as part of a class whose contribution was not justly rewarded, and he learned the basics of organizing. Once he returned to Louisiana, he frequently talked about the Scottsboro trials, a racial discrimination case that had been raised to national and international attention by the Communist Party and that symbolized its larger commitment to African Americans in the South.

But in Louisiana, Clark worked mostly alone in rural areas for almost ten years, removed from Communist meetings, discussions of issues and strategies, and probably newspapers. Some of his colleagues in the LFU, CIO unions, and the SNYC were probably party members, while others weren't. Clark's FBI file gives evidence that his work with the LFU was independent of the party's organizing efforts in Louisiana. When Harry Winson, a national leader of the Young Communist League, spoke at a meeting in the French Quarter in May 1941, a member of the audience suggested that they use Clark as an organizer: "at this meeting pointed out to WINSON that the subject, CLINTON CLARK, is a member of the Communist Party but had never been used as such in the sense of recruiting members and attending unit meetings. —— added that CLARK could probably do some good work in recruiting because he has been an organizer for five years and has a very large following. —— further added that CLARK would now have a real party built in the country parishes if he, CLARK, had been given proper consideration and guidance and sufficient funds with which to operate."[57] Other details in the report suggest a distance between Clark and Communist leaders during this year, though the deletion of names makes the record almost unreadable. At a meeting that included "the acting secretary of the Communist Party of Louisiana," someone who had attended an LFU event in Lettsworth called Clark a "phonie." [58]

After Clark's first imprisonment in Natchitoches in 1940, as he tried to continue organizing even as the state structure of the LFU disintegrated, he reestablished relationships with Communist organizations. In 1940 and 1941, the rallies of the Communist-affiliated American Peace Mobilization gave him a platform for speaking about the union in Chicago, Washington, D.C., and New York. In 1942, FBI agents reported that the Communist Party made some efforts to have Clark released when he was imprisoned again and that he sought help and guidance at the party offices when he moved to New Orleans after his release. A year later, with the help of his friend Harold Preece, a writer with Communist affiliations, Clark would move to New York. There Preece probably put Clark in touch with Communist organizations, including another workers' school.

Many years later, writing Attorney General Robert F. Kennedy from Melville in 1962, Clark would note that he was a former member of the Communist Party. "My membership were -pre- before the United State's had outlawed the U.S.A. Communist Party," he added. [59] Clark's narrative does not directly discuss what communism meant to him. When asked by a sheriff in the Natchitoches jail in 1940 about organizations that had written for his release—many probably Communist—Clark reports that he replied: "I am not family with these organization but I do know when ever any worker is organizing the poor people to better their condition and is arested these organization will fight for his freedom to the last drop." Though made under the duress of interrogation, Clark's statement is a good summary of how he saw the Communist Party—as an ally in his struggle to help his people. Clark worked with Communist organizations not for a change of government but for a change in the conditions of black people. For Clark, the Communist Party was a network of information and personal contacts from which he drew at particular moments in his organizing work, rather than a continuing source of positions or direction. With the rise of anticommunism and the collapse of the Communist-led left in the late 1940s, he would lose a network of people who had educated him, campaigned for his release from prison, and possibly found him work and health care over the years.

Clark's second imprisonment, the culminating act of his narrative, would mark the end of the Louisiana Farmers' Union. Clark and Kenneth Adams, the LFU's state secretary at the time, were arrested in Ferriday and imprisoned in Vidalia, Louisiana, just across the Mississippi River from Natchez, Mississippi, on January 5, 1941, and held there for ninety-two days.[60] Even though Clark's autobiography ends on a hopeful note, with a pledge to return to Pointe Coupee or send someone in his place, neither Clark nor the LFU would return to work in the Louisiana countryside. McIntire had been bedridden with tuberculosis for two years and was still recovering in a Denver hospital. Peggy Dallet joined him in Denver; they were married in September 1942 and began new work in Colorado. Adams was drafted while in jail and most likely left the union to enter the army when he was released. The NFU had revoked the state union's charter. Clark would spend a year in New Orleans writing his autobiography, then move north to New York. Over the next few years, the events of World War II and rising anticommunism would bring an end to this period of multiracial, left-led union organizing and transform the lives of almost everyone who had been involved. Clark's narrative unwittingly ends at the end of this era of organizing in Louisiana. In his later years, described in the afterword, he would suffer alone as the FBI and a growing anticommunism targeted the network of people and organizations that had worked for racial equality in the workplace.

Clark wrote the story of his life in organizing with justifiable enthusiasm. He had brought the ideas and resources of several organizations to Louisiana's rural black communities. It does not seem far-fetched to claim that he brought the LFU to Louisiana, just as the first impacts of the AAA hit tenant farmers in 1933 and 1934. While Clark and the LFU did not establish a lasting organization or win lasting changes in the rural economy, they did make a dollar-and-cent difference in the lives of the union members. Their accomplishments were local and tied very closely to New Deal federal programs. The detailed research of historian Greta de Jong provides measures of the impact that some of the efforts described by Clark may have made on the income of its members. In Pointe Coupee, Clark's home parish and home of some of the earliest LFU locals, de Jong finds that in 1937 blacks made up 80 percent of the Farm Security Administration clients, a much larger percentage than anywhere else in the South, and that the average net worth of the FSA clients in Pointe Coupee grew from $108 to $567 between 1935 and 1937. On the sugarcane plantations, the hearings at which LFU members spoke for better compensation resulted in wage increases for sugarcane workers. De Jong finds that wages for cutting sugarcane increased from $1.10 to $1.50 a day for men ($1.20 a day for women) after October 1937 hearings at Baton Rouge; year-round wages for working on sugarcane plantations planting and cultivating were raised slightly after the 1938 hearings. De Jong also finds evidence that the LFU was successful in filing claims for workers on plantations where wages were below these rates. Together these federal programs provided structures for assistance and compensation, while the LFU worked to make them more accessible and more responsive to the needs of black farmers and farm workers.[61]

More than these accomplishments, Clark emphasizes in his narrative his success in organizing people to work together for change. As the union's state organizer, he was to identify people in a community who would be interested in forming a union, teach them about the organization, and then set up a new local. From there, the local was guided by its officers and the state secretary, though often Clark stayed within a region and provided continuing assistance and leadership. His goal and measure of success was pulling black people together and organizing them to do something for themselves. We see this in his narrative as he ticks off the numbers of locals he set up in an area and as he describes inspiring organizing meetings. Organizing was for him both a philosophy of social change and a learned set of procedures and strategies. When questioned before a jury in the Natchitoches prison, he gave them his own summary of the work of the union: "We teach the farmer how to organize cooperative buying club and make saveing for group. We teach them health. And how to love each other in working togather." He celebrates moments when members watched out for him and protected him, when they worked together to establish cooperative stores, when hundreds of people came in from the countryside for a mass meeting he had organized.

Clinton Clark's story gives a first-person account of the lives of black people in plantation communities in rural Louisiana and Mississippi during the Depression. His story tracks the decline of wages, the hunger, and the near-enslavement of sharecroppers and plantation workers through debt and violence. His story tells how one remarkable person suffered and grew by working as an organizer, and what he accomplished as he tried to pull the resources and strategies of all these groups and government agencies to the service of sharecroppers and poor farmers. It is also an insider's view on how organizations and government programs developed over the decade and how they interacted with poor and rural people. Reading Clark's story gives us a view of organizing in southern black communities in the first half of the twentieth century, one that highlights the role played by the Unemployed Councils and labor unions. Though the overall conditions for rural black Louisianans would remain extremely difficult, Clark's work won assistance for many and may have inspired others to further activism.

Written by Himself

Autobiography has a special importance in African American literature. The narratives written by former slaves telling the story of life in slavery and escape to freedom were the first widely read works by African American writers and form the foundation of African American literature. These slave narratives played an important role in the struggle against slavery, attacking it on multiple levels. Authors such as Frederick Douglass and Harriet Jacobs documented the horrors of slavery for white audiences in the North, and they challenged their white audience's racism by showing themselves to be intelligent and fully human. For these authors, writing their own life stories was in itself a political act and another step toward freedom for themselves and all the slaves in the South. Writing their own story "enacted freedom," as William Andrews describes, as the ability to tell and publish your own story is in itself another level of controlling your own self. As Andrews emphasizes, for these authors writing the story of their lives was "uniquely self-liberating, the final, climactic act in the drama of their lifelong quests for freedom."[62] The most prominent figure in this tradition is Douglass. After escaping slavery and campaigning against it for several years in the North, he published his first autobiography, *Narrative of the Life of Frederick Douglass, American Slave, Written by Himself,* in 1845. Clark's story is part of a long tradition of African American autobiography and a tradition of "autobiography as activism," as Margo V. Perkins phrases it, that stretches back beyond Douglass and continues today.

Clark's narrative shares many of the key features Perkins identifies in political autobiographies written by black activists. Clark's narrative is as much "a story of a struggle," as it is an account of his life; it emphasizes the stories of the communities in which he works and the events in a movement over details and stories from his private life. The act of writing his own story helps his work as an organizer by documenting events in the struggle and sharing his experiences as a model and inspiration to others. Perkins's study of the autobiographies of Black

Power movement activists Elaine Brown, Angela Davis, and Assata Shakur suggests another shared reason why these black activists decided to write their life stories. Many wrote their autobiographies in prison or under the threat of imprisonment. "In making the public at least aware of their predicament," Perkins writes, "they endeavored to amass potential support and also to undermine the ability of the state to retaliate against them in secrecy."[63] Though Clark never tells his readers why he has decided to write the story of his life at that particular moment, he wrote it just after a three-month imprisonment, his second close brush with lynching in two years. Like many other black activists, Clark may have been seeking the visibility and protection provided by publishing a first-person story.

Clark was most likely inspired to write his story by *Let Me Live,* the 1937 autobiography of black Communist Angelo Herndon. Indeed, Clark's autobiography begins by following Herndon's first paragraph almost word for word. Like Clark, Herndon had become involved in organizing after attending an Unemployed Council meeting in Birmingham, Alabama, in 1930. He was jailed in Atlanta in 1932 after organizing a large, interracial rally for relief. The prosecutors tapped a law that had been originally passed in 1861 to prosecute anyone suspected of organizing a slave rebellion and ultimately charged him with "attempting to incite insurrection." Herndon was imprisoned for two years, and when he was released on bail he toured the country, speaking about his case and that of the still-imprisoned Scottsboro boys. Herndon first wrote his story in the 1934 pamphlet *You Cannot Kill the Working Class,* which was a brief and plain-style account of his life. His autobiography *Let Me Live* was published by Random House in 1937, just weeks after the Supreme Court had reversed the decision of the Georgia courts and freed him.[64]

Clark most likely recognized the similarities of his own life story to the events in Herndon's book and used it as a pattern as he sat down to the enormous task of writing the story of his life. He begins with his birth date and place, and the puzzling, unexplained memory of a tragedy that left his mother to raise her children alone. Though the unnamed experience was Clark's, he found the words to describe it in Herndon's first paragraph. Herndon writes: "I was born on May 6, 1913, in the little steel and coal-mining town of Wyoming, Ohio. My earliest recollections are wrapped in mist. It was only at the age of six that I first became conscious of the world, and the experience which initiated me into it was—tragedy."[65]

Herndon's tragedy was his own childhood illness; he begins his story by remembering his mother's prayer for his life and his family having to borrow money for his medication. Clark's tragedy, as we have seen, may have been the loss of a family member or the terrible flood of 1912. Clark's description of his childhood focuses on some types of people and incidents that are also found in Herndon's description of his childhood: an exotic grandmother, a friendly Italian grocer, an experience reciting poetry, venturing out to work at a young age with brothers. As Clark's story progresses, the similarity with Herndon's specific wording and incidents ends, though the basic plot of their stories stays the same—a search for work, discovery of the power of organizing, and imprisonment.

It is important to note that Angelo Herndon and his autobiography also provided a model and material for Richard Wright and Ralph Ellison, both African American and major American novelists of the twentieth century. Herndon's story received national attention and his autobiography was published in the years that Wright and Ellison were establishing themselves as writers and beginning their major novels *Native Son* (1940) and *Invisible Man* (1950), respectively. Wright wrote about Herndon for the *Daily Worker*, while Ellison worked with Herndon in 1942–43 on the *Negro Quarterly*. Frederick Griffiths, who has pointed out these connections, argues that, as a Communist organizer who was widely famous for a short time and then practically disappeared, Angelo Herndon "left room for the writers." Wright and Ellison could draw from his work as they wrote their own fictional accounts of men struggling with American racism and segregation at a time when communism offered an alternative vision that had to be considered. There is an intriguing possibility that Wright and Ellison may also have known Clinton Clark; more likely, they both knew of him. They may have read or heard about his organizing, or met him when he moved to New York in 1943. As Griffiths presents evidence that Ellison based Tod Clifton, the charismatic young Communist organizer in *Invisible Man*, on Angelo Herndon, he speculates that Ellison created Clifton's name from Herndon's real name, Braxton, and/or his brother's first name, Milton. It is hard not to hear an echo of Clinton's name as well. At the very least, Clark's story is a remarkable companion to *Invisible Man*, as it is a nonfiction account written from almost the same place and moment of history, a journey that parallels that of the unnamed narrator of Ellison's great novel.

Clark was directly encouraged to write his autobiography by two very different writers, Sterling A. Brown and Harold Preece, the latter a white Texan who had published activist pamphlets and written for African American magazines and newspapers. In the late 1930s and early 1940s, Preece had written passionately about the exploitation of sharecroppers, tenant farmers, and farm laborers in the South. He had worked as a writer for the Federal Writers' Project in Texas; one of his projects was collecting folklore.[66] For the *Crisis* in 1936, he had written about the strikes led by the Share Croppers' Union in Alabama as modern slave revolts answered with extreme violence. Preece says he met Clark at a Farmers' Union convention in Denver. They were both in Chicago in 1940 at the September convention of the American Peace Mobilization. Clark spoke, while Preece, according to the FBI, handled publicity for the event.[67] Preece had written about Clark in a series of articles about CIO organizing in the South published in the *Crisis* in 1941.

Preece believed that writers and writing could play an important role in revolutionary change. His sharp focus on black tenant farmers and his frequent comparisons of labor organizing in the South in the 1930s with the struggle against slavery the century before suggest that he saw himself as a modern-day abolitionist, writing about conditions in the South to bring national attention and changes to federal policy. His 1940 pamphlet, *Peonage: 1940s Style Slavery,* presents the work of the Abolish Peonage Committee (a project of the Communist group International Labor Defense) as a "new abolition movement." Comparisons to the struggle against slavery run through the pamphlet. He tells the story of a plantation owner in Georgia who bought some of his tenants off of chain gangs and had police in Chicago arrest tenants who had escaped north. Preece described the Abolish Peonage Committee as operating "the new underground railway running from the South and bringing refugees from Cunningham's Sandy Cros Plantation to the North."[68] We see this comparison as well in his first (and perhaps only) published description of Clinton Clark, in a 1941 article in the *Crisis* titled "The South Stirs": "With the financial and moral support of the National Maritime Union and other CIO organizations in New Orleans, Louisiana sharecroppers and small landowners are being organized into the Farmers Union under the leadership of Clinton Clark, a fearless Negro farmhand who might have stepped out of the pages of the slave rebellions."[69]

Preece's reference to the pages of the slave rebellions here may be telling. He may have seen the parallels between Clark's life and those of the authors of the slave narratives, and he may have encouraged Clark to see himself in the same way. In Texas, Preece may have participated in the Federal Writers' Project's effort to record the narratives of the last generation that had lived under slavery.

(Many of these narratives would be published in B. A. Botkin's 1945 *Lay My Burden Down.*) It may have been Preece, who saw himself as a revolutionary writer and a modern-day abolitionist, who suggested to Clark that writing his story was another form of activism, a way of continuing to work on behalf of his people even when it was dangerous to return to the countryside.[70] Clark had begun writing his story before he was held in the Vidalia jail in early 1942. An FBI report on his arrest notes that his only possession of value was "a package of papers written in penciled longhand, which appeared to be a possible partial autobiography by CLARK."[71] The sheriff confiscated the manuscript and gave it to the New Orleans FBI office. Clark must have begun work on his story all over again after his return to New Orleans. He mailed pages of his autobiography to Preece, who was living in New York, within months of his release.[72]

During these same years, Clark had in Sterling Brown a friend who was an English professor at a leading black university. Brown was one of the country's most knowledgeable scholars of American literature, and he was a prolific author of reviews and criticism centered on works by and about black Americans. Clark was an avid reader. Almost everyone who knew Clark later in his life remembers his many books. In his narrative, he describes reading "every good books I would get my hand on." He recalls reading along the roadside on breaks while driving from Michigan to Louisiana. Clark wrote Brown asking for books at least once. Lying sick in Natchez, Mississippi, in 1941, Clark wrote: "Here is something I would like for you and Dr. Wilkerson to do for me I will sure appreciated. if you all have any good books that I can read please send them to me."[73] Brown could have sent, and Clark could have read, works by almost any American author, black or white.

Clark began sending Brown sections of his autobiography toward the end of 1942. He first sent Brown a postcard and letter promising the imminent arrival of the manuscript:

My dear friend Mr. Brown.

You will receive the story of my work very soon, I have a friend up in N.Y. who has been working on all of my history, And I have wrote to him asking him to mail you what every parts you need to fit your book. Also I am writting up some new parts you will receive for the book If

Clinton Clark, c. 1942. Location and photographer unknown.
Courtesy Rodney Clark

you can send me some typewritting papers and ribbon it will help also
on my work.
I will be looking to hear from you real soon.

Sencerely .–Clinton Clark.[74]

Although Brown's role in Clark's decision to write his own story is unclear,
Brown gave Clark encouragement, some financial backing, and guidance. We can
hear his advice indirectly in the letters Clark wrote back to him. "Your letter and

money order was receive promptly," Clark wrote that December. "And was I to happy to get you letter, So I am going to do as you said. I will send you the story in my own words." [75] "In my own words," might have meant that Brown wanted to read Clark's manuscript, not a version edited or written by Preece. It might also have meant that Brown encouraged Clark to write in his own voice, to write as he actually spoke and not to worry about his departures from the English he read in print.

Even though Clark had distant encouragement and advice from other writers, he wrote his story alone, at night, after long days working at a New Orleans trucking company. It is important to keep Clark's circumstances in mind when reading his story and trying to understand why he chose to write it in the way that he did. He had been hard at work as an organizer in rural Louisiana for almost ten years and as a result was an accomplished speaker before he was a writer. His own sense of himself as a speaker is conveyed in his story. When recounting the occasion of his first speech in Sacramento, he breaks from straight description to portray his anxiety and the tremendous response of the crowd and his fellow workers, who crowded around him "as if I had been playing base ball. And had made a home run." He describes himself constantly speaking to small and large audiences, in California, across rural Louisiana and Mississippi, and later in Chicago, Atlanta, and Washington, D.C. Scenes of Clark talking in a church or sharecropper's shack about his trip to California and what "the working people was doing to better their condition" are repeated many times. His autobiography records many of the stories that he told in these talks and speeches. There are moments in the narrative where he describes himself telling people about events that he has written about earlier in the autobiography. The most notable is when he is given a ride by a planter who mistakes him for a preacher and warns him about "a union man coming around." Clark then describes himself telling the story to his members that night: "That was the first thing I began to talk about, I had a lots of fun with the member that night, The sharecropper laugh for more then a half hour." When he sat down at his typewriter, he was putting into writing many experiences that he had already shaped into stories for earlier, listening audiences.

There is evidence that parts of Clark's manuscript were first drafted as letters reporting conditions on Louisiana plantations to outside allies and organizations. Clark sent a handwritten version of the compelling description of the mistreatment and imprisonment of sharecroppers on the Rexmere plantation to the National Negro Congress. On this plantation, the exploitation was so extreme

that the overseer took half of the fish caught in the lake and half of the moss gath-
ered in the woods. The account in the letter seems to be a report on the plantation
as Clark first encountered it, and it ends abruptly, with the name of the plantation
owner and his mailing address. In the autobiography, Clark rewrites his earlier
account, first giving a general description of the plantation, then setting the scene
for the specific stories told to him by sharecroppers who lived there. Fewer individuals are named in the revision. Clark then describes his intervention. In fact, he
writes that one of his actions was to try to tell the story of the plantation to the
wider world: "We did began to expos the peonge plantation we send the story to
many news papers so that it could be known all over the world." The letter to the
NNC and perhaps other correspondence from his organizing efforts provided a
kind of first draft when Clark wrote his autobiography.[76]

Telling your own story, writing your own report of your working and living
conditions, was strongly encouraged by the Communist and union publications
that Clark would have read during these years. These publications encouraged
workers and sharecroppers to send letters describing their lives and work, often
publishing them under the title of "Workers' Correspondence." The Southern Tenant Farmers' Union published a pamphlet titled *The Disinherited Speak*, comprised
of letters written by members. The newsletter of the Louisiana Farmers' Union
encouraged members to write and published at least one article sent in by Clark,
which detailed the terrible poverty of white and black farmers in the Natchitoches
area.[77] This interest in the actual writing and voices of working people extended
from newsletters into the literary culture of the time. Left-wing poets wrote
poems that emulated the letters and first-person accounts of workers. Sterling
Brown himself was admired for bringing the distinctive voices of different black
communities—"the folk"—into his poetry. Part of the culture of the Communist and
labor organizations that Clark worked within was some recognition of the power
and importance of working people reporting on their own experiences.

In a letter to Brown, Clark once referred to the manuscript as "the story of my
work."[78] Reading it as a political autobiography and with awareness of his intense
experience speaking, reading, and writing within the workers' movement, may
help readers understand two features of his autobiography that may be difficult
today: his extreme focus on work and wages as he describes his life as a teenager
and young adult, and his downplaying of personal relationships and experiences.
Clark offers only a few pages describing his childhood. He later went back and,

in the only instance where he added material, wrote more about his childhood, adding two manuscript pages that he titles "Words left out of page 1." He never describes the tragedy mentioned in the opening lines of the book, which left his mother alone with seven children. Family memories and historical records suggest that Clark left undescribed even more stories of loss and personal tragedy. As noted earlier, he writes only a few sentences about the devastating flood of 1912 and does not describe the dramatic death of his older brother Walter. Clark doesn't write about his illness or medical treatments. There is no discussion of romantic relationships. His closeness to his family, especially to his mother, his sister Caroline, and his brother Roger shows throughout the story, but there are only a few scenes in which he describes experiences or times with his family in detail. The notable exception is when he tells about surprising his older sister Orelia in California. He recalls the gentle prank he played on her in unusual detail, including writing out their conversation. When she realizes who he is, he writes, she "held me for more then five minute."

In short, Clark's narrative is important because it was written by himself in words drawn from his intense immersion in union organizing in rural Louisiana. These qualities become even more apparent when Clark's narrative is compared to the two major autobiographies that have served as key primary sources for historians of labor, civil rights, and Communist organizing in southern black communities during the Great Depression. One is Hosea Hudson's account of his life. Hudson actually published two autobiographies: *Black Worker in the Deep South: A Personal Record* (Communist Press International Publishers, 1972), and the more extensive and well-known *The Narrative of Hosea Hudson: His Life as a Negro Communist in the South* (1979), which was written by historian Nell Irvin Painter from oral history interviews. Hudson grew up extremely poor in a Georgia sharecropping family; his grandmother ran the farm and his teenage aunt was the plowman. He left the countryside first for Atlanta, then Birmingham, Alabama, where, as a foundry worker, he was recruited into the Communist Party. He worked for the Communist Party in the 1930s and in the 1940s served as the president of a local of the United Steelworkers, a CIO union. As the Red scare mounted in 1947, his job and union membership were taken from him because of his connection to the Communist Party. He worked as an organizer for several years, but ultimately moved to New York and worked for eleven years as a janitor in a restaurant. His autobiographies recount in great detail the policies and strategies of the Communist Party's work in the black South. His experiences and views are similar to Clark's, although Hudson's work in an urban and industrial area immersed him much more in the thought, discussions, and community of the party. Hudson's autobiographies explore how he tried to bridge the party's theory and national policies with the priorities of southern black communities. His first autobiography was substantially rewritten by multiple editors before it was finally published in the early 1970s. When he began work with Painter on his second autobiography, he again wanted to focus on his long relationship with the Communist Party, but through her intervention he shared more of the personal experiences that shaped his life. Rather than seeing himself as created and formed by the Communist Party, through these interviews at the end of his life Hudson came to see himself more as a talented leader who developed further within the party.[79]

Another important primary source is *All God's Dangers: The Life of Nate Shaw*. This is the life story of an Alabama sharecropper who was imprisoned for twelve years after standing up to a deputy sheriff who had come to take possession of a neighbor's livestock and then shooting back when a larger force of police returned. The book was written by Theodore Rosengarten from extensive interviews with Shaw conducted in 1971. Shaw was briefly a member of the Share Croppers' Union; his membership and the union organizer's teachings shaped his response to the sheriff's deputies that day. But the resulting book, published in 1974, is an encyclopedic account of the experience of sharecropping rather than an account of sharecropper organizing. It names each of Shaw's landlords, the conditions of their contracts, the quality of crop he was able to raise on that land that year, and the play of nature, economy, and injustice that determined his earnings each year. According to Rosengarten, Shaw shared many of these details in response to interview questions. Shaw's account of his life is primarily, overwhelmingly concerned with relationships. He carefully details his relationship with each person in his community, from major figures like his father, who beat him and rented him out as a child, to half-siblings, uncles, step-parents, and in-laws. Shaw's narrative is a remarkable reconstruction of the community of Tukabahchee County, Alabama, over almost a century.

A third autobiographical work, the recently published *Witness to the Truth: My Struggle for Human Rights in Louisiana*, provides a Louisiana counterpart to Clark's narrative. Born within months of Clark and a few parishes north, African American John Henry Scott worked for decades with the NAACP to gain the right to vote for black people in his community. Scott got his first experience organizing during the late 1930s, sparked by the actions of the same New Deal agencies that drove Clark's work. Scott organized against an FSA resettlement plan that moved a black farming community off of fertile land to a more marginal area. They lost this battle and were moved, but the struggle put Scott in touch with the NAACP. Like Clark, Scott worked locally but drew from national organizations for support and perspective. His work as a Baptist pastor gave him access to educational opportunities and took him to meetings around the country, while the NAACP, which grew and then was repressed in Louisiana in Scott's time, provided a national political network. His narrative follows his attempts to register to vote and to gain the right to vote in his community, and the resulting violence directed against him and his family. His story culminates with their local victory and with the local impact of the national Voting Rights Act of 1965. Interestingly, even though the book is written in the first person and includes closing reflections on Brown's long years of organizing work, it was actually written by his daughter Cleo Scott Brown from interviews that her father did with historian Joseph Logsden.

Along with Herndon's *Let Me Live,* these works are the closest published counterparts to Clark's narrative.[80] With its focus on Louisiana and the Louisiana Farmers' Union, Clark's story adds to the stories told in these works to form a larger regional picture of the experience of sharecropping in rural black communities during the Great Depression. Significantly, that Clark wrote his story himself during the 1940s sets it apart from these important books. Although other books and fellow writer-activists influenced his choice of autobiography as a literary form, Clark ultimately decided what to tell about himself and how to tell it. Clark's narrative is fairly brief and moves quickly from event to event. He rarely lingers on full descriptions of people or places. Sterling Brown pointed toward the autobiography's constant movement between places and challenges when he initially titled his own version of Clark's narrative "Odyssey of an Organizer." Clark's authorship and his use of his own speeches and letters as sources result in a narrative that brings us closer to the kinds of speaking and writing that were present in the movement—the arguments that were made, the kinds of evidence that were presented. For example, we can see how Clark—and maybe others—interpreted ideas from Communist and union organizing in the way he uses terms such as *class,* which he understands more as a professional than socioeconomic position. With Clark's own structures, descriptions, and word choices, we can read his use of language closely for the understandings it reveals as well as for what it reveals about the use of language and writing in and between the rural extremes of this movement.

Clark's story illustrates how the denial of education and literacy continued to be a tool to enslave rural black people in the 1930s. Much of what Clark did in rural communities was write letters for people, applying for benefits that were owed to them through government programs. When wage laws were passed for sugarcane workers, LFU staff went to plantations to teach sugar workers how to keep track of their hours in writing.[81] Helping people express themselves and communicate in writing to the outside world was threatening to the control that landlords had over workers' lives and livelihoods. At one point in the story, Clark describes an overseer searching for "the fellow who was doing all that writting to the government." "Where every he see that fellow what doing all this writting he would kill him." Illiteracy made it very difficult to organize these communities into statewide or national organizations. The LFU newsletter was the main way the central office communicated to locals and members in rural areas, but the records show that it was a continual struggle to distribute it and get subscriptions when most members couldn't read or write, and issues were often stolen by planters and local postmen. Differences in the ability to read and write also may have caused internal divisions in interracial southern organizing campaigns. In at least two cases, major conflicts between local black organizers and their national affiliate arose over record keeping. When financial records of local unions weren't kept according to the standards of the national organization, it assumed that local leaders were misusing money.[82] In retrospect, these conflicts look like they were caused more by different relationships to writing than by corruption or mismanagement—the white leaders worked in a world of writing, whereas the local black leaders worked in communities where most members couldn't read or write. They were bound to have differences over what should be written down and how.

These differences between the use of writing by national and state organizers and the local leaders of unions have also left us a lopsided record of the work of these unions. Before the publication of this autobiography, Clinton Clark lay just on the edge of the historical record. He is briefly mentioned in a number of major histories of labor and civil rights organizing, but there were only scraps of evidence for historians to work from, mainly the newspaper articles in the *Louisiana Weekly* about his imprisonment in Natchitoches and materials from the campaign to gain his release.[83] The publication of this autobiography demonstrates again that writing is an important tool in gaining freedom and control of one's own life, and that writing is an important tool in gaining control of one's place in history. Writing–letters, position papers, articles, and, importantly, memoirs–leaves a record of ideas and experiences for the historians of the future. Writing at night, after a day of exhausting work, on any paper he could find, with spelling and punctuation that he figured out for himself, learning as he wrote, Clark added his own chapter to the history of Louisiana, African Americans, and the continuing struggle of African Americans for equal rights. It also reminds us how the denial of literacy has kept many, many fascinating and courageous stories out of history. We have to work hard to remember that just because these stories weren't written down doesn't mean that they didn't happen.

Clark overcame many barriers through long walks and many talks. Rural people loved to hear him talk, and often asked him to stay longer with them, most likely because he brought news from the outside world. He was a kind of living newspaper. He spoke frequently about the Scottsboro trials, which became the decade's major civil rights issue. He told people of his experiences organizing in California. During World War II, he organized people who didn't even know there was a war to help in the war effort. He provided people with contacts in New York and New Orleans, and helped them write and speak before the New Deal agencies that should have been addressing their needs. Today, that flow of information is reversed, and his narrative brings us a portrait of work, life, and the freedom struggle in rural black communities in Louisiana on the eve of the modern civil rights movement.

Notes

1. Brown, "Count Us In," 314–15.
2. Ibid., 333.
3. See ibid., 310, 312; Brown, "The Muted South," 22–24.
4. Brown, "Count Us In," 332.
5. F. G. Clark, letter to Sterling Brown, September 30, 1942, box 10, SAB. "We are exceedingly happy to know that you will be with us Friday, October 9," wrote the Southern University president. His letter includes directions for traveling to Baton Rouge from New Orleans and some coded advice on negotiating the segregated transportation system. "And here is a demand for your own comfort: Inasmuch as you are a first class Jew, you should occupy the transportation area on the bus or train which is in keeping with your ethnic background, that is the Jewish one." Brown's presence in New Orleans in

October 1942 is also suggested by a citation in one of Robert O'Mealley's bibliographies of works by and about Sterling Brown; an article in the October 24, 1942, *New Orleans Sepia Socialite* was titled "Sterling Brown defends Zoot Suit Wearers." Clark and Brown may have met initially on one of Clark's trips to Washington, D.C.

6. I owe this characterization of the region to geographer Richard Campanella.

7. Klingler, *If I Could Turn My Tongue,* 104–6.

8. Ibid., xxxiv.

9. Ibid., xxviii.

10. Though the language a person spoke in nineteenth-century Louisiana can be guessed to some degree by a person's race, class, and location within the state, it was a diverse and multilingual place, with many exceptions to any generalization. It is therefore hard to know any single person's language competencies.

11. Ibid., xxvii.

12. These quotations are reproduced as they appear in Clark's manuscript, without editing.

13. Klingler, *If I Could Turn My Tongue,* 108.

14. Rodney Clark remembers his grandmother Bridget Clark as "more Creolish than English."

15. Klingler, *If I Could Turn My Tongue,* 120.

16. Brown, "The Mississippi River Flood of 1912," 654.

17. Kemper, *Rebellious River,* 97–98.

18. Costello, *A History of Pointe Coupee Parish,* 180.

19. The 1922 flood affected Mississippi, and in Louisiana levees broke at Ferriday and at points below New Orleans, displacing a total of 70,000 people in the region. See Barry, *Rising Tide,* 156–68. As the river rose to near-record levels in April 1922, the levees had to be guarded against weakness or sabotage. As Barry explains, "If the levee yields on one bank of the river, those on the opposite bank are suddenly safe" (161).

20. Ibid., 448, note for p. 195.

21. Ibid., 164.

22. Ibid., 284–85.

23. Rodney Clark, personal communication, April 10, 2003.

24. Biles, *The South and the New Deal,* 16–35.

25. Solomon, *The Cry Was Unity,* 214.

26. Fisher, *Let the People Decide,* 39–42; Kelley, *Hammer and Hoe,* 21; and Rosenzweig, "Organizing the Unemployed," 53. On the Unemployed Councils, see also Herndon, *Let Me Live;* Solomon's chapter titled "Fighting Hunger and Eviction" in *The Cry Was Unity;* and Hosea Hudson's autobiographies, *Black Worker in the Deep South* and *The Narrative of Hosea Hudson,* by Nell Irvin Painter. Hudson describes the organization, work, and effectiveness of the Unemployed Benefit committees from the perspective of a party activist. The eviction protest of Ralph Ellison's title character in *Invisible Man* is likely inspired by Unemployed Council actions.

27. Alex Lichtenstein, introduction to Kester, *Revolt Among the Sharecroppers,* 41.

28. Naison, "Southern Tenants' Farmers' Union and the CIO," 36–41; Lichtenstein, introduction to Kester, 44–50; Egerton, *Speak Now,* 156.

29. Kelley, *Hammer and Hoe,* 161–68. Kelley devotes several chapters to the history of the Share Croppers' Union; see chap. 2, "In Egyptland: The Share Croppers' Union" and chap. 9, "The Popular Front in Rural Alabama." Kelley gives an excellent account of the relationship between the SCU and the STFU, which had discussed merging. STFU leader H. L. Mitchell ultimately backed out, suspicious of Communist influence in the SCU.

30. Johnson, interview by H. L. Mitchell, Charles H. Martin, and Bob Dinwiddie, April 4, 1976, CJP.

31. The best account of the Louisiana Farmers' Union is Greta de Jong's chapter in *A Different Day.* In addition to providing an excellent summary of the union's work, de Jong's book is a guide to the few surviving written records of the union. These include the Clyde Johnson Papers (CJP), which are held with the papers of H. L. Mitchell and the Southern Tenant Farmers' Union and are available on the microfilm titled *The Green Rising, 1910–1977: A Supplement to the Southern Tenant Farmers' Union Papers.* Johnson's papers contain letters written regularly by McIntire with news and strategy of the LFU and copies of the union's newsletters. Copies of the newsletters are also in the vertical files titled "Louisiana Farmers' Union" and "Louisiana Farmers' Union News" in the Tamiment Library/Robert K. Wagner Labor Archives (LFU-VF). A copy of what was perhaps the last issue is in box 112 of the Sterling A. Brown Papers (SAB). The union's newsletter changed names and format. The *Southern Farm Leader,* a professionally typeset and printed newsletter with national and regional news, was produced by Clyde Johnson during his short stint in New Orleans from May 1936 to 1937. The various versions of the *Louisiana Farmers' Union News,* usually a few typed pages of local and state news, were published between November 1937 and December 1941.

32. "State Charter Regained" and "The Convention," *Louisiana Farmers' Union News,* November 15, 1937, LFU-VF. This vertical file holds a number of key documents on the union: its constitution, the resolutions adopted at the 1937 state convention, buying club order forms, and a number of publications produced for the locals, including a program of readings that Peggy Dallet had prepared for the locals to use at their meetings.

33. All three issues are dated June 1, 1939, and they are numbered bulletin no. 60, 61, and 62, respectively, LFU-VF.

34. Peg McIntire, interview; Peg McIntire, letter to Liz Davey, June 2006.

35. Kirby, "The Transformation of Southern Plantations," 265, 269.

36. Peg McIntire, interview; *Louisiana Farmers' Union News,* March 1, 1938, and August 1939, CJP. Also see de Jong, *A Different Day,* 103–5.

37. Gordon McIntire relayed Clark's account to Joshua Bernhardt, Chief of the Sugar Division of the U.S. Department of Agriculture. Gordon McIntire to Clyde Johnson, July 17, 1939, and July 11, 1939, CJP.

38. McIntire, letter to Clyde Johnson, November 11, 1939, p. 2, CJP.

39. Gordon McIntire, undated letter to friends, CJP.

40. Johnson, "How to Organize," 1936. Though the description could be of local LFU leader Abraham Phillips, Clark indicates in his narrative that he worked in this part of the state—St. Landry, Avoyelles, and Pointe Coupee parishes—at this time, 1935–36.

41. C.C., *Louisiana Farmers' Union News,* June 15, 1938, 2, CJP.

42. *Louisiana Farmers' Union News,* May 1940, 2, LFU-VF.

43. On Clark speaking to the New Orleans CIO, see Margery Dallet, letter to John P. Davis, August 4, 1940, folder 56, box 22, NNC.

44. Nelson, "Class and Race," 29.

45. Wells, "The ILWU in New Orleans," 7, 11–12.

46. Richards, *The Southern Negro Youth Congress,* 107. New members went straight from the founding meeting of the SNYC in Richmond, Virginia, to organizing local black tobacco workers into a new union–the Tobacco Stemmers and Laborers Industrial Union–and helping them negotiate for higher wages and an eight-hour day. The SNYC formed over 115 local councils and held large annual conferences throughout the South between 1937 and 1948. Most writing about the group's activities in Louisiana focuses on New Orleans, which was a center of SNYC activity. A labor school was begun in 1939 and several hundred workers attended. There was a People's Community Theatre in New Orleans and in May 1941, the New Orleans SNYC council produced a play about sharecroppers, *Land of Cotton,* in Longshoreman's Hall. In 1942–43, Ernest Wright of New Orleans was a SNYC vice president, and four New Orleanians were on the national council. In June 1942, Wright and Samuel Hoskins, city editor of the *Louisiana Weekly,* would travel to Washington, D.C., to lobby for integration of the armed forces. The SNYC was active through World War II and disbanded under anticommunist pressure in 1948. As Robin D. G. Kelley notes, "a substantial portion of its membership went on to become activists in the post-1954 civil rights campaigns." See Hughes, "We Demand Our Rights," 44–45; Strong, "Southern Youth's Proud Heritage," 41, 43, 47; Richards, *The Southern Negro Youth Congress,* 50, 115; "Officers SNYC for 42–43," and Kelley, "Southern Negro Youth Congress," 787.

47. Richards, *The Southern Negro Youth Congress,* 72, n. 1; "Southern Negro Youth Congress," New Orleans, April 28, 1941, p. 4, folder 1, box 1, SNYC, FBI files, Tamiment Library/Robert F. Wagner Labor Archives, Elmer Holmes Bobst Library, New York University, New York.

48. They sent a lawyer from New Orleans to Natchitoches; he was unable to find a local attorney to represent them. "Seven refused on the ground that it was political dynamite," Dallet wrote to Davis on August 4, 1940, reel 22:0573, part 1, NNC.

49. "Farmers, Race Leaders Throughout State Rallying to the Defense of Clinton Clark," clipping from unidentified newspaper, August 7, 1940, NNC.

50. "Lynch Threat Thwarted," Press Release, National Federation for Constitutional Liberties [August 1940], reel 18:0785, part 1, NNC. The papers of the NNC also include an unsigned handwritten note that may be Davis's instructions to Louis Burnham, the NNC Youth Secretary: "Suggest person to person call to Raymond Tillman . . . Find out facts–how far to rely on Dallet. Next give facts to Press. Contact NAACP. Nat. Com. To Defend Constitutional Liberties." He suggested that the latter group could arrange a meeting at the U.S. Dept. of Justice; see 1933–47, reel 22: 0573, part 1, NNC.

51. Margery Dallet, letter to Reverend Owen A. Know, August 23, 1940, reel 18:0785, part 1, NNC.

52. John P. Davis to Margery Dallet, August 26, 1940, ibid.

53. Goodman, "Rural S.N.Y.C. Councils."

54. Clark, "Louisiana Rural Youth."

55. "Louisiana Farmers Hold Anniversary Meeting."

56. Strong, "Southern Youth's Proud Heritage," 46.

57. "Clinton Clark," New Orleans, August 15, 1941, p. 4, FBI-CC.

58. Ibid.

59. Clinton Clark, letter to Robert Kennedy, postmarked May 21, 1962, FBI-CC.

60. Notarized deposition of Kenneth Adams and Clinton Clark, April 18, 1942, Parish of Orleans, Louisiana, box 112, SAB.

61. De Jong, *A Different Day*, 102–15. With active locals in many regions of the state, many locals leaders, and the work of the McIntires, it is important to note that the local accomplishments of the LFU went well beyond Clark's organizing work.

62. Andrews, *To Tell a Free Story*, xi.

63. Perkins, *Autobiography as Activism*, 7, 27. Her concise summary of political autobiography as a literary genre is on page 7.

64. The Supreme Court justices found that owning books and being a member of the Communist Party were insufficient evidence of inciting insurrection and that imprisoning Herndon was a violation of his right to free speech.

65. Herndon, *Let Me Live*, 3.

66. In a letter to Sterling Brown about Clark's manuscript, Preece wrote, "I recall with pleasure some nice things that you said about my work when I was employed on the Writers' Project in Texas" (January 20, 1943, box 112, SAB). For a brief summary of Preece's early career as a writer in Texas, see Mooney, "Texas Centennial 1936," 41.

67. R. G. Gregg, "Communist Party of the United States of America," August 1, 1941, Chicago, Illinois, p. 16, FBI-RHP.

68. Preece, *Peonage*, cover.

69. Preece, "The South Stirs," 318.

70. Preece may have seen himself as Clark's editor, following in the footsteps of the abolitionist editors who helped bring into print the narratives of escaped slaves. In January 1943, a few weeks after Clark had sent his story to Sterling Brown, Preece wrote Brown to offer to let Brown read and copy Clark's manuscript, if he were ever in New York. "I am hoping, of course, that I can eventually find a publisher for Clint's story since I would like for him to make a little money" (January 20, 1943, box 112, SAB).

71. Name deleted, "Clinton Clark," New Orleans, March 4, 1943, p. 5, FBI-CC.

72. Pages 21 to 23 of Clark's manuscript, photocopied with the front of an envelope postmarked June 29, 1942, and addressed to Preece from Clark, are in the MSRK. There is no explanation of how Robert Kaufman, a doctoral student at the University of California at Berkeley, obtained the copies. See folder 3, box 4, MSRK.

73. Clark, letter to Brown, November 2, 1941, box 10, SAB.

74. Clark, postcard to Brown, November 12, 1942, box 112, SAB.

75. Clark, letter to Brown, December 12, 1942, ibid.

76. Clark, letter to unnamed recipient, c. 1941, reel 23:0863, part 1, NNC. The recipient was probably John P. Davis, as this letter is filed alongside a March 15, 1941, letter from Davis to Clark in Lettsworth, and an undated letter to Davis from Clark.

77. This article, titled "Down in the Red River Valley," is identified as "By C.C." in the June 15, 1938, issue of the *Louisiana Farmers' Union News*.

78. Clark, letter to Brown, November 12, 1942, SAB.

79. Painter, Introduction to *The Narrative of Hosea Hudson,* 34–35.

80. At least two other Depression-era autobiographies by black sharecroppers have been published, while H. L. Mitchell's *Mean Things Happening in This Land* is an autobiography published by the white leader of the Southern Tenant Farmers' Union. There is a substantial body of autobiographies of black Communist Party leaders, some published in the 1930s and many published in the 1970s by International Publishers, a Communist press. Harry Haywood's *Black Bolshevik: Autobiography of an Afro-American Communist* (1978) includes a chapter on the Share Croppers' Union titled "Sharecroppers with Guns: Organizing the Black Belt." Haywood forcefully describes the dismantling of the SCU as a "liquidation" by the Communist Party leadership, which in his view sacrificed a militant, provocative organization of African Americans as it tried to forge relationships in the late 1930s with unions and New Deal agencies. See also Stimpson, *My Remembers,* and Janet Maguire, *On Shares: Ed Brown's Story* (New York: Norton, 1975). The International Publishers autobiographies include Davis, *Communist Councilman,* as well as autobiographies by William Z. Foster, Hugh Mulzac, and Hosea Hudson.

81. Peg McIntire, interview.

82. See Naison, "Southern Tenants' Farmers' Union," and Wells, "The ILWU in New Orleans."

83. He is briefly mentioned in Fairclough, *Race and Democracy;* de Jong, *A Different Day;* Kelley, "Southern Negro Youth Congress"; and Solomon, *The Cry Was Unity.* Also, Dale Rosen's 1969 thesis on the Alabama Sharecroppers' Union, held in CJP, mentions Clark in Appendix E, "Organizers": "Clinton Clark, from St. Landry Parish, volunteered to organize for the SCU in Louisiana. In 1936 he worked in Avoyelles, Pointe Coupee and St. Landry Parishes. He was then about 30, literate and willing."

A Note on the Text

This text is reproduced from typewritten pages held in the Sterling A. Brown Papers in the Moorland-Spingarn Research Center at Howard University. Because it was not published during his lifetime, Clinton Clark did not have the assistance that an editor provides an author. His original writing can be difficult to read, as he was figuring out some punctuation, word usage, and spelling as he wrote. His original writing is also very moving and powerful, as his struggle with writing is a steady reminder of how much he overcame to tell his own story and to help people in the ways that he did. Reading his original writing helps today's readers more fully imagine a society where such a bright, ambitious person was prevented from pursuing an education equal to his intelligence and had to learn to write on his own. In short, the spelling, word choice, and punctuation mistakes of his original text are reminders of his accomplishment.

Retaining Clark's original spellings and usage makes reading his story a greater challenge, however. In editing his text, we have made a few types of corrections to help contemporary readers. Clark's original is written in complete sentences, but the sentences are punctuated in confusing ways, with periods and commas used interchangeably and the beginning of a new sentence not always capitalized. The periods and beginning capitalization have been regularized so that readers can more easily follow the sequence of his thoughts. Commas and semicolons that were clearly meant to be apostrophes have been changed. Some of Clark's unique style of punctuation has been left as is, most notably, his use of question marks and exclamation points. Clark used a *c* accented with a cedilla (ç) in place of the cents sign (¢) in his many reports of wages, and in two instances instead of the percent sign. We have left Clark's use of this French letter intact as a reminder of the bilingual world in which he wrote. In most instances we have reproduced his original spelling and word choice, though we have corrected mistakes that are clearly typing errors.

This handling of punctuation and spelling has some precedents. In the handwritten manuscript about Clark, "Saga of an Organizer," Sterling Brown rewrote long passages from Clark's manuscript with some editing. He corrected the punctuation of sentences but left intact many of Clark's word choices and spellings. (More recently, in bringing to print Hannah Crafts's *The Bondwoman's Narrative*, a handwritten manuscript of a novel written by a woman who had been a slave, contemporary scholar Henry Louis Gates Jr. followed a similar practice of adding periods at the ends of her sentences but reproducing her own spelling.) While our adherence to the original text makes the text more difficult for the reader to understand, it tries to stay true to how Clark worked with words and reduces our interference in how he tells his own story. It should be emphasized, however, that many small but significant editing choices have been made, and this book is not an exact reproduction of his manuscript.

The pages of Clark's manuscript are packed with print. He typed single-spaced, with almost no break in the text. To assist the reader, Clark's text has been divided into short chapters. His paragraphing and lack of paragraphing has been left as is. In different places in the manuscript, he used carriage returns or spacing to begin new paragraphs, which are shown in this copy with a standard indentation.

In bringing this manuscript to print, we did have to choose from multiple drafts of some parts of the story and also make some choices about the ordering of text. From the pages held in the Brown Papers, it appears that Clark first wrote his story in longhand, typed it, and then retyped some sections. We know that he had parts of a manuscript confiscated by police and that he also sent a copy of the manuscript to Harold Preece. Though the manuscript in the Brown Papers tells a complete story, it is pieced together from pages of different drafts. Reading through these drafts, we can see Clark learning about writing, with the mechanics (punctuation and capitalization) and style changing as he writes. However, because it seems that he was able to revise and retype some parts of his story, including the first third, a progression can't be easily seen in this reproduction. It is the middle section of his autobiography, which begins with his return to Louisiana from California, that is produced from his earliest, roughest draft.

In just one instance, it appears that Clark wanted to insert a section with additional details and events into the manuscript. There are several typed pages describing his childhood which are titled "Words left out of Page number 1." As Clark didn't mark where he wanted this material inserted, we determined where to add it.

Chronology

1942   Sterling Brown visits Louisiana in October. Clark begins send-
        ing Brown sections of his manuscript in November and De-
        cember.

1943   Clark moves to New York City in late spring. Works as a door-
        man at the Hotel George Washington and joins the Hotel
        Front Service Employees Union, Local 144.

1947   Clark loses his hotel job. Sends Brown a series of letters asking for
        the return of his manuscript.

1949   Clark is taken to Bellevue Hospital on November 6 and admitted
        to Manhattan State Mental Hospital on November 15.

1955   Clark is released from the hospital on June 9, returns to Loui-
        siana.

1960s   Clark moves to New Orleans, lives with sister Caroline.

1974   Clark dies in New Orleans on May 15.

REMEMBER MY SACRIFICE

We shall know the truth, And the truth shall make you free.
Remember my sacrifice.
— Clinton Clark

ARKANSAS

• Greenville

N

LOUISIANA

MISSISSIPPI

Wisner•

Natchitoches•

• Port Gibson

Ferriday•
Vidalia• Natchez
Sibley

• Woodville

Cheneyville• Simmesport• Torras
Lettsworth•

POINTE
COUPEE
PARISH

Ville Platte• Palmetto•
Melville•
Opelousas• Fordoche•

• Baton Rouge

Lafayette• White
Castle

New
Orleans

TEXAS

Atchafalaya River

Mississippi River

0   50 kilometers
0   50 miles

Map by Mary Lee Eggart

Clinton Clark's Louisiana

1 | We Had to Go Off from Home

I was born march the 5, 1903 on a plantation in pointe coupee parish in the little town of Fordoche Louisiana. It was only at the age of nine that I first became conscious of the world, and the experience which initiate me into it was tragedy.[1] My mother was now alone with seven children to suport, I was the youngest boy in the family.[2] Condition were just as bad with us in those days as it were in 1932. I would go to school in the little town. The school were held in a little church house. My older brothers would work out at a little stave mill for one dollar a day. I would some time play hooky in order to catch a drummer to drive for the liberty stable man, which he would pay 50¢ for one drive. I would make the 50¢ and give it to my mother to help feed our family. When the drive were to far, I couldn't get back before the school was out. The liberty stable manager would talk it over with my mother for me.

I continue going to school until I was through my grammer. My parents were anxious for me to go to school, because they wanted me to become a preacher. I had in mine to become a teacher. Our teacher would always tell us to do great things to make people like us. She would read great story of some hero. When she would be reading the story, my hair would rise on my head. I would say to myself if I could do great things like that man. Many times I would repeat the story to my parents as if I was making a speech to a large group of people. My mother is

1. The wording of this sentence is drawn from the opening of Angelo Herndon's autobiography, *Let Me Live*.

2. Bridget Lewis Clark (1870–1949) had seven children: Houston, Orelia, Walter, Arthur, Roger, Clinton, and Caroline (who was also known as Elmonia). She also raised Houston's daughter Beatrice. She spoke mainly Creole French. Her great-granddaughter Veronica Carey remembers that she could sing beautifully and was very religious, serving as a deaconess in her church. Carey recalls her great-grandmother as having Indian features and long, full hair that stretched down her back. By 1930, she had moved to Palmetto in St. Landry Parish and lived in the household of Nick Davenport, husband of her daughter Caroline, with her granddaughter Beatrice and Beatrice's husband Willie Overton. She died in Melville in 1949.

a french decent. She was born in a little town of Villeplate, Louisiana. My father who is also a french decent born in a farming town of Villeplate La. He was a preacher the pastor of four churches. He died in 1940. Thousand of poor farmers went to see him put away.[3]

I was told by many poor farmers after his death that he was the only preacher in their community that would help them to build their community up. That he would always try to help his people, so that he could have a good name in his community amond the poor farmers. At one time at his home the people in the community came to-gather to raise money to build a school house. When they called a meeting to talk over the matters of raising the money for the school, my father spoke up in the meeting and said I will write out a check for $200 for this school to be built. Every body was shocked, and wanted to know how could he do that. He was as poor as they was and a poor farmer too. Although he was a preacher, and would never except collection from his members of his churches.

Now as I was the youngest boy in the family and never had the oppertunity to see my father, but would pray that some day, I would learn to know something about his life. Our grandmother use to come home and cheer us children up. She would bring us candy. She was the mother of 8 or 10 children and she would go and stay in rotation with her children. Grandmother would come home the most of the times because we didn't have a father to look after. We was found of her because she would teach us how to talk french. She was also found of me because she said I look like a preacher. She would tell me to have faith in the lord. And said pray son. Some day you may become a preacher. And she said son, Dont never follow bad company. The people will like you. And it will be easy for you to become a leader.

She couldn't speak so well. She would talk real bad broken language. But we understood her language well.[4] And we was found of her because we thought she was so funny when she would talk to us.

3. Census records suggest that Arthur Clark (1869–1940) had left the family by 1910 and possibly before 1907, when Clinton Clark would have been three or four years old. He was ordained by the New Hope Baptist Church, under the Western Seventh District Missionary Baptist Association, on August 16, 1929. His certificate of ordination remains in the family. His parents were John and Cydalise Clark, who lived in Lafayette, Louisiana, at the time of the 1880 census. On his death certificate, Arthur Clark's birthplace is given as Broussard, Louisiana. He died in Ville Platte in 1940 of heart failure.

4. Clark's paternal grandmother was Cydalise Clark, who was a French speaker and had at least eleven children. We have not identified his maternal grandmother.

My teacher would write out peom for me to read in concerts, and I would go to sunday school and read my peom amond the other little children. This would make me feel great to have the oppertunity to stand before the other children as if I had become that great hero my teacher had being reading about in school. My grandmother would always take me to church with her. I would also go to sunday school ever sunday. My youngest sister, Caroline Clark, I would call her Carry for a short name. We would start out for the school in the morning some time with out a nickel to buy cakes for our lunch.[5] We would eat before leaving a few pan cakes. We call them flap jacks. With syrup. And that would have to last us all day. We hardly ever seen any fruit. Only on saturdays my mother, Bridget Clark, would go to the little town and bring us children back a few sticks of candy and maybe a bag of peanut. We hardly known what fruit was. Only some time when I would go to the little town and started playing with a little Itatlian boy, and he would run in his father store and bring me out a couple of banana to eat. I will never forget those days. The little Itatlian boy, I still can remember his name, Little Luke. We was good pal. We lived three miles from the Itatlian store, and at that time was the only store in Fordoche Louisiana. The Itatlian man name was John Pat. He would always pass home in his cart with all kinds of candy and fruit. We didn't have any money to buy anything from the Itatlian man when he would pass by. And my little sister and myself had to walk seven miles through the fields down a little weedy dirt road with no shoes on our feets. Some time we had to run so fast from snakes until we would losed our books, and had to get some of the grown people to go and get them for us. We was living on the man plantation by the name of Mr. Leon Porch, who at that time claim he was as poor as we

5. Clark's younger sister Caroline (Carolina in some records) was born in 1907 in Fordoche. She was his close companion in childhood and cared for him many times during his adult life. She was a petite woman with tremendous energy. When Caroline was a child, the family worked hard to see that she received as much education as possible. The 1930 census lists her as married to Nick Davenport and living in Palmetto with her husband, mother, niece, and niece's husband. She moved to Sacramento in the early 1930s, where Clinton lived with her in late 1931 and 1932. She later lived with a cousin in Chicago, where she did domestic work. She returned to Louisiana when her mother became sick in the 1940s.

In Melville, Louisiana, Caroline married her second husband, Columbus Cook, who worked in the local sawmill. For many years, Caroline wouldn't go beyond her yard. She and Clinton moved to New Orleans in the early 1960s, staying with her niece Beatrice Overton on Spain Street and later moving together to a house on Arts Street. Caroline never divorced Cook, but he stayed in Melville when she moved to New Orleans. She died in New Orleans on March 5, 2001.

was. And I can remember when we had to cook hard corn on the fire half. We didn't have no stove to cook our food on. And it wasn't much we had to cook any way. So why have a stove. And not only one time we had to cook that hard corn to eat it happen many times. Only we had a couple of good rabbit dogs, and where ever these dogs would jump a rabbit they would be sure to get him or put the rabbit in a hollow tree where some one out of the family could get him. And if we wasn't around when the dogs tree the rabbit, their wouldn't move from the tree until someone from the house would get there. These dogs had a good sign to let us know when their had a rabbit in a hollow tree. This sign was, one dog would stay at the tree and watch the rabbit, and the other dog would come home and make funny noise. And we understood their signs, and some body would leave the house, and the dog would take the lead so you could follow him. Some time my sister and myself would have smoked rabbit to take to school with us for our lunch. And the liberty stable man who was the sherriff at that time, he only had two boys to drive the buggys and carry drummers to different places.[6] And some time these boys would be going out on a drive, and there would be a drummer waiting in a hurry. I was the extria driver on my spare times, and in a case like that, we needed the money so badly to get something to eat for our family. I would make an agreement with my little sister when I would play hooky from school. I would tell her, If you dont tell on me, I will give you a nickel when I get back. The liberty stable mananger would be waiting for me out side of the school distent where the school teacher could not see him. One day our teacher did find it out and she gave me a real good punishment. I then checked up on playing hooky from school, and my mind became much closer on my books. My sister and myself went hungry to the school many days, but would never stop going to school. Our grandmother would tell me, Son try to learn all you can. It will help you in the future and you will become to be some service to your race some day. I will never forget my grandmother, because she would always tell us good thing of life. She would tell us of the slave days from away back younger. Many of her words still ring in my ear. She would say, Never say I cant. Just keep on trieing. My grandmother was full blooded french decent. Could not speak but a very little broken language. Every time she would say something to us, she would speak in

6. Clark's use of "liberty stable" for *livery stable,* a stable that rents out horses and carriages, is perhaps a confusion of French and English.

french. So we had learn to understand ever thing she would say, and that was the way the most of us children learn to speak french. When my father was the pastor of the Mamu B C Church, he had to preach to all his members in french because no one in that community could understand American english. So my father could preach to them in french. And my father was the pastor of four church and each community was all french decent. No one in the community could speak english.

In these community where my father was the pastor of those churches the big planters would work the sharecroppers for 25¢ a day. The women had to work in the planters house for $1.50 a week and one quart of milk and most of the time would have to work from 6 O.Clock until 10 P.M. And until this day the women are still getting $1.50 a week. Their have to clean the house and wash all the cloths and go in the fields and hoe when their get the work done around the house. And in these community if you dont say Yes Sir and No Sir to the White man or the White women, the mob will be sure to get you and take you in the woods and put you in a tree. At one time around Villeplatte La. one of the planter had sold one quart of milk to a Negro sharecropper and the planter claim that the sharecropper hadn't paid for the milk. And the sharecropper said he had paid the planter for the milk. So the planter said that a nigger called him a lie. The planter went home and came back with two more planters with shot guns, and kill the poor sharecroppers and left his poor widow with 10 children to suport. And nothing was every did about the matter, and no Negroes was allow to say anything about the killing. If any one would be caught saying something about this killing the same would happen to them. And if any contractor would come through there putting up some kind of job, no Negroes would be allow to work on the job. The contractor would have to hire White or the contractors would catch hell with the mob gang. So the Negroes never knew anything about working on public jobs, nothing but plantation work for 40¢ and 35¢ a day working from dark to dark.

To day around this section you cant find four Negro sharecroppers out of ever hundred can sign his own name. It just happen there laterly that they can have school for the sharecroppers children and the way the children have to go its not much they can learn in the school out in this part of Louisiana.

But the sharecroppers are still looking to the good lord. That the day shall come when the bottom rail shall come on top, and the top rail shall come on the bottom.

In 1912, it was a flood in our section of the state. The water taking everything we had and drowned out our crop. All the poor farmers was on charity. We would almost starve, because it was so little relief that was giving to the poor Negroes.[7] So after the flood, we made one more crop. And I continue going to school ever day with no shoes on my feet. I only remember having one pair shoes and I had to wear them only sundays, because there wasn't much money to keep the family living. When I was fifteen years old and had finish grammer school, my parents was to poor to send me to the high school because there were no money to pay for my cloths and transportation. I began to look for work to help support our family. And I did found a job working for a truck farmer for 50¢ a day. My brothers was working at a stave mill. And my sisters work in the field. It still wasn't much money to live on. My brothers who was working at the stave mill would only receive one dollar a day. And when the mill closed down and it wasn't no more work to do in the fields, we had to look for another job. We had one uncle living up in a large plantation section near the little town of Cheneyville Louisiana. So our uncle came and explained to our mother how we could make a lots of cotton money. So we packed up and move on this plantation and made our first crop there.[8] And when settlement times came, we still owe the planter. My older brother left to look for a job in a saw mill. When he made a couple of pay days, he came back on this plantation where we had made the crop, as he had left us on this plantation without money to live on. So as he had made enough money working at the saw mill, he move us back to our home town Fordoche La. And there we seen it was no use to farm any more. So we the boys thought to do public work. And after we moved back home, my brother taking me back with him to the little saw mill town, St. Mource La, to see if he could get a job for me doing some thing easy around the saw mill. I was only fifteen years old at that time. And in those days it didn't seem to make no different in your age to work on a public

7. In 1912, a crevasse in the Mississippi River levee at Torras, about thirty miles north of Fordoche, flooded the entire basin of the Atchafalaya River, including all of Pointe Coupee Parish. The floodwaters filled everything between the high land along the Mississippi west to Bayou Teche. Railroads and highways in the region were closed for months (Kemper, *Rebellious River,* 97–98).

8. The 1920 census places Bridget Clark and her family in Cheneyville, which is to the northwest of Palmetto and Melville, in Rapides Parish. The household included James Lewis; Bridget's nephew Wilson Lewis; her children Houston, Roger, Clinton, and Caroline; her granddaughter Beatrice; and a boarder.

jobs. My brother talked with the forman about getting me a job. The forman hire me. He give me the job walking lumber stack.

This job was a little to hard for a fellow of my age. My brother and the lumber stackers talk the matter over with the forman. The forman then agreed to give me a water bucket carring water to the workman on the job. I receive $1.65 for 10 hour day work. One day my brother layed off for a rest. And when he would lay off, I would lay off myself, because I wanted to be around my brother all the time. And my brother wanted to keep me from getting hurt on the job.

My brother Roger Clark was his name.[9] He would always draw my pay envelope alone with his pay envelope. So that was on a Friday when My brother and I layed off the job for rest. On that Saturday when My brother went to get our pay envelope, the forman started an agurement with him because he lay off the job without asking the forman. The forman then refuse to give my brother our pay envelope. My brother went to see the Supt. about the matter. And the Supt. refuse to give consideration on the matters, and the Supt. left the matter to the forman to settle. My brother went back to see the forman. The forman told my brother he would give him our money when he went back to work. My brother said its no use to continue the agurement we will leave here and go some where els and get another job. We left on a monday for McNary La, where it was a big saw mill seat. When we arrived there my brother had friends living there. So we spend the night with my brother friends and their helped us in getting a job immediately. My brother did went to work immediately. And in the next couple of days, I went to work walking lumber stack in the lumber yard. I made it pretty good for a couple of weeks walking the lumber stack, until the forman gave me a much harder job, handing lumber to the lumber stacker. My brother tried to get the forman to give me an easy job for a while. When the forman refuse to do so, my brother told me

9. Clark's brother Roger (1899–1970) was the second-youngest son in the family. As a young man, Roger moved to Melville to work at a mill. He owned a home there at the time of the 1927 flood (which they called the Melville flood). The high water forced the entire town onto the levees. In the 1950s, Roger Clark owned and operated a grocery store in Melville. He was the only African American in the area with a station wagon and ran a transportation service, driving people between towns such as Opelousas and New Orleans. He operated the local saloon, where gambling was among the attractions. The town was much larger in the 1950s; it had a railroad station and was a center of activity for the area. Railroad workers would stay there for weeks at a time while doing repairs on the tracks. Roger Clark died in 1970 in Melville.

it would be best to go back home, because the work was to hard for me. When I went home, I began to look for light work. I went to work with an Itatlian man on a ice truck for 75¢ a trip. This was a summer job. In the fall the boys from home and myself would go on the cane harvest near the little town of White Castle La. The wages was 80¢ a day from sun to sun. This was my first time to cut cane and it was very hard for me to keep up with the group. The boys from home would help me to keep up my row until I would get on to the job. I thank if I can stop remember the first year cutting cane was 1919. We would go cut cane every year. Some time we would go to different cane farm because we would look for the ones who would pay the most money for the cane cutting, where the wages would be much better. But some time would fine worst as low as 60¢ a day with one meal. In 1923 and in 1924 the standard oil Co. passed through our home town putting down pipe line. The Company was hireing every body who wanted to work cutting trees, cleaning up riderways for the pipe line. The wages were $2 a day for 10 hour hard days work. I was lucky to get a job, as in those days it didn't seem to make no different about a miner going to work on public jobs. We worked six hard months until we met with another gang who was coming from the northern part of Louisiana, then we was all layed off. For few more months, the Company would tell us that their would soon open up another job. We would stick around home working on plantation for 75¢ a day from sun to sun, until we could get back on the pipe line job again, where we could make a little more money. Only the pipe line was a part time job. The Company would hire thousand of labors so they could wine up the job in four or five months. The pipe line would always wine the job in a short time. At one time the Company had a big job up in Arkansas. The Company would get train loads of labors to take up to this job. I would always follow the gang. This job was located near the little town of Ash Town, Ark. The Company would furnish tents for the labors to sleep. We were getting the same $2 a day on this job for real hard work. 10 hours. Long days. No over time paid for your over time work. Some would dig ditches, some haul pipe and cut down trees. In this section the Negroes was not allowed to work. Those White people was Negro hater. One night a group of mobs ganged around our tents and made several shots with buck shots shell into our tents. Several workmen was wounded but not critically. The Company was forced to call out the trooper for protection, to guard the labors on the job. Things was so danger the labors couldn't go to the little town to get anything. One day the troopers taking a couple of labors to the little town to get some things their needed, and the trooper and one of the labors was shot down. It was so dangers for the Negroes there until most of them left the job. It was a small group of us stuck with the job. We drew up a plain to get togather and ask the forman for more money are else we would leave the job. So the wages was raised immediately. We then receive $3.50 a day. And time and a half for all over time. So we stuck with this job until we was out of reach of the mobs town. So the forman taking a likeing of my work. He said to me you are a mighty young man to be so brave. He then gave me a job, forman over a riderway gang. When I left this job, I had made a little stake of money to make our family happy for the winter. When I went back home it was during the winter. I went to work in the woods cutting stave bolts for $1.50 a day for a few weeks, until the sugar cane harvest open up.[10] During that time the river was rising. Every body was looking for the levee to break at any time. The Achafalaya river was a very strong courrent river. At that time the people was not so civilized. Each side of the river had to put men with guns on the levee to watch all night and day.

The planters began to get busy forceing every poor Negro and White farmers to go work free of charge on the levee. The boys and myself at our home town drew up a plan. We said, We will not work unless the planters will agree to pay us for our time we worked on the levee. The depuety Sherriff send word to every worker around the community to meet the truck to go work on the levee. We Negro worker was all ready to go work on the levee, but we wanted to see the Sherriff before we went to work on the levee. So we fine out that the sherriff was going ahead of the truck. We loaded on the truck and went to the levee. When we reached the levee, we asked the forman would we get pay for our work. He immediately became angry and told us to go to work. We refuse to go to work unless we get some consideration. One of the big planter came up to me. As I spoke up for our right, he said to me, You! S O B. You thank you are a smart nigger dont you! And rapped me in the mouth a couple of time with his fist. I immediately gave him back the same licks. One of my friend who was as big as the planter was taking my place. He pop the planter over the head with a club, then we all Negro and White had a battle for more then a half hour. One of my friend taking a piece of iron and tap the sherriff over his head. The sherriff fell to the ground, my friend

---

· 10. Stave bolts were forty-inch sections of logs that were split into quarters and then sawed into staves, the lumber used to make barrels.

taking the sherriff gun and started running. Then we all followed him through the woods. And the gang came behind us with shot guns shooting toward us. We made our exscape all night long through the woods.

The next day, we went to Baton Rouge La. That same night the levee broke and the water spread all over the country, and the Governor sent train out to get the poor people to take them to Baton Rouge where they had camps for them. Thousand of poor farmers was pouring into the refugee camps to stay until the water would go down. I was worried about my mother and sister, didn't know if they would make it safe or not. Finely when the train came in Baton Rouge one night, my mother and sister was on this train along with hundreds of others. We had relatives living in Baton Rouge, and my mother and sister moved in with them to stay until the water would go back. This flood was in 1922.[11] I found a job during that time driving an ice cream wagon for one dollar a day. When the water went back, the planters came to get the sharecroppers. Some sharecroppers didn't wanted to go back to the plantation, so the planters called a meeting on the refugee camps ground. The planters had a Negro Professor to come and make a speech to the sharecroppers on the behalf of the planters.

The Professor made a long talk to the sharecroppers. He told the sharecroppers how wonderful their could make a living on the plantation if they would go back on the plantation. He told the sharecroppers some wonderful story about a sweet life they could live if they would go back with the planters.

These words sounded so good to the sharecroppers that every sharecroppers loaded on the planters trucks and went back home to the old slave plantation to try the planters out again. We had stop farming during that time. When I went back home, I went to work helping to build the town back up again where the flood had swept all the houses away in my home town. We receive one dollar a day for this work, working from sun to sun. After that job was finish some of the home boys and myself left for the State of Texas to work on the rice farm. The rice farmers was looking for as many labors as they could find to work on the rice farms. We found a job on the rice farm near the little town of Devel Texas. The

---

11. The Mississippi River flooded parts of Louisiana in 1922; however, many details of Clark's description of the flood's effects correspond closely to records of the forced labor, displacement of families, and geography of the river's 1927 flood. See, esp., Barry, *Rising Tide*, 160–67, 282–86; Kemper, *Rebellious River*, 95–110.

wages were $1.50 a day from sun to sun, I worked a while shocking rice. One day the forman walked up to me and said, Clark, You are a good worker. I have another job for you where you want have no boss. The forman put me on a truck with the truck driver. This driver was a Negro who had been driving for several years on this rice farm.

I helped the truck driver to load the sack rice and haul the rice to Beaumont Texas, and some time giveed the truck driver a left when he gets tired of driving. When the forman found out that I could drive a truck, he bought a new truck and started me out driving the new truck, and my wages was raised from $1.50 to $2 a day. We still had to work from sun to sun. We would sleep in shacks on the rice farm. The shacks was close to the forman house. There was 50 labors sleeping in these shacks. When any of the boys wanted to go to town, the forman would ask me to drive them in the truck. He didn't give me any extria pay for this work. But he would tell the labors to give me what every they wanted to. And later on, I became the shack boss. My job was to keep the labors in line and get them up on time in the morning to get they breakfast. We would get three meals in a day plus the $1.50. When we didn't get enough to eat, I would speak to the forman about the matter. Our forman wasn't a hard man to get along with. He would tell the cook to feed the boys and put enough for them to eat on the table. From that day on our forman seen to it that we had enough food to eat. He said, I know no man can give me a good days work when he is hungry. He was a very good forman. He would work along with his labors. And didn't rush no one on the job.

I worked two season. And he taking sick and died, then his brother in-law taking the job over. His brother inlaw was as mean as he could be. And when I went back to work for this man and found out that he was so disagreeable, I left the rice farm that season and went back home. I then went to work on the sugar cane farm during that winter. On the cane farm the wages was 75¢ a day from darn to dark. We would get one meal a day and we had to sleep in some old broken down shack. If it rain in the night we couldn't sleep. During these years, I did a lots of thinking of how hard a poor working man had to suffer for his family living. Just to think of it, we had to go off from home to find jobs. The only jobs we could find was either rice plantation or sugar cane plantation. And that job was only in the fall of the year.

Are else we had to get on the slave plantation and work from sun to sun for 60¢ a day, and I had made up in my mind to never work on another slave plantation.

I would rather starve then to slave on those plantation where the ridding boss would be over you all day long on his horse keeping in step with you. Most of my sugar cane farm and rice farm work was from 1922–27–28. In 1929 I went to Texas again. I stopped in Beaumont Texas to look for work where I had some relative living. I would get up early every morning hit the street looking for work. After 8 a.m. you would have to be off the street or the police sure to put you in jail. Findly I found a job with a contractor who was building the Edson hotel. The contractors needed truck drivers to haul gravel. The wages was 35¢ a hour. So I gotten a job driving a T model ford. Some time the truck would break down, and I had to work on the truck for some time. More then a half a day trying to get the ford started again, and I didn't get any pay for the time I worked on the truck. When I protested to the forman about my pay for the time I had worked on the truck, he treated to fire me, and later on my wages was cut to 25¢ an hour. I was the only Negro truck driver. The White truck driver would get 50¢ an hour, and the Negroes had to be at speed all the time while on the job.

And if their didn't the forman would sure fire them off the job. When we would get off work at night, I couldn't hardly sleep from the rush the forman would keep us in all day.

Again when I protested to the forman about raising my wages, the next day he gave my truck to a white worker and put me on one of the hardest job. It was for the same 25¢ an hour, so I immediately quit the job. And I went and asked for my time check. The forman told me to come back saturday and get my time. That was on a monday when I quit the job. When saturday came, I went and drewed my pay envelope and taking the first train out that was headed toward my home town. And when I arrived home, the only work could be find was on the big plantation for 60¢ from sun to sun. The only chance you had getting on public jobs was when the standard Oil Co. would open up new jobs putting down pipes. Or you could go in the woods and cut trees from sun to sun, for one dollar a day. So I went to work on the plantation for 60¢ a day. I hated to do that, because I knew that 60¢ a day couldn't buy enough to eat for one person and was much harder to feed a family on that amount. And buy shoes and clothes. I had one little sister who we wanted to continue going to school. And my parents were anxious for me to go to school. They wanted us to get an education. Because during those days the rural schools terms was very short, we Negroes would only get three months schooling in each season. And too the condition were so bad for the poor farmers, because the planters would refuse to give the sharecroppers money for the crops they would make during the year no matter how much cotton the sharecroppers would make. The times was no better with the sharecroppers if the cotton was selling for 40ç a pound. The planters always had his robberserry to take what his sharecroppers made each year in the fields.[12]

12. Throughout the narrative, Clark uses "robberserry" instead of *commissary* to describe plantation stores. Planters paid sharecroppers in script good only at these stores, which charged high prices and gave credit at high interest rates, keeping sharecroppers continually in debt. The word (also spelled "robbissary") is also used by other LFU activists in their newsletter articles, one example of how the language of Clark's union organizing is present in the language he used to write his life story.

In 1930 when the depression became worst, I started traveling. I hitch hike to New Orleans, La. When I arrived in New Orleans, I went over to my aunte home.

And she was to glad to see me in the city out of the old plantation, because she knew all about the plantation system. It was time that she would write to her relatives on the plantation, and urge them to move into the city, where they could make a much better living then on the plantation system. When I began to tell my aunte about the condition on the plantation around home, she would listen with tears coming from her eyes. She would start talking angry about the plantation system, because at one time she had been cheated out of her crop by these same planters.[13]

She began to show me some hands bills that some workers had thrown on her porch. I began to read the hand bill careful over and over again. I can still remember some of the words that was on the hand bill. The first few words read something like this, The workers are not responsible for their condition. The boses are the ones responsible for the workers suffering. All workers must come to a meeting tonight. All workers must attend this meeting. My aunte urge me to attend this meeting. She also agree to go with me to the meeting.[14] The Meeting was being held in a Negro church about three blocks from where my aunte was living. My aunte and myself left for the meeting about the time we thought the meeting would began. It was 9.30 P.M. when we came near the meeting place.

13. The 1930 census records Clark's aunt as Olice Mallery, born about 1894, and living in New Orleans with her second husband, James Mallery, and her six children. She was Clark's father's sister. Rodney Clark remembers that most of his family pronounced her name as the English *Alice*, a few as the more French-sounding *Olice*. Clark's 1974 obituary names her as Alice Patman.

14. This might have been a meeting of the Marine Workers' Industrial Union, organized by the Communist Trade Union Unity League, or a meeting of an Unemployed Council, which was also active in New Orleans in the first years of the 1930s. The Marine Workers' Industrial Union led a strike of New Orleans dockworkers in February 1931; 115 strikers, mostly black, were arrested (Solomon, *The Cry Was Unity*, 125).

A mass of people was standing out side of the church looking on. We began looking over in to the group to see if the speaker would be making his speech out side of the church, just come to think of it. There was a group of cops inside of the church arresting the leader of this meeting. Also the minster was arrested. Several White and Negro workers was arested togather. They was all taking to the First preceint for investagation and was released the next day. That was one of the most excitement that I had every seen before. I never did sleep that night and many more nights for thinking what was going to bring about the new changeing world. Would the working people had to shed their blood to bring about the change, or would we have a new Governor to bring the change as Abraham Lincoln did during the civil war to free the slaves. I had no idea that the working people had to organize to bring about this change themselves.

That was one meeting I had never forgotten, because I was so anxious to get to hear the speaker. Many days when I would be walking in the street looking for work, my mind would never get off that meeting.

Findly one day I found a job with the water work Co. The wages was 25¢ an hour digging ditches for the water pipes. I worked for this Company three months. My next job was in a filling station repairing used cars. I was hired as a helper for $12 a week. I worked on this job for several months. One of the business mananger, Mr. H. Gilmore, was working for the American & Steel wire cooperative Co.

He was out of Birmingham Ala. He had been taking his car to this filling station for service. So Mr. Gilmore asked me to come to Birmingham with him to take the job driving his father. His father name Mr. J. J. Gilmore was the General mananger of the American Steel Co. at Birmingham Ala. Mr. Gilmore also own a large plantation in Ala. I went to Birmingham and taking the job driving Mr. Gilmore. He give me $10 a week. Mr. Gilmore would some time have me to drive him over the plantation section. When we would be driving along the plantation road and the sharecroppers would be hoeing the cotton, Mr. Gilmore would wave his hand toward the sharecroppers. The sharecroppers would all drop their hoes to wave back toward Mr. Gilmore. He said to me, You see, Clinton, thats the way to make them feel good and work well. Mr. Gilmore would some time have me to drive him to New York & Mich., New Orleans. I had been working for six month, and he taking sick and died with the heart attack. One week after his death, I then returned back to New Orleans and went over to see Mr. Harold

Gilmore, the son of Mr. J J. Gilmore. I went to see him about getting me another job. He then recommend me to one of his friend who was running a small animal hospital. He gave me a job night watching the hospital for $7 a week. The hospital was locate on Corondolet st.

The job was good but the wages was not enough to live on. I tried several time to get a raise. But there was a poor chance because there were several more worker there working for the same wages and did not protest for better wages. And too the Negroes at that time had no idea of what it mean to stick togather and fight for better wages. I worked in the hospital for several weeks and quit. Went to the sugar cane plantation to make the harvest. The wages then was on the sugar cane farm was $1 a day, with three meals. At that time the sugar cane worker had no idea they could get thing done by sticking togather into a union.

In the fall of 1931, the big sugar cane planters organize themselves together and forced all worker into the sugar cane fields, regardless where they would be find on the streets or the highway. And they would receive 60¢ a day from sun to sun, hard labor. At that time you could see workers from all parts of the country traveling on frieght trains going from town to town looking for work they could not find. I didn't like the idea of the big sugar canes planters forceing the workers out into the sugar cane fields to work for 60¢ a day. So one day I left out from New Orleans on a frieght train headed for the State of Calif. where one of my sister had being living for fifteen years and was a tax payer in the state of Calif.

And also my youngest sister had went over there and wrote back to me to come there, that I may be lucky enough to find a job. When I climb into a box car on the frieght train, there were several more young men on the frieght train, White and Negroes. There I met with a young White man who was from New York. We made friend immediately, because he was on his way to the same City I was going to, Sacaremento Calif. All the way through the sugar cane plantation, we had to dodge the cops, because the cops was pulling every body down off the frieght train, and forceing them on the cane plantation to work for 60¢ and one meal. We would get off the frieght train befor we would get to close to town, and walk on the other end of the town, and wait for the frieght to get a new start for the next town. My friend that I had met from New York had a lots of exsperience on traveling. He seem to know just what to do to keep the cops off of us. My friend had a little money and when we would get off the frieght in some town, he would get lunch and cigarette for both of us. I didn't know just how to take this young White fellow for being so friendly with a Negro. And as I had been hated by his kind all my life. But I had been told lots of time about most of the White worker who knowes no different in the color, and that he was one of them from New York City. When the frieght train reached Beaumont Texas, I told my friend we better get down before we get into the City limit. My friend said it was no use to get down we might get left in the town. So when the frieght train crossed the bridge into the City limit, two big cops call us down off the frieght. And fifteen other boys that was on the same frieght train. The cops taking us over to the City jail house and told us they would keep us for investagation. The next day we was released at 9 a.m. and was told to get out of town immediately. My same little friend and I hitch hike on the highway until we reach Houston Texas. Then we taking another frieght train headed for El Paso Texas. We hop a freight train that night about 11 p.m. and in a couple of days we arrived in El Paso Texas. We left the line of Texas that same day we arrived in El Paso. We then went through the State of Mexico and Arz. In two more days we arrived in Los Angle Calif. We was again put in Los Angle City jail for 24 hours, then was released and told to get out of the City in 2 hours. I was still sticking with my little friend from New York City. We was six days getting to Sacarmento Calif. where one of my sister was living.[15] We arrived in Sacarmento 3 a.m. in the morning. When we was leaving the frieght yard, there was a great big cop we ran into. He stopped us and said to us where are you boys going too. I showed him my sister address and my friend showed him some of his identification papers. The cop told us to go over to the labors centers hall and stay until day light. And there where my friend and myself split up. He grasped my hands and held them tight for a long time talking about our trip togather on the frieght train. He was such a good little fellow. I hated to depart from him. That morning when I was leaving my friend, he asked me did I needed any money. No my friend, I said to him, I have a sister living here. And I think I can get along alright now. My friend insisted and put a $5 bill into my coat pocket. I just couldn't make him take the money back. He gave me his address where he lived up in New York. He said he wouldn't be in the State of Calif. very long. And when we was leaving each other, he said, Clinton, Remember me while you are learning all you can. I said to my friend I will never forget about you. When I was walking down the street on my way to my sister house, I was trying

15. His younger sister Caroline was living in Sacramento, California.

to thank to myself. And said wonder what kind of White fellow he was. And would wonder if all the White people up in New York was the same as he was. When I reached my sisters house, she was wondering how did I made it all the way from Louisiana to the State of Calif. without money. She looked at me just as uncerned, as if I wasn't her brother. She went in the kitchen and fixed me some bath water. And after I had cleaned up, she said, Now you look like my brother, Clinton Clark. After I was in Sacramento Calif. for a couple of days, I hoped another frieght train and went to Oroville Calif. where my oldest sister was living. And too she was a property owner and tax payer in the state of Calif.[16] She had been in the state of Calif for more then fifteen years. And during all that time she hadn't seen me. She was the mother of three boys. The oldest boy was seventeen years old. She had lost her husband and was a widow. And was living on the rent of three houses she had rented out to the workers. When I arrived in Oroville Calif, I thought to have a little fun with my sister, as I know she wouldn't know me. When she left home, I was a little fellow. When I went to her house, I knocked on the door like a stranger. When she came to the door, I said hello! Mrs! Will you please give a poor fellow something to eat, I am so hungry. She said, I am sorrie mister. I dont have anything cook at the present. I will give you some flour and lard. And you can go over to that jungler over there where those other hoboes are. And cook for yourself. I said, I am sorrie, Mrs. But I can't cook. It will be no use for me to waste your food like that. She said that the best I can do for you this time Mister. She went back into the house. And one of the boys came on the porch. And I started a conversation with him. I asked him did he knew a young lady by the name of Caroline Clark. He said yes! That my Aunte. I asked him did he knew an old lady by the name of Mrs Bridget Clark, that lived way down south. He said Yes! That my grandmother! The boy immediately turn around and went back in the house and called his mother. And said mother! That man knows our Aunte and our grandmother. My sister immediately called me into the house. And said Mister, You know my mother and sister. Who is you and where is you come from any way. I said to her, I am from way down south. Some where around your home

16. Clark's older sister Orelia O'Quinn (1891–1974) and her husband had moved to Oroville, California, about sixty miles north of Sacramento, where they first worked in a cannery, then opened a general store. Orelia was widowed with two sons, Freddie and Gailon, when Clark arrived in California. The census records show that she owned her home, was widowed, had married at age fifteen, was able to read and write, and was working as a laundress at her home. She lived the rest of her life in Oroville.

town. She wouldn't take her eyes off me. She said out quick, Is that my brother Clinton Clark. I then began to smile. My sister then jump from her feet and put her arm around me and held me for more then five minute. She immediately went to the telephone and called up all her friends and told them that she would have a party tonight. That night we had all kinds of cakes chicken fruit to eat. The house was pack with White and Negroes. My sisters friends seem to be anxious to see a southrener. Every body would ask me question about the south. I couldn't tell them much because I was so excited and too it was my first time to be together with both White and Negroes dancing and playing cards together. My sister had a piano in her house and a young White man to do the playing. In this little town of Oroville Calif. both White and Negroes was friendly to each other and would always stick together much better then any other town I ever went to in the state of Calif. I spent one week in Oroville Calif. Then I returned back to Sacarmento Calif. where I was to located a job. The time when I enter the State of Calif. was the latter part of 1931. Work was just as hard to find in the State of Calif. as it was in the south. My sister who lived in Sacarmento Calif. was out of work and was living on Charity. One night sitting to our lunch table, my sister and I began discussion on jobs and the condition. She began to tell me what the White and Negro working people was doing to get some help from the relief authority. She would tell me how their get together and go before the relief agents and demand relief. And would get it. And she showed me a couple of leaflet that was thrown on her porch. This leaflet was sign by the worker unemployed council and was calling all unemployed workers to attend a meeting and to organize and fight for relief. And there was to be a hungry march very soon. I immediately began to look for the workers headquarter. One day I came back home when I had been looking for a job. My sister gave me another leaflet that she had found on the porch. This leaflet was calling all unemployed workers to a meeting that night. My sister and I went to this meeting for our first time to attend a workers meeting. When we went into the meeting a White worker met us at the door and asked us to have a seat. It was about three hundred workers in this meeting of all races. The meeting began at 8 p.m. The first speaker was a long tall White worker. He would take his time when he was talking. I liked the way he address the workers. He said, Friends and fellow workers. We are thrown out on the street to starve, when we have built the City and produced the great wealth of this country. Yes we are going to fight for our right no matter how the cause may be. If we are out of jobs it is no fault of ours. When he was talking, I was making up my mind to join with them and help to fight the battle for the working people right. When the meeting was over, one White worker came over to me and shaked my hands and asked me question, as it was his first time to see me in their meeting. I began to tell him how I enjoyed the meeting and how I could become a member. He invited me to come to workers headquarter the next day. When I went home, I could not sleep for thinking about what the speaker had said and it was true. We had built up the country to where it was and was thrown out on the street to starve, and it was no fault of our own. The next morning I went over to the workers unemployed council headquarter. When I went into their hall, there was workers of both races, Negro and White, sitting around reading and smoking cigarettes. I was walking around in the hall looking up on the wall where there was pictures of all kinds and clipping from the workers papers. One White worker came over to me and hand me over a paper to read and said to me, Have a seat this is the workers hall. I began to ask him question about the worker movement and what I had to do to join with them. He then told me that if I was unemployed, I was already a member. Then he began to tell me of the condition and what we workers had to do to better their condition. I then told him that I wanted to get relief. He said you will have to get together with more workers who are unemployed and go before the relief authority and tell them your condition. This worker gave me the imformation very clearly. When I went home this time my sister and I would talk over the matter for hours until late up in the night. We would have the workers papers to read of what was happening in other parts of the countrys, and what the workers was doing to better their condition in other parts of the countrys. I would go to the workers hall every day. And every wednesday night was the workers regular meeting night, that would be the night they would have floor discussion. Any workers regardless of his color of race, he or she could speak their opinion. I became more and more interested in the workers movement. One morning when I went to the workers hall, they was forming up a group to go before the relief agents. I was immediately elected to go with this group and was the only Negro in this group. When we went into the relief office, there stood a big belly White hair lady. She said now what you fellow wants. Our leader said we wants relief. She said, We dont have no relief today. You will have to come back another day. Our leader said when that day will be. We dont have nothing to eat now. And she said, I don't know will let you know later. We then went back to the workers hall and had another meeting. And we promased when we would go back again to not let the relief agents pass the buck over us. The next morning, we send another group, and as I again was the only Negro in the hall, I was elected. And we went again to see the relief agents. When we went into the relief office, here come the same old white hair women. I can still remember her name, Mary Judge. She said haven't I told you all that we dont have no relief on hand. Our leader said you havening told us anything about not having no relief. She said wasn't you all here yesterday. Our speaker said no. Then Mary Judge went back into the office and said something to one of the other relief agents, then she came back and call three of the workers out of our group into her office. We was waiting for fifteen minuite. When our leader came back, they had sacks of flour for each one of us. In this group we were 12 in number. We got flour, meat, irish potatoes, sugar, lard. And we left with good spirit. I then wouldn't go back for four or five days. But we would send a different group every day, to let Mary Judge know that we didn't intend to starve. Mary Judge had on her mind if she gave us some relief once we would not go and bother her any more, and we had it the opposite way. If we got relief for one group of unemployed, we could get relief for all the unemployed. And too when we won our first relief more work-ers got interested in going in group to see Mary Judge for relief. We began to send different group to see Mary Judge so regular until she began to get angry with us. She called the police on one group of workers. But I was not in this group. The polices had put them out of the relief office with clubs, so we began to work out plained. The next group went to see Mary Judge. I was elected to go with this group. Before we left for the relief office, we elected two speaker to talk. And no other one was allowed to talk. Incase the cops wanted to talk to one of the work-ers in this group, he would point his finger toward the speaker. And say there is our speaker. And I was the only Negro in this group. I was elected to be one of the speaker. And we had planed to stick together no matter what happened. So we got in line like soilders and marched to see Mary Judge. When we went into the relief department, Mary Judge immediately went to the telphone and called the police headquarter. Then she came out to talk with us. She said didn't I tell you fellow I wasn't going to give you fellow any relief unless you come here like gentel-man, one by one at the time. And as I was one of the speaker, I spoke up and said, But we are all starving together, not one by one. The big cops had came in about that time. It was twelth, 12, big cops standing around looking and ready to start something at any momment. The White speaker spoke up and said to Mary Judge,

We came for relief as a citizen of the state of Calif. We will sleep here until we get consideration. Mary Judge became angry and told the cops to get us out. One big cop put his hands on our White speakers shoulder, and said you boys get going. The speaker knock the cop hands off his shoulder and said to the cop take your hands off my shoulder you may dirty my shirt. The cop then became angry and hit this worker over his head with his club. The worker give him one lick back in his face. When the cop came up with his club again to hit our speaker, I knock the club out of the cops hands. And another big cop was standing behind me. Pop me over the head with his black jack. Down to the floor I went with blood running in my face, and I didn't know anything until the next day. And when I did come to myself, I was looking through the bars in the jail house with the same group of workers that were in the relief department. And several other workers had blood on their shirts as I did. And one of the workers was in the hospital with his jaw bone broken from a lick the cops had gave him with his black jack. We was released that morning. When we went to the workers hall, I was pretty sick. One of the workers taking me to a Doctor. The Doctor bandage my head and treated me until I was in good position and ready to go again. The next day, we receive word from Mary Judge to come over to the relief office. When we got over to the relief office, Mary Judge had all kinds of relief ready for us. And too she told us to come every week and get our relief, and she gave us a card to go to work three days a week in the aeroplane fields. We receive $12 for this three days works. And receive our relief regular. We continue to hold everything we had won, and was organizing to win more. We elected a committee of two different group to work in different parts of the City to see where there was any poor workers was in need of relief. If we would find any who need relief, we would take them to see Mary Judge and get them on relief immediately. When I had went home from the jail with the blood on my shirt, my sister like to fainted. She beg me to not go and be with the workers movement any more, because she said I would be killed. I said to my sister don't worrie about me. Thats nothing. I have just begun. The battle isent over yet. We have a lots more to do. You too will have to join our ranks. She would write letters to my mother and our other sister in Oroville Calif. and try to get them to discourage me. They would write me and tell me, Boy you better let that thing along. I wouldn't thank about what they was saying. And I continue going to the workers meeting, and would keep in touch with Mary Judge.

We began to prepare for a mass meeting to be held in the City park. It was going to be held on a Saturday. I was appointed to be one of the speaker at the mass meeting. When I went home, I would try myself out. My sister had some friends that would come set up with her some night, and I would started an discussion with them on the condition, and the Experience I had during the time being in the state of Calif. I would stand on my feet and make a long speech to them, as if I was speaking to a hundred of people. And they would be taking it in and clapping their hands, and say that right Mister. I felt with great in couragement. And continue with my speech. I wouldn't hardly sleep in the night for I was repeating my speech over and over again through the night. That saturday the meeting began at 2 p.m. in the City park. I went to the meeting well prepared with my speech. When I walk into the park, there was more then five hundred people in the park. The Chairman was calling the first speaker to the stand, I was the third speaker. Before the Chairman called my name, he made a long talk on my work sence I had been in the state of Calif. Then he said the next speaker will be a Negro from a way down south. When he was talking I was trembling like a leaf on a tree. I just couldn't make up my mind to face those people. There was a race of all kind. The Chairman said the next speaker, Clinton Clark. When I went on the stand, I began to talk with a scared voice. In two minuite my scared had pass away. And I went ahead with my speech. I began to tell the trouble we had at the relief department with the cops and Mary Judge. Every time I would get to a point, the crowd would yelled and clap their hands so loud that they would drown out my voice. The chairman would have to stand up and waved his hands to the crowd. And said let him talk. When I came down off the stand, the workers crowded around me as if I had been playing base ball and had made a home run. After that day, I had more friend then I ever had before. The next morning the Capitalistic news papers carried our meeting on the head line. They had my name and age and some of my remarks. For times, I just couldn't get no rest, I was as busy as a bee, putting out leaflet. I would go some times 80 miles to distributed leaflet. The workers open up a school. I was one of the student. Our teacher was a lady. She was from San Francisco Calif. The school would started at 9 a.m. We had raised the money for the expenses. The school would close at 4 p.m. And the school last for four months. We would eat our lunch at a workers cafe. It was during the latter part of 1931 and all of 1932 that I was in the state of Calif. I had more experience during my stay in Calif. then I had in all my life before I had left the south. My sister who lived in Oroville Calif. had an old Studerbaker car laying up that was belong to her husband before he died. And she had told me if I would get it in running condition, I could have it. I immediately put the problem before the workers in a meeting, so their agreed to help me get it in running condition. When the car was ready, any where the workers had to go, we would use the car to make the trip. I would use the car for the workers use only. We made several meeting to other towns such as Stockling Calif. Oakland Calif. We continue to have our school. We also would have court school, so the workers would learn how to act in court in case they would be arrested and went to court and face the Judge. We would go on the street every night and speak to the workers that was standing on the corner looking on. And I was elected one of the speaker to speak on the corner every night. When we would get to the corner, we would make our speach briefly, in about five minute, because the cops would usely come along and urge you to keep moving are you would be arrested for vagrancy. In 1932 was our busy year. The condition was very bad. Thousand of workers were pouring into Calif. looking for work they could not find. The workers unemployed council was busy getting leaflet out for a big hungry march. A committee went to see the relief Authority for relief to feed the hungry marcher.

So the relief Authority agreed to feed the hungry marcher three meals for one day. I was busy in my neaborhood getting out leaflet. We was preparing for the hungry march with full speed. When the day came for the march, we formed differn't group to march in differn't section of the City to draw out the workers into the hungry march. Several workers were beaten by the cops for refusing to move on when the street was blocked by the hungry marcher. At 1 p.m. five thousand marched to the State capitol. Every group was carrying differn't signs. Saying free Tom Mooney. And the Scottsboro boys.[17]

---

17. Tom Mooney was a California Socialist and labor organizer who had been imprisoned since 1916, convicted of murder for setting off a bomb in San Francisco. Labor and left organizations questioned the evidence used to convict him and protested his imprisonment for over twenty years. "The

And our demand was to free Tom Mooney and the Scottoboro boys. And $50 dollar winter relief. We didn't win our demands immediately. We did won $500 for the expenses of the hungry march, and was promised that our demands would get consideration in the future. We had a noble speaker from San Francisco Calif. While the speaker was speaking the workers was yelling from the top of their voices with high spirit. That day there was workers from all parts of the State. The next day there was several workers who had to meet court for refusing to move on. That what the police claimed.[18]

I was enjoying being in the movment for it was such a great experience for me. We again began preparing for a big demonstration to free Tom Mooney and the Scottoboro boys. The workers was preparing to make this day one of the bigest

---

Scottsboro boys" was the name given to nine black teenagers who had been arrested on March 25, 1931, in Alabama, accused of raping two white girls who had also caught a ride on the freight train. They were quickly convicted and sentenced to death, but the International Labor Defense and the Communist Party made their story a national civil rights issue and won several appeals of their convictions from the U.S. Supreme Court—only to have Alabama juries convict them again. Solomon notes that "Scottsboro and hunger became inseparable issues. Communists generalized the specter of the electric chair for the nine youths into a threat against the growing unity of blacks and whites in the fight for food and work. It was the ultimate expression of 'the capitalist offensive' against all the dispossessed" (153–54). But Clark's own story makes the connection between the racist rape trials and hunger more clear. Desperate conditions in Louisiana had forced Clinton to hop a train, just like the Alabama teenagers, looking for work. Four of the Scottsboro boys were released in 1937, while the others remained in prison well into the 1940s. See James Goodman, *Stories of Scottsboro*.

18. Two demonstrations in Sacramento resemble the march described here. During a county hunger march on October 10, 1932, protestors blocked a street in front of the courthouse for more than an hour and demanded that county supervisors provide relief for the winter. These demands were denied. See *Western Worker*, October 24, 1932, and also "County Hunger Marches So Far," *Western Worker*, October 1, 1932, for a discussion of these demonstrations statewide.

The rally Clark describes also resembles a large, statewide hunger march that converged at the state capitol in Sacramento on January 10, 1933, at the beginning of the legislative session. "Columns" of marchers had begun in six parts of the state, visiting cities and picking up more marchers on the way to Sacramento. Clark may have helped organize participating groups in other towns, as he mentions traveling to other cities to organize. The marchers' main demands included $50 cash relief for winter, legislative approval for unemployment insurance, and, as Clark mentions, freeing Tom Mooney. They insisted that there be no discrimination, including racial discrimination, "in the administration of the above demands" (*Western Worker*, January 9, 1933). The *Western Worker* estimated that 3,000 people marched in the parade on January 10, with another 12,000 watching and joining them outside the capitol (*Western Worker*, January 16, 1933).

workers demonstration ever was held in San Francisco Calif. Some of the workers was distribution leaflet and some was printing signs on banners. On the day of
the demonstration we had organized 500–five hundred delegate. My car was all
decorated with banners on each side. One was to free Tom Mooney. My car was
leading the demonstration. We left that morning just when the sun began to raise.
We arrived in Oakland Calif. 9.40 a.m. When we arrived there was thousand of
workers, both White and Negroes, waiting to cross on the boat for San-Francisco.

When we was crossing on the boat, we were serve with all kinds of lunches,
cold drinks and refreshment. Every body was in good spirit. About 2 p.m. the
demonstration had began. We march from the bay through market street. I cannot remember the exact number, but it must have been around 35,000 workers
marching in this demonstration. I cannot remember the name of the hall where
the speaking taking place. I do know it was thousand of workers there.

And I heard some of the best speakers. It was my first time to see and hear Tom
Mooney' Mother speak and a Negro speaker. I felt much stronger when I seen one
of my race making a speech in this mass meeting, when I seen so many thousand
people together at one time and fighting for the same problem. And I couldn't see
why the workers demands wouldn't be met immediately. At this meeting the sum
of $10,000 was raised for the freedom of Tom Mooney and the Scottoboro boys.[19]
I said from that meeting, If the working people down south just knew how to pull
together like the workers of the west, we would have a new south to live in.

And I said to myself if I make up my mind to go back south, I will do my part
to make it a new south for the workers. That day of the mass meeting, I had the
opportunity to meet with many Negroes who had been with the movment for
some time, and they would give me the low down on what step to take. I would
ask them many questions. Some was in a foolish way. But it was because I had
been kept in the dark all my days until I began traveling where there Negroes had
a better Oppertunity. When we was on our way from the meeting, the group that

---

19. This demonstration to free Tom Mooney occurred on November 6, 1932. Descriptions in the
Western Worker of auto caravans from all over the state match Clark's. A special "Free Tom Mooney
Ferry" was arranged to go from Oakland across the bay to San Francisco (*Western Worker*, November 7
and 14, 1932). This rally was provoked by a man's confession to part of the crime for which Tom
Mooney had been convicted. Over 18,000 people attended the demonstration, which was held in the
San Francisco Auditorium. Mooney would be pardoned and released from prison in 1939 (Georgakas,
"Mooney-Billings Case," 511–12).

I was marching with was invited to one of the workers home in Oakland Calif. We went and taking lunch at this workers home, and we met with many new friends. While being at this workers home, I would tell them about the condition down south. Some of them would tell me, If I was you, I wouldn't go back down south any more. But some would have differn't idea about that going back down south. One of the worker said to me, Clinton, When you go back south, you can teach those poor working people how to organize and fight for their rights.

You have got the experience, so when you go back south, Organize, Organize the south. We will be with you and the workers down there also. These words grew in my head like poison gas. And having never been removed until this day. While I was back in Sacramento, I began to read books night and day, getting myself prepared for the great work in the south, as I knew there where it needed to be done, way down in my old home state, in the deep south Louisiana. During this time in my stay in Calif. was my first to hear the case of the Scottoboro boys. I can remember selling 10¢ pamplets on the street of Sacaramento. These pamplets would tell the case of the scottoboro boys. Several people of both races would try to discourage me some time, but I had to come to understand who was the bosses. And who was the working class. And that I was in the working class and would stay on the workers side, as their was my class.

The workers had been giving partys and had been trying to get the Negroes of Sacramento to come out some time. May be two or three would come to the party. So I began to work direct in the Negroes neaghborhood. We give a party on the first saturday night, and on the friday befor the workers party come off, the Negroes gave a party in their community. I receive a invitation card to come to this party. When I went to the party, I asked for an oppertunity to speak. So they gave me the privilege to speak. When the crowd came in around 10 p.m., one of the leader called the house to order. And ask me to take the floor. Every body became quite. Why you could hear a pin drop on the floor. I began to tell them about the workers movment, and what the movment was doing for both races. After I had made my Speech, I told them about the workers giving a party that following saturday, and I invited them to come out to the workers party.

Many of them came over to me after I had made my speech and shaken my hands. And their all promased to be at the workers party Saturday night. When the workers party began that saturday night, many White workers was there for the first beginning. And about three Negroes was there with one girl. I had began to worrie, because I didn't wanted my races to be behine always. Then again I knew how they were down south, and how they would come out to church. The preacher down south knew just how to get us out to church on time. If the church is to began at 8 p.m. he would call them to church at 6 p.m., because he knew that some of us would be late for the church. So thats the way thing happened that saturday night in Sacaramento.

The party was to began at 8 p.m. And around 10 p.m. about 50 Negroes, women and men, came pouring into the workers party. When they came into the hall, one of the White workers came over to me and shaked my hands, and he said to me, Clinton! You ought to have been here years ago to help us to do things like that, Boy! He said thats good work. I said to him, Well all we need is the proper understanding and I thank we can do the job well. That night we had 25 Negroes to join the workers movment to fight for relief. We continued to give our party every saturday nights, the next week in the Negroes neighborhood. One White worker and myself went to investigate their condition. We found several Negro family suffering for the like of food. We formed a committee to go and see Mary Judge. When we went into Mary Judge office, we had two old Negro women along with us who had been eating out of the garbage can. I was one of the spokeman in this committee. I immediately began to tell Mary Judge the story of these old people. Mary Judge called these two old people into the relief office and immediately gave them relief and promas to pay their rent. Mary Judge told these old people not to come with that group any more. Come by yourself next time.

Dont fool with those people. We will take care of you. What did we care, just so Mary Judge listen to our demands. We didn't have no more trouble with Mary Judge. We won relief for thousand of workers in Calif. The next saturday night when we give our party, we had a Negro band that I had organize in my neighbohood. We went into the party that saturday night about 9 p.m. and took the workers with great suprise. When the Negro band start playing the music, the workers began asking question. Wanted to know who brought the suprise in the workers party. No one answered the questions. After that night I could not get out of the workers sight. The workers would get worrie if I would miss one day going the workers headquarters.

Their would began to look me up to see if anything had happinged to me. My sister who at one time had been scared for me, she became more and more interested in the movement. And she would take some friends along with her to the workers meeting on wednesday nights–Wednesday nights was the workers open forum meeting for the workers. When I had been in the State of Calif a little better then a year, I was getting ready to go back south. I spoke to several leaders about going back down south and to continue my organizing the southern workers, and the workers thought that was a great spirit, to have such a strong courage to go back south to do organizing. I knew I had something new to tell the workers way down south where I knew the planters would kill me if they knew that I had been up in Calif and had learn something and was coming back to tell the other about it. Well I said to myself it better to die trying to save the poor people life then to let all of them die at once starveing to death, and too that the south needed to be organized much more badly then the western workers. Are the Northern workers.

And the southern workers suffer the most. The last meeting I attended was in Stockling Calif. And There's where I left out from in an old Studerbaker car with one little $5 bill that the workers of Stockling Calif. had raised for me in the last meeting I had attended before leaving. The workers was giving me the go ahead signal. I left Calif with great spirit and lots of experience. When I was traveling on the lonesome desert road with a couple of thousand miles ahead of me, and only had one little pityful $5 bill. And too in a big car to buy gas for.

I travel all day and half of the night and had spent $3 and sixty cents. I parked my car way up on top of a mountain and went to sleep until the next morning, then I started traveling again through the mountain all day and night. And had spent the last $1.40 and didn't have no idea how much further I could make it. I had one flat tire and didn't have a jack to fix the flat, so there I was in a mess. I didn't know just what step to take. I would walk around up and down the road looking for a car to pass by, but no car would pass. So I study and study until my mind came up on an idea. I rolled a big rock behind the car and went inside the car and released the clutch and started the motor to running and back the car on the rock until the wheel was clear off the ground, and changed the tire and started traveling again. Mid night caught me again way up in the mountain. I parked the car on the side of the road and went to sleep until day light was near. And started traveling. When I went about five miles, I run out of gas, and no money to buy anything with. So I began thinking what to do. There I was way up in the mountain with no money. And would not see a car pass. And when a car would pass in those mountain it would be a lucky break if they would stop. So after no car passed by, I hit the high way and walked about six miles. And there I seen some old tents standing down in the bottom of the mountain.

I walked over toward the tents. I met an old White man coming out of the tents. He said to me, Mister! Are you lost. I said well! In a way, I am. And in another way, I beleieve I am lost. I am out of gas and see no chance of getting any. Ah! He said Thats Nothing, you can stay out here with me. He then called me around to the back of the tents, and taking a milk can and filled the can up with gas. And said to me will that help you.

I was so rejoyiced over this until I didn't know just how I could appreaciate the old man for this favor he gave me. He then told me that I was 70 miles from the next Town. I then started back for my car. When I made it back to the car it was 1 P.M. I wanted to make it to that town before the sun went down, so I started traveling again. Around 5 p.m. I arrived in Riverside Calif. I began to search the town to see if there was a workers headquarter. I didn't know if it were one there are not. I did find out that it was a very good Negro preacher living in this town. And that he was having a church meeting this very night. I immediately looked him up. I located where his home was and went there to meet with him. When I went into his home and met him, he began asking me question. Where was my home and where was I being headed for. I began to tell him my trouble. He was a very friendly preacher. We went to church together. When the church meeting began, the preacher interdouced me to the church members. After the service was over, the Rev. asked me to say a few words. I made a short speech. My talk was on my experience and on the condition of the working class.

I told them all about my experience that I had during my stay in the State of Calif. And why I left my home State to come all the way up to Calif. And why I was on my way back to my home State Louisiana, and what I was going to do when I get back to my home State Louisiana. Those church members give me a big hand for what I had told them. And their apprecaite my talk by taking up $6 collection and gave to me to help get me back to my home state. The preacher taking me to his home to spend the night with him. When I went home with him, he began asking me many questions about my home. And about the workers movement. I gave him all the imformation that I could thank about on the condition of the unemployed, and what they had to do to better their condition. The preacher seem to see everything clearly. And he told me that the unemployed had a hard job ahead of them. The next morning when I was getting ready to leave, the preacher shook my hand and told me to keep on praying and that he would pray for me all the way through. I filled my car tank up with gas and started traveling. I traveled all day and part of the night. And went to sleep on the side of the mountain. Before the sun rise the next morning, I started traveling. I made it to the state of Arzonia and spent one night in the salvation Army camp, and the next day I went to the state of New Mexico. And spent one night there. And there where I had give out money again. And I wasn't very far from ELPaso Texas. When I arrived in EL-PASO Texas, I went over to the Police Station. And told the cheif police that I had been up to the State of Calif. looking for work and didn't find any, and was on my way back to my home State Louisiana. And I am traveling in a car and have run out of gas and would like for you offical to help me to get back home. The Cheif Police told me to sell my car and take a train out for home. I said to the Cheif, I dont wanted to sell my car. So the Cheif turned around in his swinging chair. And he called his porter a colored boy. And gave this colored boy a ticket that he wrote for me for ten gal gas and five quarts of oil. And told the porter to go with me to the filling station. And them to fill this order out for this boy.

So the porter and I went to get the gas. And didn't have any trouble. I thinked the Cheif police for his assistence. And went over to the Negro bussiness part of town, and located some of the Negro leaders. And I had conference with some of the bussiness men, I told these Negro business men about my trouble on my way home. So one of them kept me over for the night and taking me over to the K.P. Hall where the members was having meeting. The K.P. members had organize a cooperative club to help their fellowed brothers when they get into a distress and any one passing by and need help. I made a long talk to the members of the K.P. all about my trip to Calif, and my experience and why I left my home state. I also told them what I intended to do when I get back home.

After I had made my speech they give me $12 to help me on my expense to get back home. The members told me to go ahead and keep up the good spirit. You are on the right track. I left this group with great courage, after I had spend the night with the leader of this group, and had left the next morning. I had promas to drop a card back to the leader. I wrote cards back to them every where I stoped before I arrived back home.

I wanted to asure them how much I did appreciate what their done for me in helping me to get back home in the old state of Louisiana, where I was anxious to get my people to organize and fight for their rights on the plantations. Where was taking everything the poor farmers produced.

When I had reached way down in the State of Texas, I stoped in a little town where the Negroes was carrying on a revival meeting in their church. So I went and contact the pastor of the church and joined in with them in carrying on they revival meeting. I stop over with them for three nights. We was having a wonderful time in the old time way of running a revival meeting. Every member of the church seem to enjoyed my stay.

I helped them in carrying on the revival meeting. After the meeting would be over in the night, they give me the privilege to speak to the members on my trip to Calif. from Louisiana. When I began to speak I told them about my experience while being Calif. I gave them the idea of the workers unemployed council and what the workers was doing to betters their condition through organizeing both White and Negroes together. And that was the only way we would every better our condition is for the both to come together.

After I had made my talk the preachers and the members didn't wanted me to leave. They begges me to stay with them. I told them that I was to anxious to get back home, and that I would try to get back to see them some day in the future. Before leaving the members of this church called for a collection to give me to help on my trip to get back home to get the poor farmers to organize. The collection was $5. The last night I was in the revival meeting, every member in the church prayed for me. That I would get back home safe, and continue to organizeing the poor working people. I was just to happy to be with such a strong church members. And before leaving the church every members had to come by me and shaked my hands, and told me to keep on praying. And they would remember me in their prayes.

The next morning I left for the state of Louisiana where I was born. I then never lost much time. I continued traveling and would only sleep for two and three hour at a time in my car when I would get sleepy. I could make much better time, because I had made it on the bottom land again. When I came to Louisiana, my mother had moved to Palmetto La. where her mother was born. When I arrived I immediately went to sleep, I taking a two days rest. I had came a little better then 2,000 miles and was broken down from the long drive. After I had taking my rest, I began then looking for work. Jobs was hard to find. I then went to Melville La. found a job in a garage for $6 a week, reparing cars greaseing and washing cars. I work in this garage for three month, until the manager didn't wanted to pay me the $6 a week any more. I then went back to Palmetto La. and went to work on a plantation four miles from Palmetto. The wages was 80¢ from sun to sun. There was 25 day labors working on the plantation, and the majority of these day labors was some of my relative. One of my uncle had his family out working on this plantation. When the riding boss would go to his house for something, I would tell them about my experience when I was in Calif with the worker movement and how we could get things done by sticking together. I had a workers paper along with me. I show them a cliping that was what the sharecropper was doing in Alabama. This cliping was telling how the sharecropper was organizing and had call a strike in the field for $1 for a 10 hour a day.[20] We would have meeting during the night time. In my Uncle house, we drew up a plane to call a strike for $1.10 for a 10 hour a day worked. Every body agreed to stick together and pull this strike. We was to work that week out only for 80¢. So on saturday we was to present our

20. Clark might be combining or confusing details from several different farm labor strikes of the early 1930s as he writes his memoir ten years later. In the spring of 1934, the Share Croppers' Union led a strike of cotton pickers in Alabama. As he wrote this passage, Clark may have been thinking of the 1935 strike of cotton choppers and pickers in Alabama (organized by the SCU), which included a demand for wages of a dollar per day. The union won the wage increase in areas where it was strong, but suffered brutal and sometimes fatal violence against strikers and organizers in other areas. Solomon

demand to the planter. We had appointed one of my cousin for our leader as he was one of the old hands, and he would be more cable to do the talking, because the planter was a french decent, and my cousin knowed how to place the words better then any one of us. That saturday we went all together to the planter house and drew our pay for the week work, and present our demands to him. So he went into the house, told his wife something, and came back and told us that he didn't have our money on hand, that he had to go to the bank first. So after we didn't get our money that saturday, and he didn't gave us no consideration on our demand, we waited until that sunday and sent for our money by our leader and another member went along. When they came back they didn't have our money. The planter said he had waited to late and bank had close, and that he would give it to us the next week. So he still didn't gave us no imformation on our demand. We went to work that monday and held the watch on the hours we made. When the 10 hours was we drop our hoes and taking out our team and went home, and did the same thing every day over and over again. On the last part of the week the planter became angry about, and told our leader that we woulding get paid for the time we didn't work in the field. Our leader told the planter that when we work 10 hours we had put in a good days work for any body for a $1.10 and the planter said he hadn't any money to pay that kind of wages for labor work and that we ought to be glad to get that kind of money, because it was a many poor people wishing they could get that so they would be able to get something to eat. That saturday we didn't work. We got together to go and get our money. The planter began to figure on our time that we had made. When he started to pay off, we seen that our time wasn't correct. We told the planter that we have put in the time and we wonted our money liked we worked. The planter's wife become angry. She ran into the house and came back with a shot gun, and said to our leader, You can not dispute my husband you nigger you. Our leader taking the shot gun from the planter's wife, and she just started to bustling, calling us every thing she could think of to say to us, and the planter went in the house, and began talking on the

writes that "the toll from the two cotton strikes was at least four SCU leaders killed, scores arrested and beaten, and an uncounted number of striking croppers who hid in the woods and were possibly murdered" (295–96). Clyde Johnson, the organizer for the SCU at the time, later moved the organization to New Orleans and worked with Clark. On the strikes, see Kelley, *Hammer and Hoe*, 161–68, and Solomon, *The Cry Was Unity*, 294–96.

telphone. We know he was calling the Sherriff up from Opelousas La. about 25 miles from where we was. So we left and went back home, and began discussion over the matter. About three hours later, the Sherriff came and some of the member seen the Sherriff when he was passing. As I didn't live around on this plantation, so my Uncle told me that it would be best for me to stay out of the way until they see how thing would come out. In a few minute after I had went in the woods so I wouldn't be seen, the Sherriff came and arested our leader of who was my Uncle son and taking him to Opelousas, La. parish jail. The sherriff hunted for me every where. He went to diffient houses on the plantation, so my Uncle told me that I better leave and go some where eles, until thing had blown over. That night before I had left from that section the planter had formed up a mob gang looking for me. When I got the news I took for the woods, and walk all night. The next day I made it to Torris La. and cross the river, and that was just about sun down. There I hit the bougereb swamp.[21] Just before I hit these swamp there sit an old broking down shack. An Negro man and his wife live there. I walk over to them and told them that I was hungry and that I just excape a mob gang last night. The old man gave me a piece of corn bread and a piece of smoke rabbit. Then I ask them about a place to sleep for the night. The old man didn't seem to mind it, but the old lady was afread. So the old man dirrected me to watch for a little trail in the swamp when I had went two miles up the track. As it was getting dark, I began traveling. The swamp was cover with water, the water came up to each side of the railroad track. I look and look to see if I would ever come to the old walking trail that the old man had told me about. It became late in the night, and had seen no trail yet. That was the most thickest swamp I had ever went in before. Finly I came up on some kind of wild beast laying in the middle of the track. I stop still in front of him. He made a funny noise, so I back up a little ways and then went on the side of the track, near the edge of the water, and walk easy until I had pass him. When I hit the track again and went a little piece futher there lay another one. I made a yell from the top of my voice. I thought he would move, but he didn't. He made the same kind of noise the other beast made, so I went down side the track and went by him with full speed and hit the center of the track again. And every step I would make there was some kind of beast lying on

---

21. An unfinished LFU press release, dated October 7, 1941, and copied into an FBI report, identifies this as the Bougere Swamp ("Clinton Clark," January 13, 1942, New Orleans, p. 3, FBI-CC).

the track. Some would get up and walk into the water. The ones that would go into the water seem to look like a wolf. I seen so many differen't kind of beast that night until I began to act like one myself. When ever I walk up on one beast that made the funny noise, I would repeat the same kind of noise to him. But when he would get a little louder with his noise I seen he mean real business, I became scared and went around him just as easy, and let him alone. Around about 2 p.m. that night I was so sleepy until I began to walk like a drunken man. I came across a little flat form, where the railroad men used to put their handscar when there would be a train coming by. So I layed down on this flat form trying to go to sleep. When I was just about to doze to sleep, I heard something walking in the water taking his own time. The more I would hear the noise look like the closer it would get to me. I woulding move, I just lay still to see if it would stop walking. The first thing I knew the beast was on the flat form shaking the water off of itself. The water just flash in my face. When he was through shaking the water off of itself, this beast seem to me as if it was a bear. The beast walk over to me and start smelling me all over my body, and taking his feet and turn me over and over. I never drew breath as long as he was around me. After he had turn me over several time, he then went back into the water. I continued to lay still until his sound was out of my hearing, then I jumped up and hit the railroad track and started running with full speed, until I run into another beast lying in the center of the track. When the day began to brake the track was clear. I didn't came across any more beast during day, only you would see a few deer crossing the track from long distent.

I walk that day for about four hour, then lay on the side of the track and went to sleep. Around about four p.m. I started traveling again. I still didn't see any open. When night came I became worried, because I was broken down and hungry and didn't want to be bother with any more of those beast. So I pray that the Lord be with me through the swamp safe, and I dont think I seen three beast during that night. I didnt know but I had pass the danger part of the swamp the first night. So I taking my time and walk all night weak from being hungry and tired from the long distant walk. The next day I came to an open about 11 a.m. and I still had 6 miles to walk before I would come to some house. When I first seen the open, I seen some people way up the track riding horses with guns on their saddle. I tryed to make it where they was before they would leave, but when I reach that spot where they was, I couldn't trace them. So I continue to walk. About 3 p.m. I seen an old open field and a little old shack where some cloths hanging on a line. So I hit a cow trail and went near the house and began to call, and old Negro women came out and told me to come in mister. I went over and began telling her where I had walk from without anything to eat. She said lord my son you sure are one of gods children. We have never known anybody to go in those swamp without a gun and come out alive. We have found where several people had been killed in those swamp. We have known of one Negro around here who had kill a planter, and the mob was crowding him so close until he had to make it to the swamp and he had a rifle and a sack of bullet. He killed so many beast that was trying to kill him, until he ran out of bullet and he had to come out of those swamp and let those get him. Son I know that the lord is with you. The old lady then started cooking. She said son I know you are hungry. I am going to cook you a good dinner. She gave me some butter milk and a piece of corn bread. She said son eat this, and let that hold you up until I have dinner ready for you. She went out in the yard where she had put up a few chicken up for her paster of her church that coming sunday, but she said son when I explan this to my paster he will forgive me. I asked her could I lay cross her bed and sleep while she was cooking. She told me sure, sure. When I went to sleep it was night before I woke up. She told me that she wanted me to get plenty of rest and wouldn't get me up to eat. That night the old man had came in and the old lady had told him my story. After I had eaten my lunch we began to talk over the condition. I told them where my home was, and about my trip to Calif. and what the working people was doing to better their condition. He told me that he had being farming on the same farm for 20 years and had never came out of debt, and that it was the same with all the share-croppers in that section, and that was in concordia parish. He told me that it was a many Negroes drowned in the Mississippi River because they ask for their cotton money. These old people tryed to get me to spend several nights with them. They liked to hear me talk on what I had been through. I told them that I wanted to find a job some where. And I better keep on going. The next morning I started traveling again. I walk 11 miles until I hit a gravel road, and finally caught a ride on a truck, and went to Wisner La. where there was a large slave plantation. I had an Uncle living on this plantation. When I arrive there and went over to my Uncle house, I wouldn't tell them anything about my trouble and nothing on my experience in Calif, not until I had been there more then a week. The next morning my Uncle taking me with him to the plantation lot, where all the day hand would leave out for work on truck to do day work on different parts of the plantation.

This plantation was about 50 mile square and was cleaning up wood land, and would hire any one who wanted to work for 80ç a day, and that would be from sun to sun. I went to work that morning alone with two hundred and fifty day labor. When we had started to work that morning, it was 6 a.m. and was 4 a.m. when we loaded on the truck at the lot. I notice we had 50 rider over us. Every rideing boss had some kind of pistol on his saddle, and we had to work like mules, pileing brushes and burning brushes cutting down trees. You wasn't allowed to stop only time enough to roll a cigarette. The riding boss would ride from gang to gang keeping every body moveing. There were young and old. Some of them would almost run in they work. At sun down every body would rush to the truck to see if they could get on the first truck, because some time the truck that be on the rear would get to the lot around 10 p.m. that night. We would have to go on the job at 30 minute before the sun rise every morning, and the rideing boss would see that the sun was well down before he would knock us off work. That first day I worked it was 10 O.Clock when I went home that night. I was so tired I couldn't sleep well that night. I would tell my Uncle how it was ashame for the working to stand for such a hard punishment and want rise up about it. He wouldn't say a word. It seem like he was so use to such treatment until it didn't worried him. It was a many more like him on that plantation. I was afread to tell my Uncle much because he was born a few month after the slave time, and was much use to that kind of life and wouldn't change a bit. I did run across a few good boys that had the right idea about what the worker should do to better their lots. Every chance I would get on the job, I would talk to the ones that I could trust. I would tell them how we could get thing done by getting ourselves together and force the planter to raise our wages. If I can remember the year I work on this plantation was in the latter part of 1933. I began to make so many friends on this plantation until they would come some night to get me to spend the night with them, to get more imformation on how to organize. I would go to church on sunday and would make the sunday school at the same time, and had the opportunity to speak on the scottoboro boys case every sunday. The sharecropp became so interested in my speach until some would come from other town after me to make an address in they church. I had about 50 day labor organize on the job and was trying hard to get the majority of the group that I was working with, and then we would call a strike, for more money. But there was so many stool pigon on this plantation until you would have to be very careful. Ever once and a while I would get the news what some stool pigon had said to the boss about me. I could see the rideing boss look-ing suspicion when he would come to our gang. When he would ride off a piece he would be looking back toward our gang as if he was listen to hear if I was tell-ing the labor something. Some of my friend was on to him and would tell me what to do. We stop talking about organizeing on the job. We would do that when get off or on saturday night have a place to meet, also sunday would be a good day to get together. I began to slow up speaking in the church. We found out that was where the stool pigon hang out to carry the news to the boss. On this planta-tion you wasn't allow to lay off one day. If you did layed off or be late for work one morning you would have to leave the town, because the plantation owner own the little town. One saturday when we was getting our pay envelope, the rideing boss told me I was fire and to leave the town, not let the sun rise catch me in Wis-ner sunday. Some of my strong friend told me not to leave that they would go down with me. Then some told me it be the best to leave, because there had been so many poor Negroes killed for nothing and nothing was done about it, and we want you to live. Some day you may have the power to do the goods for us. One of my friend had a car, and he taken me to Alex. La. that same night. Three more of my friend went alone for company. We discuss on the matter on our way. They degreed to go back and keep the people together that we had already organize. I spend that night in Alexandria La. The next day I started traveling, headed for Baton Rouge La. I wanted to stop off in Palmetto La. But I knew that I just excape the mob in Palmetto. I arrive in Baton Rouge that evening, went over to see my relative there, to see if they could tell me where I could fine job there. Thing didn't look so good in Baton Rouge. The next day I started hitch hikeing toward the Mississippi line. The first day I walk fifteen miles while walking and talking to ev-ery poor farmer I could see near the highway. I couldn't hear a good word about no kind of work, and most of the farmer I seen would tell me that they was starve-ing. They couldn't get relief, and the landlord would only give them a little meal, a little piece of salt meat, a half gal. syrup. And that they was selling their chicken and hogs off they yard to buy the cloths and soap and other little things they need. When the sun went down, I was still on the highway. Ten o.Clock that night I was still on the highway. Around one o clock I went to sleep on old highway bridge. The next morning at 5 a.m. I arise up and went down a little stream of water and wash my face. And started hitch hikeing up the Mississippi highway. I met an old Negro farmer. He was on his way to get a bucket of water down the stream. We started to talking. My talk seem to suit him well. He then invited me over to his house. When we went in his house his wife came and met me with great enthusiastic. There were 11 children. The oldest one seem to be nine years old, they were all looking hungry. When the old man began to tell me how they was liveing tears were almost comeing out of his eyes. The women ask me did I wanted her to cook me something to eat. She said we don't have much but you are welcome to such as we have. I said to her, Sister? I have walk since yesterday 26 miles. And I have not eaten anything, but god knows I wouldn't want you to take bread out of your children mouth for me. She then said my dear Brother? That is right what you said, but I look at it on the opposite way. These same children of mine some day may have to come to your house and ask for a piece of bread. So Mr you just sit there and keep my husband company until I get you something cook. Before I left I gave them the address of the unemployed council headquarter, and told them to write to them and ask them for imformation on how to organize the farmer to fight for relief. I walk about 6 more miles before I stop again. I then came across a thick community of sharecropper. I went in the field where I seen a couple of them plowing. When I reach where they was one of them said to me, MR, you wants a job, I can work you, but I cant feed you. I told him, I may like your job, but I cant work and Starve too. We then Laugh the joke off and began to talk business. He ask me question about the present condition. When I out lined the matter to him he beg me to spend the night with him. I was much enthusiastic over the offer until I ask him to get some of his neighbors to come over to his home that night and that I would give them some new idea on the condition. He degreed with me and send me over to his home until he would quit work for the night. After we had our lunch that night the sharecropper began pouring in his house. In less then an hour there were fifty sharecropper in there both men and women. We all were laughing and talking for a while. The house man then call the house to order. He standed on his feet and repeat the lord prayer, and made a long talk. He told them we have here with us tonight a stranger who wants to talk to us and he said it want cost us nothing, because you know how our people is. They are quick to say, That fellow is just here to fool us poor folks out of our money, and at the same time we dont have nothing for nobody to fool us out of. The boss have taken everthing we have made, and its nothing left for anybody eles to beat us out. Then he gave me the floor. I said to them, I dont think its much left for me to say, because that man have told you the god truth. May be I can tell you all some of my experience that I have been through dureing this depression.

I gave them the full detail on the scottoboro boys case. When I was thourgh with my speach, every sharecropper in the house began to tell hard story of they life. Some would tell how many bail of cotton he had made during his life farming and didn't have a decent bed to sleep in.

I had been on the highway one week when I made it to Woodville. Miss. and stop for one night to see if I could fine a job. I went to church that night, and made a long talk on the scottoboro boys case.

From there, I went to Sibley Mississippi. And stop off there for a few days as there were a large plantation with hundred of Negroes there. I had stop there to make a few days work, so I could make a few nickel to help me until I could fine a better job. The wages there were 40ç a day. It was raining every day while I was there. I made several speach in differen't churches on the scottoboro boys case. The poor farmer were starveing in this section.

When I was leaveing this section, I came across another large plantation down by the Mississippi River. I began to talk with a sharecropper when he was out of the field for dinner. We had long talk on the condition. When some sharecropper seen there was a stranger talking, there come about ten more to see who he was, then I began to talk to the group. A few minute later, here come a rideing boss and he call one of the sharecropper out from the house apiece, and ask him who is that fellow and what is he talking about. The sharecropper told the rideing boss he didn't know the man but his talk is good. The rideing boss then told the share-cropper. Tell that fellow to come here.

I immediately went to see what he wanted. He said to me, Say fellow what you selling. I said nothing. He said, You just going around here fooling these nigger. I said No. This is my race and I am telling them how to live and what they should do to protect their liveing. He then said to me, What way you come in here. I told him where I had came from. He said get going the way you come. I then became angry and said to him, I have a right to go where I please, but if this is your land I will get off of it. He said this is not my land, but I will protect my niggers. I then turn around and went back in this sharecropper house, and continue with my talk. He left on his horse. He had a long gun on his saddle, and he was just about drunk. Before leveing he said something to the sharecropper very low. The share-cropper said to me, we are not studying about that fellow. All he want is to keep us in the dark.

The next town was Natchez Mississippi. There I had conference with a couple Negro Doctor and a few more business man.

And the next town was Port Gibson Mississippi. I spend three hours there, I talked with several Negroes there. The poor people there was almost starveing and couldn't hardly get on relief and those that did get on relief didn't get enough to live three days.

When I hit the highway again, I walked about five miles when it began to get dark. I had talked to several poor farmer and every one that I talked to, he would tell me how the planter was treating him. And they couldn't get on relief. I would give them the address of the unemployed council headquarter in New York City. I think I can remember giving two thousand poor farmer this address, because I had taking that many address. And every one I would get his or her address, I would give them the address of the unemployed council.

It became darker and darker. I stop to talk with a Negro sharecropper just before dark, and when I had told him how far I had walked from, he was so sorry that he couldn't fix a place for me to sleep. He then gave me the name of his brother who lived three miles farther up the Mississippi highway. I still can remember his brother name, it was John. He had dirrected me to his house.

When I reach to correct spot, I seen a light in a house that look like the right place. When I came close to this house the dog began to bark. After then the door flew open and there came a white face with a shot gun in his hand, and said its no John live here. We dont allow no stranger around here keeping moveing. I said to him, Thank you Mister and went on. I went two miles farther and made a fire side of an old log and went to sleep.

When the sun rise the next morning I had walked four miles. I seen a big born over in a field, where there was several Negroes getting some mules togather. I walk over to the born where they was, and ask the rideing boss about getting a job. He ask me where I came from and what kind of work could I do on a farm. I told him any kind that is to be found. He then said I can give you a job cleaning out dithes in the field. I ask him what was the wages. He said 40¢ a day. I said, I am sorry, Mister, I have to suport my mother and that want get bread for her. When I was leaveing he told those Negroes, That fellow dont want to work. I continue traveling night and day telling poor farmer I would see to organize and fight for relief. I was so angry about how those poor farmer was being treated, until I had in mine to organize every poor farmer in the state of Mississippi and march to the state capitol and demand relief. When I had reach Greenville Miss. where I made my stoping place, I was told by the people there that I had walked the distance of three hundred miles. I had walk from Baton Rouge La.

5 | We Continue Organizing the Sharecroppers

I began to look for work immediately. The only job I could get was working on a plantation for 65¢ to work from sun to sun. I went to work on a large slave plantation for this wages. I began immediately talking to the sharecropper to get togather, only you had to pick your sharecropper to talk to, are the boss would know it before the days was over. I would go to the churches, and speach on the scottoboro case, and Angelo Herndon case. When I was in this section two month, we would have the churches to take up collection for these two cases and send the money to the I.L.D. in NEW YORK city. I began to make friends with the best preacher and the Colored business man in Greenville Miss. The first local I set up was 6 miles from Greenville, on the same plantation where I was working as a day labor for 75¢ a day.

On this plantation the sharecropper had never had a settlement with they planter. On another plantation near Greenville the planter was paying his day labor with watermelon; the way he would do, he would give them the watermelon, but when they come to get his pay the planter would take pay out of his time that he had work.

The poor farmer was almost starveing. Many time I have seen some poor farmers going into the grave yards picking pepper grass to take home to cook for the family to have something to eat, because they couldn't get no relief. We would write and get imformation from the unemployed council and ask them how to organize the farmer and fight for relief. They would immediately write to us and give us the imformation. I wouldn't miss one night of being in some place where I could talk to some group and get them to organize a local council in they community. I had went so many places and had made so many friends until the minster would invite me to come and make a talk in their churches on Angelo Herndon and the scottoboro boys cases. I think if I can remember we had set up 20 some council in different community. We had five set up in the city of Greenville.

We had set up so many council until the member told me, we will suport you, Brother Clark, if you will stay here with us, and take the lead. I gave them my word that I would do my best, if I didn't find a better job soon. Finely I move into the city of Greenville. One day I went into the Greenville post office to get my mail. And I had receive a letter from the I.L.D., and I was standing in the post office reading this letter when a couple of planter was standing behine me reading my letter at the same time. When I was through reading, one of the planter said to me, Boy, thats the thing raiseing all that hell up in Alabama, Ant it. I said to him, That Right? and went out of the post office.

Dureing my stay in Greenville was the latter part of 1933 and the first beginning of 1934. While my stay in Greenville I could hear some of the most meanest story of how the planter had killed some of the poor Negroes farmer because they wanted to move from the planter farm, and at one time while my being there, it happing that one sharecropper wanted to move because the planter had refuse to give him a settlement. The sharecropper had went to get a truck to come and move his furniture. When he came back with the truck, the big planter had send one of his Negro stoolpigon to watch the house. The stoolpigon told the sharecropper that the big planter told him to not let anybody take anything away from that house unless they come see him first, and that not to go in that house. So the truck driver said to the sharecropper, if that the way thing is, I better not fool with the furniture. It may get me into trouble. It was getting dark. The sun was just about down, so the truck driver told this sharecropper it will be best for you to go and come back tomorrow. So the truck driver and the sharecropper left. When they had drove about 3 miles from the farm, the sharecropper became angry, and told the truck driver to stop that he was going back and see about his thing. So the truck driver tried to get the sharecropper to not go back. But the sharecropper said I have my best gun left in my house, and I am going back and get it. So the next day you could hear it all over the country that this sharecropper had been killed and takeing to a white undertaker. I know of a Negro who tried to get the matter investigate but never heard of the matter any more. So I began to get busy haveing meeting in Greenville in different section of the city. Every night some where we would have a meeting some where in the city. I had began to live in the city. Some I would make speaches in the churches. I had made friends with a Negro black smith. He would ask a many question about our set. I would tell him of our work in and around Greenville. I thank I had been in Greenville Miss. about six month. We had been haveing meeting in my room for more then two month, before we had made up our mine to change the meeting. The night we had change our meeting, it was so late when the meeting was over, one of the member ask me to spend the night with him. So I did spend the night with him.

The next morning about 8 A.M. my landlady came to the house where I had spend the night. When she came in the door, I could see something had happeing, the way she was looking so excited. When she came in she began to tell me the story, that a mob had been in my room looking for me. She said it was two police and five other alone with the cops. When they inter the house they began to ask who was the fellow what live here with you, look like you gave him your best room to sleep in, he must be an importain man, Ant He? They look on the wall and seen a large picture of Tom Mooney sign by the I.L.D. and said are you a member of that thing. The landlady said yes?

The cop said where is that fellow dont you know where he went last. The land lady said no? So they left out and went to several more houses looking for me. I was told that the Negro black smith who I had made friend with was the one who did the job as a stoolpigon. When the land lady brought the news and the mob was crowding me so close I got into the land lady car and she drove me to one of the council and I contact my member and report to them. And they had one white member in this council. That night we call a meeting and the member apointed the white farmer to go in town to see if they could fine out what it was alabout. And the member keep me in a safe place until this committee fine out something about the matter.

When the committee came back, thing was so hot on my trail until the thought to send me out of the county until thing blow over. They immediately put up $20 and takeing me to the first train leaving for New Orleans La. It was mid night when the train arrive the little town. The next day I arrive in New Orleans and there hunt up the worker headquarter. When I found the worker headquarter I told them the story and wrote the story into the Unemployed Council in New York City. I was to glad to get in contact with the worker movement in New Orleans, because that we could cooperative togather. I spend a few night in the city. Then went back to Palmetto La my mother lived and to there I had almost been lynch once.

I spend a couple night with my mother. From the time I had left Calif and left Greenville Miss. it was a very little sleep I would get. I would read every good books I would get my hand on. When I wasn't reading a book, I would sit down and study how could I get every poor farmer in the south organize and make all the big planter and big boss come across with the good that they had takeing from us, and that we had been a slave all our days and it was the time for our freedom. I would study so hard some time until when I would start out getting the farmer togather. I tried to do the job over night. I had made up my mine to get the word to every poor farmer that I could reach in the south. And if every worker and poor farmer in the united state would have under my aim and give me the proper suport, its no telling what could have been accomplish for the good of all.

When I left Palmetto La. started traveling again. You still couldn't get job easy around the country, only you could get plantation for as low as 60ç a day. I went over the Achafalaya river into point coupee county where was many plantation and thousand of poor white and Negro sharecropper slaveing and almost starveing. This was in the latter part of 1934. My first stop was Legonier plantation. I call a meeting one of the sharecropper house, then I went to the next plantation section Lettsworths La. I call a meeting in another sharecropper house. Every night we had a meeting in different sharecropper houses. We had about five hundred who had sign his name to join hand with his fellow sharecropper to fight for they right. The night when Huey Long was killed we was holding a meeting in the Negro odd fellow hall in Lettsworth La. with about four hundred sharecropper in the hall.[22]

I met a blind preacher one day in pointe coupee county. When I began to tell him about the worker movement, he told me a little story, to asure me he beleave in the poor people getting togather. I can still remember his name. It was Rev. D. H. Hunter. His story went something like this. He said the old times clock went something like this, take, your, time, take your time? take your time? The new clock went like this, Get togather? Get togather? Get togather?

Every meeting and every poor farmer I would talk to I never would forget to speak on the Scottoboro boys and Tom Mooney and Angelo Herndon case. I had the facts of these cases and would let them know how the boss framed up the worker, and that the same would happen to them unless they would organize and fight to stop it.

I had been in this county for about a couple week when I had receive a lots of little pamplet to give away to the poor farmer and one of the planter had put his hand on one of them. The planter got busy looking for the one who put them out. When I would come in the county I would always cross the Simmesport bridge over the achafalaya river. The planter formed up a mob group to meet me at the bridge with they gun to kill me and put me in the river. One thing happen, one of the sharecropper wife was working as a cook for the planter that was the main

22. Louisiana senator and presidential candidate Huey Long was shot in Baton Rouge on September 8, 1935.

leader of the mob gang. When she came home she immediately told her husband about the matter.

I can remember the sharecropper name. It was Willie Finley. He knew where to fine me so he came where I was and taken me back with him, left me at his house and went to the bridge to see if they would be there. When he went to the bridge he seen about ten planter there with gun in they hands. He then came back to the house and takeing me to where he could get me cross safely. And he did get me over safe, he takeing his rifile alone with him in case he had to use it.

I then began to organize the sugar labor. From Simmesport to West Melville La was the distent of 35 miles. I would walk this up and down untill I had reach every sugar cane labor up and down the achafalaya river. When I left this county of avolle, I went to Opelousas La., St. landry county.

I immediately went to work speaking in the churches. I was calling meeting in every community in 9 miles from Opelousas La. At one night we had call a meeting in a Negro school house, we had four hundred farmer to attend this meeting. We had school teacher and Negro business man also to attend, and they also made speach in the meeting.

In less then three month we had organize more then one thousand sharescropper into the unemployed council. We was organizeing so fast until an state organizer was forced to come in and organize a state office, and in a little while, when the organizer came we receive a state charter from the Farmer Education and Cooperative Union of America. The state organizer was a very good organizer. He was a young man. His name was Claud Johnson. He would organize the white, while I would organize the Negroes.[23]

At one time in st landry county when I had wrote several letters to the resettlement administration in Washington D.C. asking for imformation about

23. Clyde Johnson (1908–94) was the organizer who moved the Alabama-based Share Croppers' Union to New Orleans in 1936. Soon after the move, Johnson orchestrated an affiliation with the Farmers' Educational and Cooperative Union of America, which was also known as the National Farmers' Union, and brought in Gordon McIntire to serve as secretary. This was the beginning of the Louisiana Farmers' Union. Johnson soon moved to Washington, D.C., to lobby for the Wage Hour Act. The correspondence between McIntire and Johnson comprises much of the written record of the Louisiana Farmers' Union (see CJP).

Johnson was born in northern Minnesota. He became involved in radical organizing when he joined the National Students League (NSL) while studying at City College of New York. When he took over

teams, and about getting loan to buy teams with,[24] the planter wanted to know who was telling the sharecropper how to write to Washington D.C. That they could run their part of the country themselves. One night when I was at a meeting of one member house in st. landry county, three white planter came to this house and call the sharecropper out in the yard, and ask him to tell that fellow Clinton Clark to come out. The sharecropper said to the planter, What you all wanted with him. Tell me and I will tell Clark. The planter said no, we wants to tell it to him. The sharecropper then said, No? sir? I am responable for Clinton Clark, and if any body wants to talk with him while he is in my house they will have to see me. I will died for Clark. The planter then seen that the sharecropper mean real business. They then told the sharecropper what they wanted.

I still can remember the sharecropper name, J.B. Richard, a french decent.[25] The planter told richard, tell that fellow, Clark, to leave the county as quick as he can, and let those white people come and organize they own organization,

---

the SCU in 1935, he was already a veteran of southern labor organizing and actions. After his years with the SCU, he worked for the United Cannery, Agricultural, Packing and Allied Workers of America (UCAPAWA), a CIO-affiliated farm workers' union, first as research director and editor, then as the international vice president. He organized beet workers in Colorado, pecan workers in Texas, and flour mill and cotton compress workers in Houston. He worked for a number of labor publications and organizations up until the 1950s, when the McCarthy era forced him to work as a carpenter. He resumed union work in California in the late 1960s, when he became business agent of the Millmen's Union Local 550 in Oakland. In his later years he wrote extensively on labor history. See Kelley, "A Lifelong Radical"; Kelley, *Hammer and Hoe;* de Jong, *A Different Day.* The guide to "The Green Rising, 1910–1977," which contains the CJP, has a brief biography of Johnson.

Clark's misremembering of Johnson's first name may be a misspelling, or he is possibly confusing Johnson's name with that of Claude Williams, a white Arkansas minister who worked with the Southern Tenant Farmers' Union.

24. The Resettlement Administration was a New Deal agency created to address the needs of tenant farmers, especially those who had been displaced as a result of New Deal agricultural policies. Among other programs, it made loans to small farmers. It became part of the Farm Security Administration when the FSA was created in 1937.

25. John B. Richard was elected vice president of the LFU at its November 1937 convention. He was described in the union newsletter as president of Local #1 and "a faithful and outstanding leader of the colored farmers of St. Landry parish and one of the leading farmers in his community" (November 15, 1937, p. 2). Kelley describes Richard as the leader of a sit-down strike in St. Landry against the eviction of tenants from an FSA plantation (*Hammer and Hoe,* 169). He died in Arnaudville, St. Landry Parish, on April 13, 1992.

because he may get kill at any moment. Richard told the planter we will take care of Clark. When the planter was leaveing they told Richard well tell Clark we have warning him.

Mr Claud Johnson, the white farmer union organizer, made a tour over the state. He visitor every local I had organize. He didn't miss a one. Many days I went hungry. I knew that was a shame, but when I came across so many poor farmer almost starveing to death, didn't even have bread to eat in their house, then I became maddied and maddied. I became much busy organizeing those poor people of my class. I knew then if I had to work on a farm to starve, I would just as well sit under a shade tree, then to work on one of those slave plantation. I knew if all the poor farmer would organize and stick togather they would win better condition for all.

Then I would feel much better working on a farm. In those days the poor farmer was the forgotten man. In 1935–36 I continue my organizing in st. landry county; avolle county, pointe coupee county. In the latter part of 1936, the planter began to search for me in every fields. They had their stoolpigon out in every fields to locate me for the planter.

I knew then if I didn't stay out of the way for a while I would be killed. I then started traveling. I went to Dallas Texas, and found a job for the winter working in a garridge washing and greaseing cars, alone with ten others, for $1.50 a day. At lunch time I would get this group togather. I would tell them of my experience in Calif. and what the other worker was doing to better their condition, but they didn't seem to see into the matter so well. While being in Dallas I met with many white and Negroes union member, I also had the opportunity to see the white women worker of the Dallas laundary company pull a strike, and seen when the cops taken a group of them to the jail.

They won the strike. I will say these women had a strong picket line. When one day they had a bloody fight the cop jailed about 50 of them. I think it was two scabs killed.

I worked on this job in Dallas all the winter until 1937.[26] I was working as a extra man on this job. I left dallas in the first month in 1937–Headed for a big job I

26. Clark applied for his social security number (what was then called an "account number") while living in Dallas on January 6, 1937. His application lists his address as 2710 Union Alley in Dallas; he was working at the Fifteen Minute Auto Laundry at 813 Pearl Street in Dallas.

had been imform about in Niles Mich. I hitch hike on the highway until I made it to the state of Tenn. I then hop a frieght train and went to Chicago Ill, and spend three night with some of my relative there, then went to Niles Mich.

When I arrive in Niles Mich., I found a job helping a truck driver to haul gravel for a few week. When that job wine up with the gravel, I immediately found another one, working on a lake where the big business men would spend the summer. My job was to take care of the boats and cut grass around the yards. I would receive $8 a week to look after the boats and watch the water pump. I would get paid extria for the grass cuting work. When I had work for six month I bought a ford pick up and then began to make extria money, hauling junk from all over the city. When the summer was over and there was nothing to do any more, I had an oppertunity to continue hauling junk from the city of Niles, but as there wasn't enough junk to make a liveing during the winter, and to I wasn't use to the snow, I began to pack up, load up my truck, and started traveling for the south again. I had a lots of books that the business men had given me. I would read these books at all spare time. All alone the highway when I would stop for a rest, I would continue to read these books. This was my first time to read business guard on the world history. How to control your business. While being in Niles Mich, I had the oppertunity to meet with hundreds of the C.I.O. member working in plants. In the plant there was Negro and White worker. I went to several meeting of the C.I.O. and A.F.L. while being in Mich. Before leaveing Niles Mich. I had made many friend of these two union. They gave me the same encuragement that I had receive from the worker of Calif. They told me when I go back south dont stop until I get all the worker organize in the state of Louisiana, and in every part of the south where ever I would stop. When I arrive back in Louisiana, my first stop was in Palmetto La. where my Mother lived. And there was where I had been almost lynch once. It was in November 1937 when I arrive in Palmetto La. My brother Roger Clark was then out of a job and had a family to support. When he told me of his trouble, I immediately gave him my truck and told him to get out in the woods and make what you can to support your family. He was so happy over this until he didn't know did I mean this are not. He drove the truck home that eveing. The next day I left Palmetto La. headed for Natchitoches La. where I had been imformed of a big job was open. When I arrive in Natchitoches, I found a job. It was an extria gang takeing down the railroad fense. This job was just about to wine up. The wages were $1.50 for ten hour work. In two more weeks this job close down. I then went over on a large plantation just across from the line of Natchitoches county into red river county. The planter gave me a job immediately cutting down trees cleaning up new ground. The wages were 60¢ from sun to sun. On this plantation there were Mexican and Negro sharecropper. 96 farm family was on this plantation. The owner of this plantation live up north. The manager would go around to each sharecropper when the crop was layed by, and make an agreement with the sharecropper to buy his crop just as it stand. He would give him an offer for his crop. He would never offer no more then $10, no matter how much cotton you had. And if you refuse to sell your crop, you would fine yourself in debt when the time come to settle. No sharecropper ever knew anything about a Government check. I began to have secret conference with the best sharecropper on this plantation. One sharecropper ask me to write a letter for him to the A.A.A. department about his check. I immediately wrote this letter for him. In 8 days he receive a letter to call at the local office of the A.A.A. The sharecropper immediately takeing his letter to the county agent for advice. When the sharecropper arrive to the county agent office, the county agent ask the sharecropper did he work his crop and gather his crop. The sharecropper told the county agent yes, Sir? The county agent then said, Well if I was you, I would let this thing along, but you can do as you please about it. But the best thing to do is to let this thing. The county agent then made the sharecropper a promes. He told the sharecropper if he go back home and talk thing over with his boss and let the matter along he would fix him up the next year. The sharecropper went back home depending on the promes of the county agent. This sharecropper have never heard from the county agent any more. The sharecropper went to see the county agent many time on the same matter. Ever time the sharecropper went to see the county agent, he would hear the same story. Let this matter along. Are move to some other plantation if you cant get along with the one you living on. I would stay from the county agent office and would give the sharecroppers advice when they would go to see any of the Government agents, because these agents would work hand in hand with the planter. And I didn't want to be spoted out until we had a strong organization to protect ourselves. We never lost one minute. We continue organizeing the sharecroppers.

6 | Who Sent That Man Here?

We then drew up a plan to write a letter to the worker unemployed office in New Orleans, La. In six or seven days we receive a letter from the Louisiana Farmer Union sign by the state Sec'y Gordon McIntire, giving us all imformation how to set up a farmer union local in our community.[27] We immediately call a meeting and read the letter to the interested farmer. At that time we had to organize fifteen head of a farm family in a local before we could get a local charter. That night we set a meeting to get our number. We would have meeting with the best farmer ever night in different section on the plantation. Eaght days after we had our last meeting, we call another meeting to get our correct number to send for our charter. When this local was set up, we began to work to set up another one in red river county. Inside of three months we had three local organize on different plantation.

27. Gordon McIntire attended Commonwealth College in Arkansas, where he was recruited to the LFU by Clyde Johnson. McIntire was the secretary—what we today might call the executive director—of the LFU from 1937 until 1940. He was the main contact and support of a network of local groups of small farmers and sharecroppers across the state as well as the liaison to the National Farmers' Union. From New Orleans he organized locals around the state, visited them and spoke at their meetings, established and maintained cooperatives, monitored policy, wrote protest letters, testified at hearings, and wrote a newsletter that was sent to members across the state. He was frequently jailed and shot at. He was the secretary of the Southern Organizing Committee of the NFU, working to expand the union across the South.

The union had many successes under his leadership. In 1940, McIntire was diagnosed with tuberculosis. "He ran himself into his sickness," remembers his wife and one-time assistant, Peggy Dallet McIntire. Bedridden for over two years, McIntire stayed first in Charity Hospital in New Orleans, then in Sarnac Lake (New York), and finally in the National Jewish Hospital in Denver, Colorado, where the NFU had its headquarters. As he finally regained health, McIntire tried to reconstitute the union from his sick bed. He wrote a six-page letter to union members and friends, trying to reconnect them with each other. The letter closes with a sense of how much had changed and how much he had lost: "I am glad to have been able to write you all. I should like to hear from each of you but I cannot promise to answer your letters due to my health. I wish I could see and talk to each of you. You are the best friends I have ever had. I enjoyed working with you. My only regret is that I was not a better leader" (letter to Members and Friends of the Farmers' Union in Louisiana, March 10, 1942, CJP).

Our state sec'y Gordon McIntire made a tour up in Natchitoches county and red river county. He visit my local. Said we was doing a good job keep it up. McIntire went to some white farmer and organize them into the farmer union. After McIntire left, the sharecropper became more and more interested. They would come after me to make talk in their churches from all over the county. I would set meeting some time 25 miles apart. I would start walking that morning in order to make the meeting that night. We would have a meeting ever night some where in the fields. When the first three local was set up, I began to put in full time in organizeing. I would set the meeting in rotation, Wed, Thur, Fri, so I would have something to do three night in a week. When we had seven local organize, I would have seven nights to make a meeting in differient community. I had to walk ever step to make these meeting. My closed walk I had to go to a local meeting was fifteen miles. I would go to these meeting rain or sunshine. Many time I went to a meeting almost drowned. The member use to tell me, You better take care of yourself, You are doing more for the union then you care for yourself. I would tell them, I have to do this if I don't somebody will. Because we don't have no time to lose. The planter began to listen when some stoolpigon had give them the news about our union meeting. One planter went to one of the sharecropper house where we had our meeting some time. The planter told the sharecropper that it was a mob gang looking for that fellow Clark. And told him that if he didn't keep that fellow Clark from his house, the gang will get him too. And that he didn't wanted no lynching on his plantation. Another plantation in red river county where we set up

McIntire married Peggy Dallet in September 1942 and entered Denver University in a city management masters' degree program. Later he worked as city manager of Colorado Springs, and in Washington, D.C., he worked with the Bureau of the Budget and the Pan American Union. In 1952, he accepted a position with the Food and Agriculture Organization of the United Nations and relocated his family to Rome. Hours after his ninety-day provisional period had ended, he was fired without explanation. A long struggle to clear his name followed, during which the family's passports were revoked, leaving them stranded. They ultimately learned "that everything that was against him was McCarthyism" (Peg McIntire, interview).

McIntire built a business selling *Encyclopaedia Britannica* and *World Book* across Italy. Though he visited the United States, even returning in the 1960s to Louisiana, which he found disappointing, he did not want to move back. From Italy, he closely followed the U.S. civil rights struggles and independence movements in Africa. He traveled internationally and died unexpectedly while visiting Pakistan with his children in 1970. "Peg's Family's Reflections"; Peg McIntire, interview.

a local, we was haveing our meeting very close to the planter house, when he got the news about it. One saturday when the planter was paying the day labor their little saturday night money, he told them Now boys don't take this little money and give to that union fellow, so he can send it to New Orleans, La. to some union and made them rich. One time we had call a special meeting way back in the cotton field, where no cars traveled. The planter got the news from some where. About 8 p.m. that night, here come a long school bus with ten planter and a few school children, pretent like they were going fishing. Two of the planter came over to the house like they wanted some water. When the planter seen several more sharecropper in the house, they ask one of the sharecropper, What kind of meeting you all haveing here. The sharecropper said, No, we just visit our old friend as we usely do all the time go and see one another once and a while. The planters went down in front of the house where there was a stream of water. While they was out there talking, we drew up a plan. We had one old lady and one old man to go on the front porch and start singing a church song, and while they began to sing, we slip out the back door and went to another sharecropper house about a half mile away and carry our meeting on. When the planter left, we had our meeting and had maded back to our house and going to bed. The member had made up in they mine to stick with me no matter what happen. One planter had sent word to me by his sharecropper. If I didn't leave the county he would kill me where ever he see me. One day as I was hitch hiking to Powhattan La. from red river county, a big car drove up side of me and there was the planter who said he would kill me where ever he see me. He said to me, Get in here preacher. I said to him, Yes sir boss. I had a little hand bag in my hand. He seen the bag. He said to me, Are you a preacher? I said to him, Yes sir? He then ask me a few words out of the bible. I answer his question correct, and he ask me what church will I be to that night. I told him what church I would be, but I didn't give him the correct church that I would be, because I thought he would bring his mob gang to get me out. He then told me to get all the member of the church to know that it is a union man coming around. And if they should happeing to see him, they better not fool with him, because that union will get them into trouble. IF I get my hands on him it will be to bad for him. He will never fool with another union any more soon. I said to the planter, Yes Sir? I will sure get them told. And I will keep you posted of that union man too if I can see him. I continue my discussion with him until I get out of his car. When I went to the meeting that night, that was the first thing I began to talk about. I had a lots of fun with the member that night. The sharecropper laugh for more then a half hour. They thought that was the funnest thing they ever heard of before. All of this was doing the year of 1938. During this year I set up ten new local or more. I was busy as a bee, walk in rain in mud ever where I could reach the member. Some places when it would rain to much, we would have get boats to go to the meeting. It didn't make no differient. I would urge the member to get the boat, because I had made my promas to the member that I would never disapoint them. And I had give them my word to be at all meeting unless something happen, and if they didn't see me in one meeting, they better get on they horses and look me up and see what has happen to me. In the fall in 1938, McIntire sent out bulleton calling all local to send delagate to the state convention. We elected five delagate to go alone with me. We ranted one of the member car to make the trip. We had our problem all made out to take to the convention. When we arrive to the state convention, our state Sec'y McIntire had several government offical there to give imformation and answer question. There was also a couple hundred of sharecropper from all part of the state, giving some hard story of differient kind and they was true story. Our Natchitoches county Problem was, It was a large plantation up in Natchitoches county that belong to some big company up north and want to sell. When we put our problem before the state meeting, our state sec'y McIntire put it up before the state dirrector of the F.S.A.[28] And he gave us the proper imformation. He told us to go back to Natchitoches county and take up the matter with the county F.S.A. Supervisor. When we went back to Natchitoches county and made our report to all the local, we taking up how much each family own in stock around his house. We appointed a committee of five to have a conference with the F.S.A. Supervisor. When the committee went to see the F.S.A. supervisor, he gave the committee a promas to take up the matter and give it to consideration in a few days, and would let them know when to come back to talk the matter over. About two week later we got the news that the F.S.A. had bought this plantation. Most of the member receive cards from the Supervisor to come to his office. In the began of 1939 on this plantation the F.S.A. had 47 farm family to move on this farm. There was a oppertunity for the sharecropper that they had

28. The LFU held its 1938 state convention in Baton Rouge. The Farm Security Administration was created in 1937 within the U.S. Department of Agriculture to administer programs to help small farmers, especially displaced tenant farmers. It gave hundreds of thousands of dollars in loans to small farmers for farm supplies and equipment, and gave millions of dollars in loans to help families purchase land.

never had before in life.[29] After that victory was won the sharecropper became more interested. We then set up five more new local. Every sharecropper you could meet he would be talking about the farmer union, telling the other sharecropper that he better join that farmer union are they wish they had after while. One sharecropper came from a plantation in red river county one day looking for me as he had heard that I could tell him how he could get his Government check. He ask me if I could come and have a meeting in his community. I told him sure, Nothing would hender me from coming to their community. He went back and round up several sharecropper togather to meet in his house one night. This plantation was located in red river county and part of this plantation also was locate in Natchitoches county, 250 sharecropper family on this farm who had never heard of a government check. The first night I went on this plantation to have a meeting only about 25 or 27 sharecropper came out to hear me speak. We held our first meeting at one of the sharecropper house. I had every one to write a statement of how much cotton he had made from the begining of the A.A.A. We then set another meeting to get more sharecropper out. The next night we had 75 sharecropper to attend our meeting. When we had over a hundred sharecropper to write his statement on his back crop, we immediately forward these statement to Sec'y Wallace for consideration.[30] In fifteen days later every sharecropper on this plantation receive a letter from the A.A.A. department telling them how much they check would be. When every sharecropper receive his check it was a great shock all over the plantation. They wanted to know who sent that man here. Some said god must have send him here. And some would call me a government man.

29. Clark had earlier written this story in a letter that was published in a special edition of the LFU newsletter for cotton tenants. His letter is similar (and probably served as source material for the narrative) but includes names. The families were resettled on what was known as the Allen Plantation, located in Natchitoches Parish. Representatives from Long Star Local #38 had met with H. G. Swander, assistant director of the state FSA program, at the LFU state convention in Baton Rouge. After the convention, a committee elected by the local met with the parish FSA supervisor, R. D. Prothro. See "Union Members Start Cooperative Farm (Letter from Clinton Clark)," *Louisiana Farmers' Union News,* June 1, 1939, bulletin no. 62, p. 4, LFU-VF.

30. Henry A. Wallace (1888–1965) served as secretary of agriculture in the Roosevelt Administration from 1933 to 1941, implementing the agriculture programs of the New Deal, such as the Agricultural Adjustment Act. He would later be Roosevelt's vice president (1941–45), replaced just before Roosevelt's death by Harry Truman. Wallace ran against Truman in the 1948 presidential election as the Progressive Party candidate.

Many of them came over and hand me $2. $3. $1. I refuse to except they money but they insist on me to take the money and told me to buy a suit of cloth to remember them. The sharecropper was so happy over this victory. I think they talk a little to much about the matter until the news reach the plantation owner, and the rideing boss began to get busy looking for the fellow who was doing all that writting to the government for these nigger he said. The rideing boss told some of the sharecropper he didn't beleave it was a nigger doing that. He said must be some white yanke from up north doing all this mess. He told the sharecropper they didn't have to write to Washington D.C. He was going to see to them getting they check. He began to ride his horse ever day with his gun on his saddle. And told his sharecropper where every he see that fellow what doing all this writting he would kill him. No matter what the rideing boss said the sharecropper would bring me the news and put me on the spot. We continue with our meeting secret, every night we would meet some where. By getting these check for these sharecropper the news spread all over the plantation belt. The sharecropper would come from miles looking for me to get imformation how to write to the government for their checks. On this large plantation in red river county, every sharecropper had to sign a fake contract, where they had to give so many free days work and only allow to have one milk cow. If you get over his number you would have to sell out are pay him $5 a head for each month you keep them on the plantation. And such as a garden you would have to give him half of every thing you planted in the garden. If any work need to be did on the road are fix a bridge you would have to help fix the bridge and the road. If it take a month you would have to work free of charge are move to some other plantation. I would stay out of sight. I would stay at one of the best sharecropper house in the day time so no one would see me. If the rideing boss are a stoolpigon would pass by the house, I would go inside of the house and stay hid in the house until they would get out of sight. And when it would get dark, I would start out for the meeting place. Some time I would start out that night after the meeting way up in the night walking to be at the next meeting place. I would have to do most of my sleeping in the day, because the planter was hot behine my trail. And I couldn't work on no more plantation in that section. No planter wanted me on his plantation. They said I had a racket that was no good for the people up in red river county. They would lay for me every where they thought I would pass. They even had some of their stoolpigon out carrying guns with them to kill me where ever they see me.

But my good member were on guard for me. They would keep me posted.

In 1939 I had made up in my mine to build the union so strong that when the planter would rise up and try to stop our union, they would meet up with such a strong force that the fear would be in his eyes. I would contact ever school teacher and good preachers, ask them to cooperative with our union. The teacher and preachers began to get interested. The preacher would let us have his church to have our meeting. And the teacher would let us have the school houses. Many teacher was elected to hold some office in our farmer union local, as most of the teacher husband was farming. We then organize a county union with County President, County Sec'y, Tres, County Board members, and had rented the mason hall to have our county meeting twice a month. We had rented an office in Natchitoches for our offical business. I never lost one hour during this time. I contact all the Negro business men in Natchitoches La. Coushatta La. Campti La. and in many other city around where ever I could reach them. About the middle of 1939 we had around fifteen local. I would have to make two meeting a night in order to keep the union rolling. I hardly would ever get to ride to a meeting. Some meeting would be not less then 25 miles apart. But regardles what happen I wouldn't miss one, because the sharecropper would always be exspecting me at they meeting. Many time I would be sick and broke down from walking so much. But in order to not disapoint them, I would walk if it would be 25 miles. Our state sec'y Mr. McIntire had organize a buying club in the southern part of Louisiana, so the member could buy cooperative and make a saveing. As soon as we receive this imformation we began to organize a buying club in our section. Our first order we send in to our state sec'y was a little over a hundred dollar from one local. Another local send in a little over twenty five dollar. When our state sec'y seen that we was getting down to real business up in Natchitoches county, McIntire get in his car and drove alway up to Natchitoches from New Orleans, a distence of a little better then two hundred miles. When he came up he immediately contact the wholesale Company in Natchitoches La. and made arrangement for our local to buy dirrect from the Natchitoches wholesale company. After Mr McIntire giveing us our start, we was busy makeing our order ever two week.[31] We contact another

31. To help members buy goods at better prices than the plantation store demanded, the LFU provided order forms for farmers to buy groceries and household supplies at wholesale prices. Clark's locals in the Natchitoches area carried the cooperative principle much further. Here is Gordon McIntire's

wholesale Company up in Shreveport La. to buy our fertilize. We would buy so many ton of fertilize from the wholesale Company at one time, and the wholesale Company would deliver our fertilize without cost. When the plantation owner heard the news about our buying club, they ask the member question. Wanted to know where they was buying their supplies from, because they didn't see them any more at the robberserrys. The planter threaten one of our member to kill him because he refuse to give him the imformation he wanted. The planter made two shot in this member house. This sharecropper was forced to leave his home and stay away for some time, and when he did come back he would have to slip to see his wife. He had seven children also. The planter was looking for me ever where. We was building the union so fast until the planter was telling all the sharecropper if they join that union they would have to look for another place to move. The planter had they stoolpigon out in ever fields, and we had our stoolpigon out in ever fields to keep me posted of how the planter had they trap set for me.

I knew the planter would kill me if they layed their hand on me. The fact [was] that the sharecropper was unimform of the Government checks, and never knew what they cotton was selling for. And many of them never had a settlement from his planter for crops he has made for years. On one plantation near Natchitoches the sharecropper are not allow to go visit the next owner plantation. If he do go without promisson, Mr. Taylor will use the whip on his naked. If a sharecropper would get a Lawyer in around that section, they would be getting the planter Lawyer.

The Taylor plantation was very large. He used his sharecropper like slave. Until to day he haven given his sharecropper a settlement for they crops. Mr. Taylor dont allow his sharecropper to talk to each other when they are working in the field. No visitor allow on his plantation unless they get permission from Mr. Tay-

account of the Natchitoches buying club: "I had an interesting experience at Natchitoches where three Locals had sent in a combined order of more than $200. My original thought was that the orders would not be more than $15 or $20 and that I could carry the merchandise in my own car on a regular trip. Since this was impossible we were forced to make arrangements with a Natchitoches wholesale and found that the manager got his start in merchandising some 80 years ago with the old Farmer Wheel and one of its local cooperatives up in the Ozarks! I haven't advertized this latter fact but at least Mr. McKern showed himself very willing to deal with our colored members directly and they are handling the whole business at this time without any orders or correspondence coming to this office" (letter to Clyde Johnson, November 11, 1939, p. 2, CJP).

lor first. Mr. Taylor used his whip on his sharecropper when they get to be bad nigger he said. One time he started to put the whip on one of the sharecropper wife while she was hoeing in the field. Because Mr. Taylor said she talk back to him when he told her to move on. But the sharecropper wife taken Mr. Taylor on a suprize. She raised the hoe up in the air to come down on Mr. Taylor head. But Mr. Taylor excape. He took to his heels. And never came back in the field for a few weeks, until he thought the sharecropper wife had cool off. There was another plantation about 12 miles from Natchitoches. The onwer names Mr. Timon and Judge Cunningham. The two planters had an different way of whiping they sharecroppers. Judge Cunningham, he would call all his sharecropper out of the field into his yard. Judge had a box in the yard. He would stand on this box and make long speeches to the sharecroppers. The judge speeches would sound good to these sharecroppers untill no sharecroppers would dare to say that judge Cunningham beat them out of they crops. Judge Cunningham was a smart man. He was a lawyer and used to be the judge of Natchitoches county. When every another small white planter would beats his Negro sharecroppers out of his stocks are crops, Judge would take it up for the Negro sharecropper in court aganist the small white planter and would win the case for the Negro sharecropper. But things never turn out in the Negro favor. What ever the judge would collect from the small planter, he would keep it for himself and this Negro sharecropper would have to move on judge cunningham plantation. If he didn't stay on judge cunningham plantation, Judge wouldn't get him out of trouble anymore. When judge cunningham would be making his speeches to his sharecroppers, he would preach to them like a Negro preacher. He would show them how easy they would get to heaven if they would keep praying. Don't never worrie about anything down here on earth. If they do they would be show to go to hell and be burn to dust. Most of the sharecroppers fell for judge cunningham because judge would get them out of trouble and would not let the other fellow take anything from them and would always preach to them how to be safe. But on the other hand judge was bad then the other fellow. These sharecroppers has never gotten a settlement from judge cunningham until this day. Many sharecroppers are afread to protest to the judge cunningham because he change they mine when ever he preach to them. These sharecroppers forget about the settlement when the judge preach them the way to go to heaven. Judge Cunningham had two big farm that he had taken from some Negro youth. The Negro youth father had died and left this farm from them.

Judge cunningham claim that they father owes him some money way back and these youths didn't know anything about the matters. But the judge framed up with other ring group in the court. And taken the farm from the youths. There was the Timon plantation would used a little different way to take from the sharecroppers what ever their made in the fields. He would buy each sharecropper a pair mules and ever thing they need to work with. But they would have they life time to pay for the mules and other things. Well he said they will never pay for them. They will die in debt with Mr. Timon. He sell all the cotton with his name on the bail. Mr. Timon has a robberserry. They get all they food out of Mr. Timon Robberserry. Only on Xmas when the sharecroppers see a little money to make a little sweet bread. And buy a little wine and a cigar. And sing his little song. Xmas don't come but once a year cheer cheer. In red river county there was a Dr. who own another large plantation. He would keep all the Negro sharecroppers afread of him. He shot his nourish that work in his office. She was a beauty young white girl. He was a drunker. He kill three Negro sharecropper had no excuse to do so. One time one of his sharecropper was hoeing in his corn field. And this Doctor son came in the field where this sharecropper was hoeing his corn. He told the sharecropper to leave that corn along and go in the cotton and hoe. The sharecropper refuse to do so. The sharecropper told the Doctor son that he had already work in the cotton. And it was time to work in his corn. So the Doctor son became angry and left on his horse and went to tell his daddy that a nigger talk back to him. The Doctor came back with the sherriff of Coushatta La in red river county and three others. And taking this sharecropper out of the field into his house and made him take off his cloths and layed him on the floor naked. And the sherriff put his feet on his head and taking a big rope and cut into his meat. Blood ran down fast. This old man was 75 years old. Until to day this old man is not able to walk. This Doctor taking everthing this old man had, two mules and all his chicken, hogs, and told him to leave the county at once. When I gotten the news, I immediately wrote the matter to Mr. Gordon McIntire, our state secy. of the farmer union. When Mr. McIntire wrote back for full imformation, the Doctor had a mob gang out looking for me all over the fields. The Dr. said I will show that nigger how to run other people business. Some of his Negro stoolpigon had told him that I was writting this mess into the news paper. For days I had to stay out of sight. He even had some of my own race carrying gun to kill me where ever they see me. But My best members had them posted and also the gang. They kept me in a safe place and would let me know where ever they would be are what was said about me and we also had our guns ready for the mob gang when ever they would attact me. We thought it was a god blessing thing they didn't meet together with my group. All the rideing boss would carry their guns on they saddle telling all they sharecroppers that they just wants to lay they eyes on me. One of the rideing boss said, If I see that nigger, I bet he want go around here fooling these niggers anymore. I will put him in the right place. Many days I work in the cotton fields side by side of my fellow sharecroppers telling them that we had to get to gether to get our justice from the planter. If it cost blood we had made up our mine to organize and forced the planters to give justice to the sharecroppers all over the cotton fields. At one time this Doctor was rideing in his car from town as drunk as he could be. Two old Negro farmer was laying down side the highway. The Dr. stoped his car and order these two Negro to move off the highway in a hurry. The two Negro ask him what was his trouble. The Dr. fired two shot killed both of the Negro. And he went and order the Negro off his plantation to hook up the wagon and get those two nigger off the highway. And it was nothing ever did about this killing. Once again on one saturday a group of Negro sharecroppers was gathering around the big plantation store.

Two of these Negro started playing with each other. The Dr. son went out where these two Negro was with his pistol in his hand and said to them, You nigger stop that fighting around here. One of the Negro said we are not fighting we are playing. Without another word the Dr. son shot and kill the poor Negro. And nothing was said about this are give justice to the Negro in red river county.

Another thing when ever a sharecropper went to sign any papers with the F.S.A. are the A.A.A. and the planters know anything about it, this sharecropper would have to move immediately. Before any sharecroppers went to any government office, he would have to ask the planters could he go. If the planters didn't agree you would have to stay where he tell you. When ever your government A.A.A. check would come to you on some of the plantation and you got the check and didn't bring the check to the planters big store you are subject to be killed. And it did happen that way one day when two sharecroppers receive they check and had bought their ticket to ride the train to town to get their check cash. The planter heard about the matter just before the train came up. The planter went to the depot and didn't ask the sharecroppers one word. He shot them both. The train agent called up the sherriff from Coushatta La. When the sherriff came he taking the two Negro sharecroppers to the Dr. and order them to stay out the county when they get the Dr. treatment. After that happen many sharecroppers wanted to move but the planter lock the gate and told them if they wanted to move just give him $50 and they could move. So no sharecroppers had that amount of money to pay so they stay on the plantation for another year and suffer hard. Ever one was afread to say anything about moveing any more. But the union began to grow fast in red river and Natchitoches county. Because the sharecropper was getting aganist the planters with all they might.

7 | They Sure Wants to Kill You Bad

In the summer of 1939, McIntire our state secy of the Louisiana farmer union called me down to New Orleans. At that time the Government offical was having a sugar cane hearing in Baton Rouge La. The big cane grower would be there to fight the cane labor wages. So McIntire round up the cane labor both white and Negroes. McIntire taking me up in rapee county to organize the Negro cane labor in Lecompti La., about 19 miles from Alexandria La.[32] When Mcintire was leaving in his car to go back down near Baton Rouge to organize a group of white labors to take to Baton Rouge with him, he told me, Clark get them together. I know you can do it. If anything happen you know our telephone number called up our office. My first night in Lecompti La. I round up five sugar cane labors and explan to them how importan it would be if we get a group of cane labor to go over to the sugar cane hearing in Baton Rouge. So we set up a plan that night to get the church the next night and get a large group out so I could make a speech to them. So we had ever thing arange o.k. for the meeting. The next night we gotten out 75 cane labor. Most of them had been working on the cane farm below the sugar cane wages that was set by the Sec'y of Agrul. Wallace. The wages was set at $1.50 for men for 10 hours and $1.20 for women for 10 hours. The planters was only paying the men $1 and the women 90¢ for 10 hour. So the 75 cane labors filled out blanks that McIntire had made up in the proper form. These blanks would be filed to McIntire and he would forward them to Washington D.C. for consideration. So we set another meeting for the next night in the same church in Lecompti. About two hundred came the next night. One hundred and fifty filled out blanks that night. We also elected five delegate to go to Baton Rouge for the sugar cane hearing. The money was raised in this meeting to pay the delegate fees. We rented a car to take the delegate to the sugar cane hearing. The next morning we left out

32. The Sugar Act of 1937 had established minimum wages for workers on sugarcane plantations; the LFU regularly spoke at state hearings to determine the wages and conditions of compensation of sugarcane workers. "Rapee county" is a reference to Rapides Parish, just southwest of Natchitoches, La.

in the car for Baton Rouge, where we would meet McIntire with the white cane labors. When we arrive in Baton Rouge, McIntire had a truck load of white cane labors there in the sugar cane hearing. The meeting was held in the L.S.U. at the University La. of the Agrul Dept. At first they didn't want Negroes in the meeting. But McIntire protest that they let the Negro come in and testify. So they did let us in to testify. I will have to say a few words in congratlation on McIntire work. He was the best white worker I ever work with. He was cool headed. He knew just how to go at the work to get the job done. Where ever he went to put over a good job, he did it. And it was a good one too. All over the state of Louisiana you can hear the sharecropper speaking about Mr. McIntire work. Even the landlord are glad that he taking sick. Because he kept them straight when ever they tried to put they crocket work on the sharecroppers. At one time the landlord was talking about killing McIntire where ever they see him. When McIntire heard about what the planter said, McIntire went to talk it over with the planter. The planter seen that McIntire was a brave man. And was not afread of them. So the planter invited McIntire over to their home for a friendly discussion. One time McIntire had called a mass meeting in Pointe Coupee county to organize the white and Negro sharecroppers. He had put out hundred of leaflet all over the county. And hundred of sharecroppers both white and Negroes came out to hear him speak. The plant-ers had organize a mob gang to break up the meeting. But McIntire went to the county court and seen the high sherriff. And the sheriff taking his dupitys alone with him and seen that this meeting went through. Good work for McIntire. So now after we left the sugar cane hearing, when I gotten back to Lecompti La. I immediately started organizeing the sugar cane labors. McIntire had file our claim for the back pay. But it wasn't long the planters got the news that it was some smart guy up there trying to run their business. They began to organize they mob gang. One of the big planter called all his sharecropper togather one morning just before they hitch up they mules. He made a long speech to them. He said to them, Boys they telling me it is somebody around here trying to run our business. Now I want to telling you all it is no body up in Washington going to run our business down here. We will take care of the south ourselves without the help of the offical up in Washington D.C. Now if it is any one of you belong to that union, you better pack up and move immediately. Are it going to be to bad. The next morning one of the sharecropper that had filed a claim against the planter and myself went to the post office to get our mail. This sharecropper receive a letter from the sugar division in Washington telling him where to meet the Government offical to investagate the matter. So while we was reading the letter in the post office, there was ten planter in the post office sizeing me up from my head to my feet. I wasn't noticing them. But my friend was. My friend said to me very low, Look how those people looking after you. Then I began to watch them to see if they realy was looking me over. And that what they was doing. We walk out of the post office and the planters follow us out step by step. So my friend and I split up. He said you go one way and I will go another and watch them to see what they are trying to do. So I went around the corner to one of the cane labor home. And the planters gotten into their cars and follow me to see where would be my stoping place. Before they just past by the house looking toward the house where I had stoped. So when they gotten out of my sight, I immediately went way back in the field where there was the complete plantation had join in with me to build the union. That night the planters and the sherriff and city police went to the house where they had seen me and search the house looking for me. And went and question my friend what was along with me in the post office. And they question every Negro in the little town of Lecompti La. About two hundred mob gang the highway from Bunkie La. to Lecompti La., a distent of 35 miles, searching for me. That night about 12 O.clock my friend came back in the field where I was and told me to lay quite until the matter blow over and we can get you out of here, because they sure wants to kill you bad. All the sharecroppers on this plantation came togather with me and surrounded the house with old piece of shot guns, sticks and bottle iron to fight the mobs gang if they did attacted me. All night long the sharecroppers stuck by me. The next morning two sharecroppers went in the little town to see what was going on. When he went into the town, he seen a preacher. This preacher said to him if you see that fellow Clark, you better tell him to get out the way in a hurry because the mob is sure looking for him to hang him. And they are threaten to kill all the sharecroppers that join that union. So the sharecroppers came back and told me the story. We immediately wrote a special deliver and send one sharecropper to mail it on the train where the planters woulden see him getting the letter off. And I stayed hid in the field until the next day. And one of the sharecropper went and rented a car from a good Negro preacher. And five sharecroppers went along in the car with me. They taking me to Alexandria La. where I wire our state Sec'y Gordon McIntire and told him the whole trouble. And McIntire immediately forward the matter to the sugar cane division in Washington

D.C.[33] And he send me Money to go back to Natchitoches La. and continue my organizeing work. So I went back to Natchitoches and started working immediately. I went to every local and told them we must get busy. We started our meeting to going in a rotation. We would have three meeting in one night. In two week we had five new local set up and five others waiting for me to come and explan to them how to set they local. I didn't lose one second, worked night and day organizeing every new community that I could reach. We began to set up buying club in ever local. The planter began to spread the news to all the planters to watch for the union organizer. Telling all the sharecroppers that they better let that union along if that union fellow come by and ask you all to join that union. Because that union is going to get you all into trouble. I went to every community and organize every school teachers and preachers. We started having our meeting in the school houses and the churches. At first we were having our meeting in the sharecroppers

33. The planters were striking back at Clark and union members for filing for back wages owed under the Sugar Act of 1937. The LFU had created a small booklet to help workers record their time and payment. (A copy of one of these is in the LFU-VF.) On July 1, 1939, the union had sent a demand for back wages to the Agricultural Conservation Associations (the local parish committees) in all the sugar parishes, demanding that the AAA payments be withheld from the plantations that owed back wages. Some of the members of the parish committees were planters who were on the list as owing back wages. "Immediately upon receipt of the wage claims in the office of the Agricultural Conservation Association," McIntire wrote to Gardner Jackson of the Washington-based Labor's Non-Partisan League, "terror broke out in Rapides Parish, where one of the big landlords against whom we had entered several claims, was Chairman of the Parish Committee" (July 17, 1939, CJP).

On July 11, 1939, McIntire wrote to Joshua Bernhardt, chief of the Sugar Division, describing the threats made on the lives of Clark and union members who had filed for back wages and urging the agency to protect them. McIntire was trying to push the federal agency to intervene at the local level to ensure that the law was enforced. In his letter McIntire quotes an entire letter that he received from Clark describing the incident; unfortunately the microfilm copy is difficult to read: "Now this is the way it happened. Those wage claim blanks were mailed to [name unreadable] committeeman of Lecompte and he told all the landlords about those wage claims. And they went hogs wild about this. They began to question every Negro they saw about it. They also sent the law looking for me everywhere they thought I had stayed a night. They have notified every law and landlord from Lecompte to Bunkie. I know this because a preacher came to Lecompte and told us about it. He told us to be careful" (CJP).

Historian Greta de Jong has found evidence that the FBI and Department of Agriculture did send agents out into the Louisiana countryside to investigate these complaints in August and September 1939. "The FBI's involvement was reluctant, and its agents showed more sympathy with plantation owners than with sugar workers" (*A Different Day,* 112 and 248–49, n. 85).

shacks. Several teachers and preachers join our union and taking lead in their community. The union began to grow so strong until the planters began to get afread and worry.

So we started organizeing for a big mass meeting. First we called all the offical of the parish union to discuss on how we should organize our mass meeting. We contact with one of the Wealthier Negro business man. He was the owner of a large masonic hall. He rented this hall to our parish union. This Negro business man, his name Scott Lewis. He had a Brother by the name of John Lewis who own a very large plantation himself. But these two brother cooperative with us in many ways in suporting us. There was also a Negro Dr. name Johnson. And a Negro F.S.A. Agent they also cooperative with us. These Negro business man told me many times, We know these planters are not treating these sharecroppers right. And for many years being cheated out of they crop and Government checks. Also many of the white sharecroppers had lean they suport to help build the farmer union. The white sharecroppers were being treated just as bad as the Negro sharecroppers. And some time worst. When we held our first meeting in the masonic hall, the wholesale Co. send one representer to explan to us how we could make a big saving if we continue to buy our food cooperative. And we did continue buying our food cooperative. Every two week our local would send the wholesale Co. one big order. But the planters could not stand for this to continue, because it would close the planters robberserry down. And the planters would not have the chance to steal from the poor sharecroppers any more. We continue perparing for our big meeting to come off in july 1940. Every member was perparing to bring a basket with chicken and cakes and many other good farmers foods. I had distribute one thousand leaflet for the purpost of this mass meeting.

The planters gotten hold of the leaflet. And too we taking a committee to see the mayjor about getting a permit to have this meeting. We explane to the mayjor about our buying club and what the meeting was called for. He agree for us to have the meeting without a permit so long as we having this meeting in the day time. Our main reason for taking this committee to see the mayjor was because Scott Lewis called me in his office one day and told me that the planters told him not to let us have this meeting in his masonic hall. But Scott Lewis told me if we go and see the mayjor and get a permit we could go ahead and have the hall for our meeting. The planters send all kind of threat to me trying to get me afread and leave the town. Before the day for the meeting, Mr Taylor the Negro slave driver would ride up and down the gravel road all day long stoping every Negro that would pass him asking them for that fellow Clark. He told the Negroes that he would kill Clark where ever he see him. Mr. Taylor stoped ever Negro Insurance agent he seen rideing in a car, as Mr. Taylor was imform that Clark was rideing in a V8 car. And when ever he seen a Negro rideing in a V8, Mr. Taylor would stop him and ask him his name. And told the insurance agent that he was looking for that nigger you call Clark what going around here fooling these nigger in that thing they call a union. Mr. Taylor called all his sharecroppers one morning and ask them how many of them belone to that thing. No sharecroppers give him any answer. And that made him much angry. He told his sharecroppers if he knew any one of his sharecroppers who belone to that thing it will be the last of them. And he said that thing is going to get some of you nigger neck broke. Mr. Taylor had his stoolpigon watching all his sharecroppers to see if any one went to the farmer union meeting. He had also warned them not to attend the parish union meeting what we was planing to hold in july. Mr. Taylor and his stoolpigon neather one stop the sharecroppers. They continue going to they farmer union meeting ever other night in the school house one miles from Mr. Taylor plantation. At one time when the America youth congress was having they convention up north, we had elected four high school studen to go to this youth congress convention to represent the farmer youth in the south.

Mr. Taylor and some of the other big planters heard about these four Negro youth going to this meeting. The planters didn't like it. They tried all they could to find out how did those kid get to this convention.[34] The planters called a big meeting in Natchitoches town and they envited Scott Lewis, Dr. Johnson, and several other Negro Leader of Natchitoches. The planter was trying to get these Negro leader to get me out of the parish. But it didn't work like the planter wanted it to work. Most of these Negro leader kept me imform of the trick the planter was

34. The American Youth Congress (AYC) was the national federation of left student organizations founded in 1934. The organization proposed and lobbied for the American Youth Act, a New Deal aid bill for low-income and unemployed young people, which did not pass. Robert Cohen summarizes the rest of the organization's agenda: "The movement's activism on behalf of domestic reform also included free speech fights on many campuses, support work for the Congress of Industrial Organizations' blue-collar organizing, the establishment of campus cooperatives and student labor unions, and campaigns against racial segregation in college area stores, services, recreational facilities, athletic teams, and in university admissions" ("Student Movements, 1930s," 801). It was the son of local black businessman Scott Lewis who attended the AYC. See Margery Dallet, letter to John P. Davis, August 4, 1940, folder 56, box 22, NNC.

trying to play them aganist me. Dr. Johnson, Scott Lewis, John Lewis, these three Negro leader of Natchitoches County said to me in a conference we had togather one day, Clark, We know these sharecroppers has been treated unjust on these plantation. The planter wanted us to join hands with them to brake up your union. We appreacated you being in our county getting these sharecroppers togather so they can get justice from the planters.

Many times before our meeting came off the planter layed for me where they thought was my pass way.

They were in the right pass way at all time. But our membership was so strong, the news would get to me befor I would ever go through the pass way. The planters and the sherriff had spoted my rooming place and they even layed out there for me several night as I was out to my meeting places. But I had been imform of their tricks. And would never let them get close enough to me in the night. So they never did have the chance they wanted.

After the planters seen that all their threats couldn't get me afread, so I would leave that meeting alone and leave the county, they had all the leading Negro school teachers to call me togather and have a conference with me. So one morning about five O.clock, one hour befor the sun rise, I was awoken by one little school kid, handing me a letter that the princble of the Natchitoches high school had send me. He was asking me to call at the high school for 5 p.m. As it was very importian conference he wanted me to be there without a fail. I was already perpared for anything, regardles what it would be, meeting are anything that may come up. So I went to this meeting without a fail. When I went to this conference, there was five of the most importian leading teachers there. More was supose to be there but some way they fail to show up. This conference taking me to a much suprise. When the chairman open up the conference, he said this meeting was call to get imformation from Clark about this union that has the whole country stirred up. He ask me to tell them some about the union. What is the aim of the farmer union. Is it the C.I.O. are is it the A.F.L. So I began to explan to them what the farmer union stand for. I told them that the farmer union was a organization for the poor class of farmer, education for the poor farmers so they may be able to do busines as the big farmer are doing. We are teaching them how to buy they food cooperative. And how to plant plenty of food stuff in their garden to put up for the winters. And what they should eat for they health. And how importian it is for them to learn to pull to gather and love each other.

So the princeble ask me was that meeting going on any way. I said to him why sure its going on. He said to me, You said Clark, you have seen the mayjor about giving your meeting. Well supose the major be out of town. And one of the planters come over to this meeting on his horse with a gun and get down and walk into your meeting and shoot you down. I said to him, Well no doubt it may happen. But still I do know I am right and we not going to put this meeting off on no bluff. And another Teacher who stand for the planters aganist the sharecroppers, Mrs. Breader Lewis, she said to me, My young fellow I can do you good and I can do you harm. Before she could get the word out the princeble said to Mrs. Breader, We didn't come here for that. When she said that question to me, as I know she was the Bosses stoolpigon, I told them a little story. Some thing like this. I said do you all know who made the first train. It was Stevenson. Many people said he was crazy. They said he didn't know what he was doing. When the day come for stevenson to try out his train, every body came out to see if the train was going to run. And when Stevenson had the train running, they said you never stop it. Well the planters said the same thing about the poor farmers. They said the sharecroppers was lazy, they would never organize. So today we are organizeing the sharecroppers. And you will never stop them from organizeing to better their condition.

I said they may kill me. But that will never stop the poor people from organizeing to improve their condition. So one of the leading teacher said to me, Well you know we live here. And if we wants to continue to live here we will have to stay in our place. So again they ask me how long had I been organizeing in Natchitoches county. I said to them three years and one half. Mrs. Breader the planters stoolpigon, she wanted to continue to ask question about the union. But the princeble of the school rejected and said Clark have to go to his meeting now. We will close our conference. Just before inter the conference I had told the teachers that I had to make three meeting that night. So I left in my car in a hurry to make those three meeting.

Mrs. Breader also left in a hurry. She went to let the planters know about our meeting.[35]

---

35. An August 31, 1940, *Chicago Defender* article about Clark's release identifies her as Mrs. Beatrice Breda and reports that she "agitated and caused his arrest." The article identifies principal Gaddis C. Hall and principal emeritus J. W. Thomas.

That was our last night before the big meeting would come off. Mrs. Breader told the planters and the planters organize they gang with their big guns laying for me to come from the meeting that night so they could kill me before the big meeting come off the next day. But I was imform about them before the sun went down. And my members and I went perpare for them at all our meeting. And I didn't went to my room that night.

We had three big meeting that night. And told all the members that we was not going to let the planters brake up our union. In the meeting ever member said No, No, We going to roll our union over them. We have our right to organize to better our condition in a union. Just as the planters have their union to fight us, to keep us from getting our right. Ever members in the meeting had something to say that night. They told me that they was 100% behine me. And said they will go down with me if it take blood to keep you here with us to keep our union rolling so we can get our justice from these no good planters. They have been robbering us out of our crops and labors long enough. And we are getting dam tired of it. We rather died then to continue to living this way. We are not a bit better than our grandfather. We are slaveing for them and getting nothing out of our crops. Ever new year we are still in debts to them. Just look what happen on Mr. W. Prince plantation. He call all of us togather last year to give our settlement. When we went to get our settlement he gave each one of us one gallon of port wine for our settlement. Yes we going to build our union and fight for our right. We going to have our meeting tomorrow. We don't care what the planters say. Everbody was strong with great spirit in the meeting the night before our big mass meeting. Most of the members did not sleep that night so they could get perpare for the big meeting for the next day. Because we was looking for some visites from the C.I.O. of New Orleans, La. When I was in New Orleans, I had invited two of the Negro leader out of New Orleans, Willie Dorsey, Pres. of the I.L.W.U. and Earnest Wright, a papers writer. And four other members of the I.L.W.U.[36] And

36. President of a New Orleans warehousemen's union, Willie Dorsey was a New Orleans colleague and counterpart to Clinton Clark in the later 1930s and early 1940s. He was president of the International Longshoremen's and Warehousemen's Union (ILWU) Local 207 when he traveled to Natchitoches for the mass meeting. He would later represent the CIO at the LFU fifth-anniversary celebration in Torras, Louisiana. Like Clark, he was active in the SNYC.

Dorsey was from rural Louisiana (Lumville), was a speaker out of the Baptist church, and, like Clark, worked in tandem with white, left, and Communist labor organizers who came to Louisiana in the later 1930s. When the ILWU tried to organize New Orleans longshoremen in 1938, Dorsey had

ever farmer union members was perpareing to bring a basket alone with them. And thats why they was perpareing they basket that night so everthing would be pleasent for the next day. When the visit would arrive to our meeting.

The night before the meeting, every local were having meeting so to be ready for the big mass meeting. We had change our meeting from the masonic hall to the church, because the planter had threatern to burn the masonic hall down if this meeting would be held in the hall. So we send a committee to see the pastor of the baptis church and he agree to let us have our meeting in his church. The Saturday night before the mass meeting we were busy as a bee perparing for the big. The planters were the same as we were. They was busy as a bee perparing to brake up our meeting. The planters lay for me all that night trying to get an oppertunity to kill me. But our membership was so big until every thing the planters tried to do against us we know it before the planters moved. I didn't go to my room in Natchitoches the night before the meeting.

---

been working on the riverfront for over twenty years and became a spokesman for the CIO union. Bruce Nelson describes his charisma: "A lay preacher and spellbinding orator, Dorsey was also a physically powerful man who became an instant legend when he flattened a notorious AFL goon with a single punch and routed his gun-toting entourage" (Nelson, "Class and Race in the Crescent City," 29).

After the ILWU lost the 1938 election for representing the longshoremen–a campaign marked by violence, arrests, and police confiscation of records–Dorsey went on to lead Local 207 and its remaining membership of warehouse workers. Dorsey's poor financial management and failure to pay dues to the ILWU International provoked it to investigate and to attempt to restructure the union. The resulting struggle between Dorsey and Harold Goddard, the International's representative and a veteran of the Abraham Lincoln Brigade in the Spanish Civil War, became a struggle over the Communist Party's influence in the union. Much of Goddard's criticism of Dorsey seems a stern reaction to a New Orleans style of political leadership, as he criticized Dorsey's spending on "dances, raffles, festivals and other petty rackets" (Wells, "The ILWU in New Orleans," 18). David Wells's master's thesis tells the story of the dispute, which drew in local priests and courts and was a major New Orleans labor issue while Clinton Clark was working there, writing his memoirs and preparing to move to New York. Ultimately, the International suspended the local leadership of Local 207 and kicked out Dorsey. He began organizing for the CIO Retail Workers Union, Local 389, and attempted to recruit workers away from the ILWU locals.

Ernest Wright (1909–79) traveled to Natchitoches as an SNYC representative. Wright had been a social worker employed by the *Louisiana Weekly,* the New Orleans African American newspaper, in its Community Responsibility Program. Within a month of returning from prison in Natchitoches, Wright led black insurance agents–the majority of black office workers in New Orleans–in a strike against the black-owned insurance companies that employed them. During the strike, police arrested Wright on assault charges related to violence against strikebreakers. One of the four insurance companies ultimately

Five O. Clock that sunday morning four member of the farmer union and myself got into my car and we went town to get everything ready for the meeting. We went to the most importian Negro leaders to get donation to buy ice and soda water. They give us money to buy what ever we needed.

The labor union group arrive early that morning for our meeting. We all got togather and went over to our parish union office to have a conference before the meeting. I gave them all imformation of what had taking place before the meeting. So Mr. Wright and Mr. Dorsey subjected that we go see the mayor and having him to come to our meeting. So Wright and myself went to see the mayor. When we went into his office, the mayor never wait to see what we had to say. He said to me, Boy? You better get out of town as quick as you can if you know what good for you. If it would not been for me the planters would have kill you last night. But I kept them off of you. The first thing you know you will find yourself flooting in that river in a sack. I didn't know you had invite those C.I.O. members here in this parish. If it was the A.F.L. members you had invited here it would have been alright.[37]

---

settled with the union. The strike made Wright a highly prominent labor and civil rights leader; when he was released from jail, a crowd of 5,000 attended a parade on Canal Street and a rally in Shakespeare Park (now known as A. L. Davis Park). He would work for the CIO in various positions through the 1940s, including serving as general secretary of the New Orleans Industrial Union Council-CIO, a council of twenty-eight unions and 35,000 workers, as well as holding office in two civil rights organizations, the NAACP and the SNYC. In 1942 Wright was also deeply involved in the People's Defense League, a civil rights organization that ran voter registration drives and protested police violence. The People's Defense League registered almost 5,000 black voters in New Orleans in 1946 and grew to be a statewide organization. In his account of Wright's life, Keith W. Medley attributes the downfall of the PDL to Wright's involvement with Earl Long and "the seamy world of party politics." "Wright hoped to use the alliance to liberalize the voter registration office so more blacks could be added to the rolls, but his abandonment of his mass base in favor of a much maligned political faction caused his influence to deteriorate" ("Ernest Wright," 55). Wright stayed in the labor movement and civil rights organizing throughout his life. He experienced anticommunist scrutiny of his 1940s labor organizing work when the Louisiana Committee on Subversion in Racial Unrest investigated him in 1957. Wright ran as a candidate for governor in 1963. Medley writes, "People remembered that it was Wright who pushed back the mountains to plant the seeds of black political participation" (55); he received almost 40,000 votes. See also Fairclough, *Race and Democracy*, 54–55; Ward, "Class Conflict in Black New Orleans."

37. The older American Federation of Labor, which organized segregated unions of skilled workers, was much less threatening to the status quo than the new Congress of Industrial Organizations, which was formed in 1935 and organized multiracial unions of all workers–skilled and unskilled–at a site.

Mr. Wright ask the mayor if wanted to see the farmer union charter. The mayor said know. I dont want to see nothing. The best thing you fellow can do is to get out of town as quick as you can. So Wright and myself left to go see Mr. Scott Lewis the Natchitoches Negro leader on what step we should take. Scott Lewis told us it would be better if we call the meeting off and noteify the offical of the farmers union. That was around nine O.Clock in the morning. About eight hundred farm family was in town in the broken down wagon and buggys and old cars. The church was pack and all around the church on the street in the church yard ever where they could find a place to stand. On our way back to the church in my car, we met the cheif police and one of his helper alone with him. When we pass his car he turn around and came behine us with full speed.

8 | What One of You Is Clark?

When they over taken us, the chief police order me to stop my car. When the cheif was blorn his car horn, Mr. Wright look back and seen it was the police. He told me to stop the car. So I stop immediately. Then the two police jump out of they car and began searching both of us all over to see if we had a gun. The cheif said what one of you is Clark. I said this is him. He said Ah you are the fellow going around here making all this trouble ant you. I said I am not making any trouble. I was trying to stop trouble. What was already going on around here. The cheif said Oh yes. Well we see who was making the trouble before this is over with. Then he ask me, Clark where is that big fellow Dorsey. Then he drove us over to the church and pick up Dorsey and the other three fellow that was sent from the C.I.O. of New Orleans. All the sharecroppers came out of the church to see what was happen. The cheif had Dorsey and his group to get in they car and drive it over to the city jail where they put us in jail. Ten minute after they put us in jail, ten planters was in there to see us. The cheif police would point his finger at me and said to the planters, That big B. . . one is Clark. He is the organizer. The police taking several sharecroppers into the police station to question them about the farmer union. One of the member the police had taking in the police station. The police ask him was he a member of the union. The farmer said yes and gave the police his membership card. The police taking his membership card and look it over carefully. When the police was through question the farmer, he ask the police was their through with him. The police said yes. So this farmer said give my union card back to me. The police said what you going to do with it. You dont need it any more. The farmer said yes I need it because I want to know when to pay my dues again.

The police ask the farmer what good have the farmer union been to him. The farmer said it have save me a lots of money. I have paid high price for my fertilize befor the union came here now sence the union have organize the cooperative buying club, I have save from $5 to $6 on a ton.

So the police gave him his card and told him he could go home. The offical question many sharecroppers during the day. The planters tried to get the sharecroppers afread but the sharecroppers was ready to started a war aganist the planters for stoping our big meeting. The first night we were in jail we were taking out and question one at the time. I was taking out and question twice the same night. The cheif police wanted to know how many member the farmer union had in Natchitoches parish and how long I had been in the parish. When I told him that I had been in the parish four years, it took him to a suprize. He didn't wanted to beleave that. When they was question me the first night, they threatern me with the lynch mob. The cheif told me that I would be a dead man before the next day, that I would never see the outside world again.

All through the night some of the planters would make around in the jail looking after us. The first thing the next morning, the cheif unlock my cell and called me out and question me before a couple of planters. He tried to make me tell him how many members I had organize in the parish. When I couldn't answer that question, he club me over the head with all his might. And as he struck me over the head, three more police was standing up with their pistol in the hand. All had their eyes on me looking just as mean as they could. Then the cheif open the cell and knock me into the cell and said to me go back into that cell and come back and tell me how many members you had in that union.

Then the cheif called out Dorsey and question him about the C.I.O. and next Earnest Wright. Some how they was a little afread of Wright. The high sherriff would tell the planters that nigger there is from New Orleans. He is that smart fellow, he is a paper writter. He is also one of the leader of that NAACP. When ever they would ask Wright a question, Wright wouldn't bite his tounge. He would talk dirrect to the offical with out holding back with his voice. All that monday the planters was coming into the jail looking afters us. The planters was taking in his hold family into the jail to look me over. When ever the planters would come into the jail the sherriff would point his finger and said that the organizer. Clark. That big b. . . one over there. One planter said to me while been in jail, Nigger you will be hanging in a tree before the next twelfth hours. You been going around here fooling these nigger. We will never let you get by with that mess in this part of our country. During that time our state Sec'y McIntire was sick in the hospital. A young white girl by the name of Peggy Dallet was acting Sec'y.[38] At one time she had came up to Natchitoches to make a tour over the parish. We had set meeting all over the parish in ever local.

38. Margery "Peggy" Dallet (1910–) was acting secretary of the Louisiana Farmers' Union when Clinton Clark was imprisoned in Natchitoches in 1940. She had assumed leadership of the union when Gordon McIntire was hospitalized with tuberculosis in January 1940. From the LFU's New Orleans

Peggy Dallet had invited a White organizer to come over and make the tour with her. When Peggy came we had one of the sharecroppers wife to meet her. And a couple of sharecroppers and myself met the white organizer. We held meeting all over the parish in the churches and school houses and in different sharecroppers shacks. When the D.A. was question me that was the first question he put to me before several planters. Clark? What you doing rideing around here with that white girl in Natchitoches parish. Dont you know it is aganist the law to ride with a white woman after dark. Exspecial in Natchitoches. Dont you know we will hang you in a tree. I said it was a white man rideing along with this white girl. The D.A. said it makes no different who was along, you had no business rideing with them after dark.

The five Delegate from the C.I.O. who was in jail along with me was released inside of three days and was told not to return back to Natchitoches parish anymore. After my friends was released the offical began threatern my life, telling me

---

office, she organized the effort to gain Clark's release. She hired a lawyer, set up a Clinton Clark Defense Fund, worked with the Negro press to publicize his story, and urged liberal organizations to investigate his imprisonment and lobby for his release. Her memo in the HLP outlines her actions and savvy strategy, which included delaying publicity to the press just long enough to give the Natchitoches district attorney a chance to release Clark in response to their initial inquiries. She wrote leaders of national labor and civil rights organizations and wired U.S. Attorney General Jackson. Clark's memoir notes that they had met before when she had visited him on an organizing trip; their car trips together would later be used to threaten him with lynching when he was jailed.

Dallet was raised in Woodmere, a Long Island suburb, and was a student at Vassar College before marrying her first husband and moving to New Orleans in 1937. They were living in Torremolinas, Spain, when the civil war began and chose New Orleans for its similarities to the Mediterranean artistic community they had left. As she traveled to New Orleans, she learned that her brother Joe had been killed in Spain while fighting for the Republic with the Abraham Lincoln Brigade. Her brother had done extensive labor work, including organizing steelworkers for the CIO in Youngstown, Ohio. Arriving in New Orleans, Dallet looked for a way to continue his work, and, after attending the meetings of several unions (finding the longshoremen "too rough" and the teachers "too stodgy"), she heard Gordon McIntire speak about the Louisiana Farmers' Union at the YMCA. She remembers that he wouldn't say *union* out loud, instead calling it the *onion:* "I almost think I fell in love with him that night." After the meeting she offered him the one skill she thought she could contribute–typing–and started by typing the union's constitution.

She progressed from typing to attending meetings, answering calls and letters, serving as liaison with French-speaking members, and producing the union newsletter. The conditions in Louisiana shocked and transformed her. "I had known of my brother's activities but I hadn't felt them," she said in an interview. It was a union, she remembers, so attentive to the different needs of its locals that it produced three different versions of its newsletter. She saw the union as an effective local strategy for addressing global

that I would be hang at any hour. The planters was waiting for me out side of the jail house. Three time a day the offical would take me out of the jail house and question me about the union. Several telgram was sent to our union meeting but the D.A. taking them and never did return them to me. And several sharecroppers came to see me, but the offical would not let them in the jail to see me. Drove them away from the jail and told them they didn't want to see that no good nigger he will be dead for the next morning. After the members of the C.I.O. had been released from jail, the offical gotten busy, because Wright and Dorsey spread the news all over the state. The sharecroppers send telgram into Peggy Dallet, our Acting state Sec'y. Our state Sec'y of the farmer union was sick in the hospital at that time but was still giving advice to the farmer union in Louisiana. While being in jail the planters would come into the jail by groups with they wife and children to look me over. And the jailer would point me out to the planters. Some of the planters asked me what was I doing on they plantation. Dont you know it is against the law to go on another man farm to organize these nigger. I said to the planter no sir. I didn't know that. The D.A. and the sherriff was rideing all

injustice. "I think we felt almost that we were—you know how the Jews say they're the chosen people? We were lucky that we had this tool to work with, that we found a way of achieving what we thought was right, and I think that's where the optimism came in." Dallet and McIntire fell in love, and Dallet began what McIntire would call in a letter to Clyde Johnson "a Louisiana divorce."

When McIntire was hospitalized, Dallet assumed a leadership position that few women had held. McIntire would later write, "She was naturally handicapped but made a marvelous effort and even extended the organization into the Florida parishes." Shortly after Clark's release from the Natchitoches jail in 1940, Dallet's mother was killed in a car accident. She left New Orleans and the LFU to tend to her father, who had survived the accident. She later organized credit unions in New York. In 1942, she moved to Denver and married McIntire. She worked for the National Youth Administration in Denver and for the Office of Price Administration and the National Education Association in Washington, D.C. In 1952, Peg and Gordon and their two young children moved to Rome, where Gordon had taken a position with the United Nations' Food and Agricultural Organization. After he was abruptly fired, she supported the family as a typist, translator, and tennis instructor. Together the McIntires later built a successful business selling *Encyclopaedia Britannica* and *World Book* across Italy.

Gordon died in 1970, and Peg returned to the United States with her son and daughter-in-law in 1980. She became an active member and officer of the Florida Coalition for Peace and Justice. As a peace activist she has opposed the expansion of the arms race and weapons testing, playing a key role in civil disobedience at military facilities in the Gulf South. She has fostered educational programs and institutions that promote democratic and nonviolent solutions to conflict. She serves as the resident grandmother at the coalition's summer youth camp. Peg McIntire, interview; "Peg's Family's Reflections"; Gordon McIntire, letter to Members and Friends of the Farmers' Union in Louisiana, March 10, 1942, CJP.

over the parish trying to get the sharecroppers to tell them that I had promas to take the land and the mules from the planters and give to the sharecroppers. The planters threaten to lynch the sharecroppers if they didn't tell them that I promas to give them mules and land. The sharecroppers refuse to do so. The D.A. and the sherriff and the cheif police threaten to let the planters lynch me if I didn't tell them that I had promas the sharecroppers mules and land. When the D.A. seen I wasn't afread the following day they called all the jurymen in the jail to question me. The room was full of all kind of businessmen and planters to question me. They wanted to know about my schooling. How long had I been organizeing the farmer in Natchitoches parish. How many local was organize. And what part did the teacher played in the farmer union. Also the preacher. And they also wanted to know what labor union did the farmer union affiliate with. So they give me the floor. I said to them the farmer union is not a labor union although they both struggle for a living. The farmer union is class organization just as any other class organization whoes members are limited to those of that class. The banker union. The Doctors' union and the Lawyers' union. The merchant union. They are class union. The farmer union are a class organization. We teach the farmer how to organize cooperative buying club and make saveing for group. We teach them health. And how to love each other in working togather. One of the planters tried to cut me off when I was talking. He was asking me some kind of funny question. But I didn't hear him. When one of the jurymen said to the planter, Let him talk.

Let him talk. So the planter didn't say anything anymore. One of the planter looking in one of the farmer union books that shows the farmer union program. And he said Clark. I see in this constitution where the farmer union affiliate with the C.I.O. One of the jurymen said no, this is not the constitution. After the D.A. seen that he couldn't fram up a good charge against me. And he had tried all kind of ways, bringing in differen't planters to ask me all kinds of funny question, trying to trick me into a fram up charge. At one time it was one old age sharecroppers had join the farmer union. He had been trying to get on the old age pension but the relief agent refuse to even take up his case. He had made several trips to see the relief agent for relief. The relief agent had drove him from the relief office ever time he went there. So when he join the farmer union, he explan to me his condition and how many time he had went to ask for relief and was run out of the office. So he ask me to write a letter for him to Washington D.C. So I wrote two letters for him. One to Baton Rouge La. and one to Washington D.C. In a few weeks he receive a letter from both places telling him to go back to the local relief agent. So he did go back to see them.[39]

When he went to the local relief office, the relief agent ask the old farmer why did he wrote that letter to Washington. The sharecroppers said he couldn't write and he didn't wrote the letter. The relief agent ask the old man well who wrote this letter for you. The relief agent talked so frighten to the old man until he was shakeing like a leaf. The old man said a union man wrote that letter for me. The relief agent said was he a white man are a colored man. The old man said he was a colored man. The relief agent said how much you paid that colored man to write that letter for you. The old man was so scare until he was talking out of his head. The old man said I? I? I? paid him two dollar. The dues was $2 a year for any farm family. This old man had join his family into the farmer union for two dollar. But the relief agents wanted to say that Clark had collect money on false. So when the D.A. seen he couldn't get any of the members that had some understanding to tell a lie on me, the D.A. went to this old man house and threaten the old man if he didn't tell that Clark had promas to get him on relief for that $2 the old man had paid to join the farmer union. The D.A. taking the old man in the city jail into my cell. And the D.A. said to me Clark. You know this fellow. I said why yes. He is one of my member. Then I shake hands with the old man and ask him how was he felling. The old man was shakeing like a leaf falling of the tree when the wind was blowing in a strom. The D.A. said to the old man, Say old man. Didn't Clark said he would get you on relief if you join the union. The old man was so scare until I felt like crying and knocking the D.A. cold. But I know the big gun man was watching every move I would make. The old man was talking with a trembling voice. Ah, Ah, He said. Two dollar to join the union. The D.A. said again to the old man, Didn't he said he would get you on relief if you join the union. The old man started with his trembling voice. Ah, Ah, He said if I join the union he write for relief for me. Then the D.A. said thats all I wants to hear you say, thats all I wants to hear you say. And the D.A. told the Sherriff take him over to the parish jail. The sherriff then taking me over to the parish jail, where they feed you only syrup and bread and boil potatoes twice a day. The sherriff put me a hot cell for 36 hour. And the planters would come and look through the hole at me with

39. An article about Clinton's release on the front page of the *Louisiana Weekly* on August 24, 1940, repeats this story of an older man coerced into accusing Clark.

they family. They would look at me like they was ready to get me out at any moment and hang me. One day one of the sherriff taking me out of the cell to take my finger print. While he was taking my finger print, he was moveing my hands a round. When I was slow moving my hands, the sherriff said to me, move your fingers like I tell you. I said to him all right. He said dont tell me alright nigger. Tell a white man yes sir and no sir. I then said to him O.K. He then said dont say O.K., tell me yes sir. I said again to him O.K. He said look here nigger. I will rap this gun over your head if you dont listen to me. I never said anything to him any more. One day the jailer came to me in the cell where I was and said to me, Clark dont you know these Negroes are getting along alright. We give them every thing they need. They dont need no union in this parish to organize these Negroes. I have a farm. I give my Negroes every thing they wants. The sherriff said to me Clark. You see those union people are way up north sending telgram down here demanding your release. And you are in jail. They want come to see you. Now they are sending thousand of telgram here demanding your release.

One day when the D.A. was question me, he said to me, Clark dont you know you are taking a chance with you life going around here organizeing these farmers. Dont you know these planters will kill you. Dont you know it is aganist the law to go on these plantation unless you get permesion from the planters. I said to the D.A., No I didn't know it was aganist the law. One of the planters said Clark had his meeting on my farm at night. For three years Clark was organizeing on my plantation. He never give me any trouble. The sherriff came in my cell one morning and said to me Clark. Do you remember that day you and McIntire held a meeting on that bridge and you and McIntire had those saw off shot gun watching. I said to the sherriff, No I dont remember nothing like that. McIntire and I never had any meeting on any bridge togather. And we never did carry any saw off gun to do our organizeing. Clark, if I was you I would let that union along and let those people come here and do they own organizeing from now on. You see no one come here to see you while you are in jail. He said Clark, what did Scott Lewis and Dr. Johnson got of the union dues for helping you to organize these farmers. I said not anything, these people didn't help me to organize. They just beleave in justice for the poor farmers and had nothing against the farmer union for organizeing them to better their condition. He said how come you take in those teachers in the union. I well most of the teachers husband were farmers. And when ever any head of a family join the farmers union, ever one in the family become a member. The Supt. of the school houses had taking all the keys from the teacher to keep the union meeting out of the school houses. The planters said they pays the taxes on the schools. And it wasn't going to be any more union meeting in the schools.

One day the sherriff came in my cell and said to me Clark, You realy had you eyes open. You show know what you was doing around here. I said to the cheif police, as he was in the cell at the same time, I ask him what kind of charge they had on me. He said to me I better pray that they do get a charge on me, because the planters are waiting for me outside. He said it was two hundred planters come to get me out last night and they kept them from getting me out last night.

When they first put me in the parish jail, it was four other men in jail with me. They gang around me to question me. They wanted to know what they put me in jail for. After I had explan to them why I was put in jail, they said to me, These planters sure going to hang you for doing that work around here. We know of three they have kill for telling these sharecroppers to get togather. If I was you I would pray to the lord ever hour and ask him to spare me to get out of this jail alive once more. And promas him you will never do that kind of work any more. And tell the sherriff you will let that union along and if you do that they may let you lose.

I said to my friend, You may be right. But I know I haven done any kind of crime. I had the right to organize the poor people to better their condition. The Government had give the people the right to organize. Why should we give up our right to the bosses, when we been slaveing for them all our days. It is better to stand up for your right now while we have this oppertunity to do so. Before I was released, these boys wanted to know how could join the union when they get out of jail. They become real friends to me. They push me on many question about the union.

Several morning when the boys get up out of the bunks, they would tell me that they could see that it was a new day coming for the poor people. One of the boys had kill a white fellow. It was three white boys drunk one saturday night. This Negro boy was talking to his girl friend. And these drunking white boy taking a club and knock this Negro boy over his head and taking this Negro girl from him. It happen that this Negro boy had a pistol in his pocket and pull it out and start shooting the drunking white boys, killed one of the white boys and wounded the other two. And the Negro boy went and give hisself up to his boss at a saw mill Campti La. His boss taking him to the parish jail. His boss had promas to get him out as soon as the matter would cool off.

This Negro I can still remember his name. It was John. He would read the bible morning and night and pray all day long. When I had explan to him what the union mean to the workers, he said to me one morning, Mr. Clark, I seen in my bible just what it is all about. It says the day shall come when the bottom rail shall be on top. And the top rail shall be on the bottom.

On the day when the offical decited to release me, the sherriff came to my cell and had a talk with me. He said Clark, we have decited to let you go if you will agree to stay out of the state and not come back here any more. We have fix up your car. Fix the tires and put gas in your car. We will take you to the Texas line and protect you out of the state until you get to the line of Texas. I thank the line of Texas is 40 miles from Natchitoches. Clark, that union is just going to get some of these nigger kill around here. And if I was you I let that union along. You are to smart of a fellow to let those people use you like that. Why dont you get you a good job some where. You can do it, I know. All the question the sherriff asked me, I never give him no answer. I just let him talk until he was tired. Then he told me to get my cloth togather by the time he get back. When he came back he asked me some more question about different organization that he had received from asking for my release.

I said to him, I am not family with these organization but I do know when ever any worker is organizing the poor people to better their condition and is arested, these organization will fight for his freedom to the last drop. He said to me, but they are a long ways from here to fight your freedom when they just sending telgram demanding your freedom. I didn't say anything as I know those telegram had taking afect, because if they didn't they wouldn't been so anxous to release me. Then he open my cell and said lets go. And he taking me down in the court room, where the D.A. and a couple more offical was. The sherriff said to me, Clark meet the D.A. The D.A. said Clark knows me. Then the D.A. ask me to sign some paper before leaving. Before signing I look the papers over carefull. If couse I didn't realise it was a peace bond until I had reach New Orleans.

It was in the after noon when the sherriff came and taking me out of my cell. And said lets go Clark. I am going to follow you to see that nobody do you any harm. When we went out where my car was, it was already to go. I gotten in my car and the sherriff follow me until we reach the Texas line. When we reach the Texas line the sherrif stopped his car beside of my car and told me good by and let that union along. At the time we was talking a big planter walk up to the sherriff car and ask the sherriff who was that fellow. The sherriff said ah he is just going on. I started traveling when the sherriff said good by. I went to the nearest town and contact a Negro school teacher and had him to send a wire to the Louisiana farmers union office in New Orleans to imform them of my released. Our Acting State Sec'y didn't realy beleave that it was true so she send me another telgram asking me to call her on the long distent telphone. So I did call her on the phone. After I had explan to her about my released the C.I.O. was having a meeting that night and Peggy Dallet the La.F.U. Sec'y explan to the C.I.O. members about my release and raise enough money and wire it to me for my exspense to get to New Orleans.

All along the highway where ever I met friends, it was a great suprize rejoyce to see me alive and safe from Natchitoches parish jail. Because their know what those planters would do to me if it wound'n been for the labor union and the progressed organization fighting for my freedom. When I arrive in New Orleans all the paper writers was in the farmers union office waiting to see me to get the story about my case up in Natchitoches parish.[40]

While being in New Orleans I found out that the C. Liberty for the people right had made a very strong fight on my case as well as many other organization.[41]

40. Clark's release was a front-page story with a photograph in the *Louisiana Weekly* on August 24, 1940. The paper had published several articles on his arrest and imprisonment. A story about his release also appeared in the *Chicago Defender.*

41. From New Orleans, the Louisiana League for the Preservation of Constitutional Rights sent a letter to the Natchitoches district attorney protesting that Clark's arrest before the rally and imprisonment without charges violated constitutional rights of peaceable assembly and due process. Harold N. Lee, a professor at Newcomb College and member of the executive committee, also attempted to raise money to send a team to Natchitoches to investigate. Lee wrote Samuel Zemurray about the case and asked for a donation. Letters Lee received on the case and carbon copies of the letters he wrote are held in his papers at Tulane University. Lee's letter to District Attorney H. L. Hughes provides a window into the approach and tactics of this liberal white organization. Lee denies that he objects to Clark's arrest because it is a race or labor union issue, but by doing so he ensures that these reasons for Clark's arrest are mentioned.

> The Louisiana League for the Preservation of Constitutional Rights is not interested in this case because the proposed meeting was to be held by a labor organization . . .
>
> Neither is the League interested in the fact that the proposed meeting was to be held by Negroes. The Constitution respects neither color, race nor economic beliefs in its guarantees of rights. One of the most fundamental doctrines of constitutional democratic government is that all persons are equal before the law, and are all equally under the law. The League is interested in this case only because of the denial of the right of peaceable assembly and due process. At this time of national emergency, the principles upon which our government is founded must be guarded jealously. (August 7, 1940, HLP)

Clark might also be referring to the National Federation for Constitutional Liberties, which in Washington, D.C., lobbied the Department of Justice to intervene for his release. See National Federation for Constitutional Liberties, "Lynch Threat Thwarted: Farm Union Organizer Released after Delegation Visits Department of Justice," reel 18, part 1, NNC.

9 | Escape from Peonage

After my released from Natchitoches jail, I had the oppertunity to go up to Chicago and make a speach to 20,000 workers in a big mass meeting. When I was making my speach, I told them that I may be lynch but I was going to return back south and continue with my organizeing. The writer for the Chicago defender taking my picture and taking notes on my speach. The following week the story was publish in the Chicago defender.[42] The planters receive the news. And was hot as fire because their didn't get me the first time before they had arrested me. When I left the mass meeting at Chicago, I travel with a group on the highway to Washington D.C. and had the oppertunity to speak in several churches and in many others places all over the city. Also went with a delgateion and had a conferences with one of the United state sentor—visit the home of Frederick Douglass and many other importain places.[43] And went to Balmore Md. and made a speach

42. This was the national convention of the American Peace Mobilization, a short-lived group that opposed U.S. entrance into World War II in 1940–41. Estimates of attendance àt the rally, which was held in Chicago Stadium as the Congress was considering a draft bill, were 11,000 to 20,000 (Walker, "Communists and Isolationism," 3). As the organization had significant Communist involvement, many attribute its antiwar position to the fact that in August 1939 the Soviet Union had signed an agreement with Nazi Germany to not attack each other. However, this interpretation neglects the legitimate reasons Americans feared entering a war. Many African Americans were nervous about the draft bills, remembering the treatment of black soldiers in the segregated armed forces of World War I (see Herndon, "Negroes Here Oppose Conscription Bill"). Many reconsidered their antiwar positions, of course, in 1941, when Nazi Germany invaded the Soviet Union and Japan attacked Pearl Harbor.

On September 14, 1940, the *Chicago Defender* ran a large photograph of Clark speaking at a rally under the dramatic headline "I MAY BE LYNCHED." The caption briefly told the story of his imprisonment: "CLINTON CLARK Organizer of tenant farmers and sharecroppers, who was jailed in Natchitoches, La., last month, is shown addressing the Peace Mobilization meeting at the Chicago Stadium, Sunday. Clark told the group that he was going to return to the southland and continue organizing farmers. 'I may be lynched,' he yelled, 'but I am going to return.' Clark was arrested when attempting to call a meeting of Natchitoches farmers. He remained in jail 20 days and was then escorted out of the state under threat of being mobbed."

43. Immediately after the convention in Chicago, a delegation traveled to Washington, D.C., to

in another big mass meeting. And came back to Birmingham and made a Speach to the members of the S.N.Y.C. at another big meeting. When I came back to New Orleans, I immediately went back in the fields and started my organizeing the poor farmers again.

I went to Lettsworth La in pointe coupee parish where the first farmer union local was organize and had been 500 strong and was well organize. And our state sec'y Gordon McIntire had been sick for some time and no leader had been with them for some time. That reason the members had died down. So while I was in Washington D.C. the committee to aid Agriculture workers had give me $200.00 to buy a car to continue my work. I travel all over the parish in my car, calling meeting in ever community getting the dead local alive again. In three weeks time we had ever dead local going with full speed again and two or three new ones on start. I would travel night and day working to build a strong union all over the state. We would go and have conferce with the F.S.A. and the A.A.A. agents and invite them to our meeting. And when ever the F.S.A. agents would have meeting in the parish, I would always attend their meeting and make speaches in their meeting. And would have all the members of the farmers union to attend these meeting. Dureing my organizeing in pointe coupee parish, I came across a large plantation by the name of rexmere plantation. About 75 sharecroppers family living in peonage. The onwer of this plantation live up in Chicago. This plantation was surrounded with bob wire fence. A big gate kept lock at all time. No one was allow to enter on this plantation unless they get the permisson from the plantation boss.

And no sharecroppers was allow to come off the plantation unless their get permesson from the plantation boss. On this plantation there was one of the most beautiful fishing lake in the country. When ever the sharecroppers went fishing on this lake, they would have to give one half of the fish they get to the plantation boss. And if there was no work to be done the sharecroppers would some time

lobby against the Burke-Wadsworth conscription bill. Fifteen hundred people demonstrated on the evening of September 5, 1940, and were roughly handled by police. The bill was passed the next morning (Walker, "Communists and Isolationism," 4–5). Clark's FBI file records part of a speech he made in Washington on the evening of September 6: "We oppose conscription because we don't want to go to war. We want to stay at home and get something to eat, a decent place to live. We want this nation to abolish the poll tax, pass the anti-lynching bill and educate the mass of ignorant people of the South. If this is done I can express the will of the people of the south in saying that you won't have to pass the conscription bill to get us to stop bullets. We will volunteer" ("Clinton Clark," August 15, 1941, New Orleans, p. 3, FBI-CC).

go in the woods and pick moss to sell. They would also had to give of the moss they pick to the plantation boss. Also the plantation boss would buy each family his house hold goods and have them to pay for them out of their crops. But when the sharecroppers was ready he would have to leave the household goods on this plantation. And it was no way for the sharecroppers to run away because he had to go through the gate and the plantation boss had the key and they sure had go by him because he live near the gate. And no visit was allow unless he get permisson and had to tell who he wants to see and what for and if he get permesson he would be limit. And this rule was the same on the sharecroppers.

Also there was a big store on this plantation where the sharecroppers had to get they food and pay double price for what ever they get out of the big store. And no sharecroppers ever know what a government check was alabout. The plantation onwer would go back and forward to Chicago. He had a beautiful home on this plantation. He had a united state flag hanging over his home. When ever he would be going to Chicago the flag would be hanging up. And when he would be at his plantation home the flag would be down.

The name of the onwer was Sentor Wood. Here is a story of familys that exscape from this plantation. Leon Smith Negro sharecropper tell the story of how he and his family and friends exscape from the peonage rexmere plantation. Leon Smith said the overseer hit my son and put his pistol in my daughter face. My son went to work one morning and the overseer wanted to force him to work in water and my son refused to work in the water because he just gotten out of bed with the flue. When my son went back home, he went to the plantation store to get a package of prince albert tobacco. After he had gotten the tobacco and started out of the store, he met the overseer. The overseer called him back into the store. The overseer told him, how in the hell you come to the store and take up tobacco and dont want to work. How do you expect to pay for the tobacco. My son told the overseer he had been paying for what he gets out of the store.

The overseer told him you are just going to get this dam club over your head. At the same time the overseer let the club went down on the boy head and across his back. The boy name is Charley Smith. So Charley ran and gotten out of the overseer way. And at the same time Charley sister was in the store, so she ran and screamed. The overseer over taking her and put his pistol in her face and told her to tell that S.O.B. husband of yours he better not be caught on this plantation anymore. If he do he better bring his coffin with him. So after that trouble come up several family wanted to move. Their went to see the onwer and told him they was going to move. The onwer told them if they move just give him $200.00. And if you move without my concent, I will pay $200.00 to see you set in jail where I can come and look at you. After these sharecroppers seen that they couldn't get away with their household goods by the planter, about midnight four family exscape through the woods. They taking a few cloths in a sack. They walked five miles through the swamps in water. When they came to a gravel highway, they find a sharecropper with a car who taking them to Lettsworth La. And there where they tell the sad story how they was treated by the planter on this plantation.

Leon Smith and Nelson Connady said, If the sharecroppers would work six days in the week, they would always be short of a day when they goes to get they pay. And when they would go to the Overseer and ask about they time, the overseer would tell them that he was going to pay them what was on the book. And at the same time the overseer would get angry. Some time the sharecroppers would work until 10 O.Clock at night and would not get any pay for the over time they worked. When it would rain the overseer would have some of the sharecroppers cleaning the tracter and greaseing the tools and would not get any pay for this work. When the sharecroppers would protest about pay for this work, the overseer would tell them that a man has the right to clean his tools what he worked. One of the sharecropper started his crop. He hoe the crop, plow the crop and layed it by. The overseer said to this sharecropper his crop was not going to make anything. So the overseer had his crop plow under and planted peas for hisself so the sharecropper didn't get anything for his crop he had worked. The overseer forced the sharecroppers to sign over their government checks to him. One of the sharecropper tried to get away with his house hold goods one day. The sharecropper had his furniture all loaded on the wagon ready to move. The overseer seen the sharecropper coming to the gate before he could get out of the gate. So he didn't get the chance to exscape with his furniture.

So after the sharecropper seen he couldn't get away with his house hold goods, he exscape with his family in the night, went through the woods with his children in water and mud, travel all night long with five little children. This sharecropper didn't owe the planter one penny on his house hold goods but that was the planter rule. You didn't have to owe him anything. But he held the book on the sharecroppers and you had to obey his law are els. The owner of this plantation had a large plantation store. Some time he would called all the sharecroppers to his store to make a speach to them. One of the sharecroppers tell the planter speach to them. The planter said to the sharecroppers All he wants the boys to have is a good pair of shoes on their feet and a good ax in their hands. He said if you boys work two hours one day dont look for any pay for it. Also he said if you boys wreck any of the tools you work you will have to pay for the tools, regardless if it is good are bad.

Now if you boys don't work, I will get along some how. Because me and my overseer will be eating fish and beaf stake, while you boys will be on the other side of the lake eating snow balls.[44] The planter had a sign by the store for speed limit. If you had a car you had to stop by the store and get permisson from the store keeper before enter the gate. After this plantation was explaned to our farmers union members we organize our best leader. And we went in my car to the rexmere plantation and gotten in contact with some of the sharecroppers that live near the plantation. And midnight I crawl over the fence and went to one of the family house that I had his name. And we gotten severl of the sharecroppers togather that night and had a meeting. Eight sharecropper sign their name to join the union. And they set up a local on this plantation. But they had to be very easy. They had to talk very low about the union, because the planter didn't want the secret of this plantation to be known. And if he know the union was there the news would soon spread all over the country and he couldn't do as he been always keeping the sharecroppers in slave. We did began to expos the peonge plantation. We send the story to many news papers so that it could be known all over the world.[45] About ten family made their exscape from this plantation. All of them came to Lettsworth La. where we had a large parish union set up. We taking this group to the F.S.A. department and ask for some attention for them. The F.S.A. taking this group incharge and each family was giving 40 acres of land to work. Today these family are living a better life then they ever live before. And are prode to be in the farmers union to fight for a better life. In union there is strengh.

44. A *snow ball* is the Louisiana name for a snow cone–ground ice with sweet flavoring added.

45. Clark also sent an account to the National Negro Congress office in Washington, D.C. His handwritten account of this incident is held in the records of Executive Secretaries Correspondence, 1941–42, NNC. This section of his autobiography seems to draw from this earlier handwritten account.

After I had gotten a car to work with, I began to organize a cooperative store in Lettsworth La. where we had a strong farmers union to do the job with. We call a meeting with the leader in the parish union and they agree to put up chicken, corn and hogs to help build the cooperative store. I went around to all the members house and taking up the chicken, hogs and corn and everthing that would help build the store. We had elected a committee to be responsble for everthing that was collected for the cooperative store. So everthing I would go to the members house and get. I would bring it and turn over to this committee. I didn't lose one minute working to build the cooperative store. The planters fought aganist us hard to keep us from building the cooperative store. But we never notice anything. We keep on working to build the cooperative store. We were organizeing three parish at the same time. Each parish we working togather to help build the cooperative store. I went to Franklin La. where there was a large sugar cane plantation working the labor under the wages hour law. I began to get a local started. We were organizeing in secret because the sugar cane planters was doing everthing their could to keep the labor unimform of the wages hour law. Many of the labor was paid below the wages hour law. I travel all over the cane belt and find the same condition on ever cane plantation. The planters was aganist the wages hour law. They would have the big store to get even with the labor when they would come to the big store to get their food. Very little cash the labor would have when they would get their pay envelope on pay days. Mr. McIntire our state Sec't of the La. F.U. had collected thousand of dollars for the sugar cane labors in the cane belt. He even fought hard to get wages hour law to act for the sugar cane labors and was success to get it to act.

McIntire never lost one minute fighting for the poor farmers while he was in the fields. Many night he slept in his car on the high way waiting for the day to brake so he could have a meeting on some case that the poor farmer had give him to take up with the government offical in the county seat. And we have to give it to him, he never lost a case that he taking up if it was a true one. All over the state of Louisiana in the cotton patch you can hear the poor farmer asking where is that man, Mr. McIntire. He sure know what to do with these big planters when they are stealing from us poor farmers. The planters dont like him because he stood up for our justice and kept them from taking government money from us. But we love mr. McIntire for what he did for us. We pray to the lord that he will soon recover from his sickness and come back and help us poor farmers again. These planters are glad that he are sick so they can keep on stealing from us. May god bless Mr. McIntire to come back to Louisiana again.[46]

McIntire was well known by both the planters and the sharecroppers for his good work for the sharecroppers. And the planters know him because McIntire kept the book on them ask well ask the planters kept the book on the share-croppers. And wouldn't let them get away with their tricks on the sharecroppers. At one time the planters wanted to raise the rent on the tenant in pointe coupee parish. The tenant send a telagram to McIntire to come at once. And that was in the midnight when this telagram reach him. McIntire went to these tenant aid at midnight to fight aganist the rent rise. When McIntire arrive in pointe coupee par-ish he called a committee of the parish union togather and taking up the case. And McIntire jump in his car and went look up the State dirrector of the F.S.A. and other government offical. In a couple days McIntire had a meeting togather with the planters and the government offical. The tenant stuck with McIntire. And the rent rise was stop. And the government offical gotten the planters to agree to rent the land to the F.S.A. And the F.S.A. rent the land to the tenants. This is a remem-bers of Mcintire work in the fields that will never be forgotten.

The sharecroppers are still talking about how the planters was talking about killing McIntire and tried to bluff McIntire but their couldn't do that. McIntire stood on his ground for the right of the sharecropper. McIntire lost his health by staying out night and day fighting for the right of the poor farmers both White and Negroes. When the rent rise was stop and the back money was collected, it was collected for both White and Negroes.

McIntire layed in bed in the hospital for more then two years down with the T.B. All the sharecroppers missed him for his good work in the cotton fields. Most of my best experence came from McIntire. He would never let me miss an op-pertunity where ever it was a chance for me to get some experence. My first trip to Washington D.C. McIntire had the La. F.U. to send me there to the agriculture department to tell the condition of the poor farmers in the State of Louisiana. There must have been the sum of 37 tenant in the agriculture department from the south. We had conference with the head of the A.A.A., W.P.A., F.S.A. and the re-lief agents and many other government offical in Washington D.C.[47] When McIn-

---

46. When McIntire was moved to New York, LFU president Charles J. Gille sent a letter to locals, asking them to help raise funds to pay McIntire's hospital bills (June 5, 1940, CJP).

47. These are the Agricultural Adjustment Administration, the Works Project Administration, and

tire taking sick, I work hard as a bee to hold the farmers union members togather along by myself. Had a couple of union members to come and take McIntire but was unexperence and the job went bad for a while.[48] But I never lost one minute fighting to keep farmers union rolling.

When I had went to Washington and told the Government about my work in the fields in Louisiana, they told me to go back to Louisiana and keep up the good work. I will say that was a good incouragement to me. When I came back, I speed up with my work. I travel night and day working to build the farmers union. I also had to oppertunity to make the National farmers union convention in Denver Colo. where there was five hundred delagate at that convention. I happen to be the only Negro represent the poor farmers from the south.

I was treated fine. It happen that I just had bus fare to get to this convention and I was allow to make a five minute talk. And when I was through talking ever body yell and taking up a large collection for my trip back home. I will never tell all my experence that I have had sence the last twelth years. Because it will be hard to remember ever thing although will get real close to all of it. Many time I have been offer another job and a good one two if I would let that union bussines along. I know if that was did it would mean that I had sold my class to the boses. Like Judas did Christ, sold him out for a piece of sliver. I know that I was in the working class and will always stay in my class. Many times the planters had threaten to kill me and also McIntire. We never stop because they threaten our life because we know we was on the right track. Our work was for justice and not to penetrate our class into the bosses class.

---

the Farm Security Administration, all federal agencies created during Franklin Delano Roosevelt's administration to increase incomes and jobs during the Great Depression. The date of this trip to Washington is unknown.

48. First Roald Peterson and then Kenneth Adams led the LFU after McIntire was hospitalized and Peggy Dallet moved to New York in the fall of 1940. Peterson, who had been a part of the Farmers' Union growing up in North Dakota and who had been a volunteer in the office under Dallet, took over the state office in fall 1940. Kenneth Adams, who seems to have been from the area and who spoke French, became secretary when Peterson left for a job in the Soil Conservation Department in Texas in June 1941. Adams was called by the draft board while he was imprisoned with Clark in the spring of 1942 and was probably drafted after his release (Gordon McIntire, letter to Members and Friends, March 10, 1942, CJP; Kenneth Adams and Clinton Clark, notarized statement, April 18, 1942, box 112, SAB; and Gordon McIntire to Clyde Johnson, July 15, 1941, CJP).

In 1941 we had a school in the rural to educate local leader. The school last for more then three week. It went fine. The leader liked the school and learn a lots out of the school.[49] After the school was out, I taking sick and had to lay up for a while. I tried to contain taking rest.[50] But when I was not organizeing I couldn't rest until I would be in a farmers union meeting some where. So I travel in a new section up north Louisiana on the Mississippi river, Ferriday La. in Concordia parish, where the farmers had being asking for the farmers union ever sence 1939. When I gotten there I was still sick. I travel all over the parish investagateing the condition of the poor farmers. I would cross the Mississippi river and go into the State of Mississippi and investagate the poor farmers condition there too.

I never lost one minute going from one State to another. I start organizing local in both State. That was in Sept. 1941 when I landed in Concordia parish. Along about Xmas I had three local in Concordia parish and in Adam county Mississippi. We had three local in differen't community in Mississippi. I had a conference with the Adam county F.S.A. Supervisor. He thought it was swell to organize the sharecroppers in Mississippi. So I went in ever church and made speach to the poor farmers and made friends with all the preacher. In Natchez Miss. there was a special Headquarter where all the Preacher hang out during the week. When I know of this, I set a date to meet them all. I went there and made myself known to them. And got up on the floor and made a speach to them. I told them what it mean to them if the poor farmers would organize. Most of them degree with me and invite me to come over to their church and make a speach to their members.

49. McIntire wrote to Johnson: "They have (Bob and Lem) agreed to send down a teacher for three training schools one week each in Washington, Pointe Coupee and Natchitoches parishes. I think Lem has in mind one of Rob Hall's friends from the northwest Farm Holiday movement" (July 15, 1941, CJP).

50. On November 2, 1941, Clark sent Brown a letter from Natchez, Mississippi, that began with the news that he had been sick for two months. "But it seem like I cant stop. for looking at the condition of my people in Mississippi," he wrote, "I have organizer three new local for the farmer union sence I been here in Natchez Mississippi in my sick bed" (box 10, SAB).

I contact all the Business leader in that section and had them to know what my business was to be up in their part of the State. Ever one I talk to said that the union was much needed in that section of the State and told me to try to put my work through.

One day in Sibley Mississippi I went to one of the big planter store. It happen that it had rain that day and all the poor farmers was hanging around the big store. I went in this store with a suit of cloth on my back and a clean shirt. When I first went in the store all the sharecroppers was talking. Ever body stop talking looking back at a stranger coming in the store, exspecial a Negro with a suit of cloth around a plantation store. I had in my hands a farmers union Paper. I said to the planters, This is Clinton Clark, the organize for the farmers union. I am trying to get these sharecroppers organize so they can buy cooperative from your store. All the sharecroppers was standing and looking dirrect toward me and the planter as if the planter was going to lynch me for telling him that I was going to organize the sharecroppers in his community. The planters listen to what I had to say carefuly. And taking his own time to say something back to me. When he did come out with a word, it was a good one and help me to get the farmers to cooperative with me.

He said well I will tell you. All over the world the labor is organize. And ever body is organize but the poor farmers. I thank it couldn't be a better idea that the poor farmers get to gather as soon as posable and as quick as they can. After I walk out of the store all the sharecroppers came out behine me and ask me to give them my hands and told me, Mister you are a brave man of my race. And many of them invited me to spend the night with them. I want to leave for the next community but these sharecroppers worrie me so until I decited to spend this night with them and pay another visit to their community later. That night a Preacher was having a big meeting in his church, and the sharecroppers invited me to attend this meeting and their give me the oppertunity to take the floor to speak to the farmers on the farmers union. I talk on the labor union and what they was doing to improve their condition and how it was more importan that the poor farmers organize into a union of their own. When I was through talking, the church members give me a big hand and ask me to talk some more. The preacher then got up and said to the members, Now we have another moses here with us again. We should be prode to have some one to come here and open our eyes. Now dont go and tell the planters that we have some one in here telling us to organize, and before we can get togather the planters will beat us doing what we trying to do. Let us learn what is good for one of us poor farmers is good for all of us. And what is bad for one of us is bad for all of us.

So lets us put God in front and stick togather and fight for a better condition. God had send moses here to open our eyes. We oughtt to be prode to have such a brave man in our community.

When the meeting was over the sharecroppers was pulling on me, asking me to come spend the night and take dinner with them. We set a another meeting in the church as the preacher give us the church to have our meeting any time we wanted.

The next morning I went back over the river to Ferriday La and started organizeing all the small farm owner into the farmers union. My first local was organize in around Vidalia La. The local was set up about 15 miles south of Vidalia down the Mississippi river. There was tenant and sharecroppers living along the river side on several plantation on the Mississippi river. The planter had their own store and was charging the sharecropper double price for what ever they get out of the store. There was a gravel road on the missisippi levee and the only way you could get to these plantation it would be to walk it or try to get a ride with the mail man. He would make one trip a day on this rout. And if he didn't know you it would be hard to get a ride with him unless some of the farmers would recemend you to him and then you had to pay him 75¢ for the one way trip. Several time I had to walk this 15 miles some time 25 miles to reach the sharecroppers. At one time when I had got a ride with the mail man and was on my way to investagate the condition on two plantation, one of the planter was setting in his car side the road where the mail man had to pass. When he seen the mail man was getting close, he jump out of his car and came to the mail box where the mail man had to stop. And walk up to the mail man and said to the mail carrier is you got those check. The mail carrier said yes in a draging way. The planter said give them to me. The mail carrier seem like he didn't wanted to give him the check before me. But he findly give the check to the planters. At first I didn't understand what the check was all about. But that night when I was amond the sharecroppers, I find out that the check was for the sharecroppers send by the Government from their cut acres of cotton or the peas they would plant in the cut acres land.[51] And the planters would get all

---

51. In order to raise farm prices, the AAA guaranteed payments for farm land taken out of cotton production. Here Clark witnessed the theft of these payments, as the postmaster gave the sharecroppers' checks directly to the plantation owner.

these check and forced the sharecroppers to sign the check over to him for what they would buy out of his store. And he would only let his stoolpigon have a few dollar cut of their check for keeping him imform of what was going on around the plantation amond the other sharcroppers. The sharecroppers on this plantation are afread to tell you any thing about what was going on the plantation. The only way you could get anything about the plantation you would have to go to the next plantation and the sharcroppers would tell you everthing what was going on. The next night I walk to the next plantation and there where I got togather five good head of a family togather and had a meeting in one of the sharecropper home. We talk until two O.Clock in the morning and decited to set up a local. And each one had pick out the one who would be trusted to join in with them and would have them in the next meeting ready to set up the local. In a couple of weeks time this local was set up. After this local was set up, I then went to Ferriday and started organizing a new local. In a couple weeks time I had one set up there. After this local was set up, we had a preacher elected for the local president. And he had a church down the black river. One sunday when he went there to preach, he told his members about the farmers union and told them how it was very importan that their put up a local in their community. And he told them if they would set a meeting, he would bring a man to talk to them and tell them about the farmers union. So his members was to glad to hear about the union and told him to bring the union man in their community immediately. So on the following sunday we rented a car and a group of members went to our preacher members church, and when we reach this church there was 75 sharecroppers there waiting to hear the speaker. Before open the meeting, I sing a few union songs for them. I can still remember how it went something like this.

> Bank head cotton song.
>> Poor old farmer done forgotten
>> Made his little crop and cant sell his cotton.
>
> Chorus: Oh my lord, Oh my lord
>> What a fix we're in!

When this meeting was over many question was asked. And the local was set up the same day, paid their dues immediately. The farmers union dues was $2 a year for each head of a family. So when this black river local was set up, that made three local set up in concordia parish. Then we organize these three local into a parish union, with a parish President and Sec'y Tres, and parish board of dirrector. And three local was set up in Mississippi over in Adams county. When the Japs Attack the United States, I was having a meeting Ferriday La.[52] We started organizeing to help win the war. I went to ever meeting the F.S.A. would have and help the F.S.A. Supervisor to tell the poor farmers how importan it was for them to plant more food to help win the war. We taking a committee to have a conference with the F.S.A. Supervisor on getting land for a group of farmers. This conference last for more then a hour for the Supervisor was very interested in our plans. He taking out a map and show us the land that he would give to us if we would organize the family to put on the land. And he explan to us how much money was on hand to build the houses for the family when their would be ready to move in. The Supervisor even told me to go around and tell all the farmers when ever they would need imformation about the F.S.A. that the office was open for them at any time. When we was having this conference with the Supervisor, I remember he told us a little story. When something like this. He said one time there was a man who was a good whip man. He could take that whip and knock down flies and bugs and pop a cigarette out of your mouth without touching your skin. One fellow told that whip man to go over to that tree and knock that black thing down. The whip man said no. The other man said why. The whip man said because that is a harnest nest. And their are organize. And the Supervisor said to us that what I wants to see you boys do, get organize.

Again the Supervisor told me how he had organize five good family to put on a very good farm under the F.S.A. And these sharecroppers had filled out they blanks and was excepted on the farm. So he told me that the planters had slip around and filled these sharecroppers head up with bunks. And when the Supervisor was ready for the sharecroppers, they refuse to move on the F.S.A. farm instead their had listen to the planters. So the Supervisor ask me to talk to my people and tell them not to listen to what those guy said, for them to come to his office and he would then tell them the F.S.A. program. So I did just what he told me. Every church I went to I got up and made a long talk on the matter and told them how long their had been listen to the planters and had never gotten their condition any better from the planters good words. And now our Government is trying to help

---

52. This of course was the attack on Pearl Harbor, December 7, 1941.

the poor farmers to get back on his feet again through the F.S.A. program. Why we ought too sure them we appreciate their help and take this oppertunity while we have it. And try to make it better.

The following week we called a parish union meeting with the board of dirrector. In this meeting we set our plan to get up scrap iron to give to the defense program. We had elected one member who own his little farm to keep all the scrap iron in his yard until we would have enought saved to turn over to the defense program. Ever member would have to bring the scrap iron to this member farm once each week, not only scrap iron ever thing that would help to win the war. And also we had elected a committee to go over and see the post master on how we could buy war saveing stamps and bonds cooperative. The post master give us all imformation and we was to start in the week when I was arrested and put in the Vidalia parish jail.

Each member had degree to put up 25¢ a week to buy the defense bonds and stamps. And we was to start saveing funds on the Russians China Britain defense. We was calling meeting in the churches ever night to explan the dangers of the war if we didn't do all we could to help win this war and too defeat Hitler. Not only was we planing to buy the defense bonds and stamps cooperatively, we had plan to put up money togather to buy seeds of all kinds to started planting more food to help feed the army. We was going to buy thousand of chicks so by the end of the year we would have eggs by the thousand and chicken by the thousand to turn over to the defense. We had started puting up the funds for our problem already. We had went to the F.S.A. Supervisor for more imformation about the food program.

The F.S.A. Supervisor giving us all the imformation and was glad of my help in the parish. He would invite me to all of the F.S.A. meeting to speak to the F.S.A. client. It was time I couldn't get rest because the farmers would look me up day and night to go to different places and speak to the poor farmers on the war program. I was glad to go with them at any time to asure them that my heart was right and ready to do anything that would open the people eyes to help all they could to help win this war. I never lost one minitue. Ever oppertunity I could get to speak in the churches, school houses, I would make it if it was posable to do so.

On sundays we would have speaking in the churches letting the farmers know how importan it was to save all scraps for the defense to help win this war. We had the news spread for 40 miles up and down the mississippi river to rigister with the civilian defense and to cooperative with the F.S.A. to plant more food to help win the war. Many of the poor farmers was unimform of what it mean to help win the war. To make them understand I would go through the fields to their shacks and sit down and explan the war matters to them over and over again so they could see clearly into the hold matter.

When ever body was registering with the civilian defense, many of the poor farmers was afread to go to the school house and register. So when I was imform of that I immediately went to the churches and explan the matter to my people. And had them to march with me to the school house on the monday when the civilian defense was registering. Then the poor farmers became more and more interested in doing their part after I had going through weeks talking to them. Many time some of the farmers would walk up to me and say Mr. Clark, you sure has open our eyes sence you have being in here and explan so many true thing to us about the war and how we should live togather. I will say the Lord must have send you in our parish. We need many more like you to come in our parish and sure the true light to these people, because their have been in the dark so long until they think it is not no light for them in this world down here on earth. We hope that you will put some thing in them that they will see the true light. And we can get out of this old bad living we are in now.

I happen to go on a large plantation where the planter didn't allow the share-croppers to plant anything but cotton. For years this plantation didn't allow the sharecroppers to plant anything but cotton only and was not allow to have a cow are chicken on they yards. Most of the sharecroppers wanted to move but their find it was no use. The planter was all in the same union aganist the sharecroppers. The other planters would have to find out why you move from the other planta-tion and would find out from the planters, and he would be sure to see that he didn't take him on the other plantation.

One day I went to post office to get my mail. When I went in the post office there was around 15 planters standind talking about the war. I was reading a letter and at the same time listen to them. I heard one of the planter speaking aganist President Roosevelt. He said President Roosevelt had taking all the Auto tires and all the Car from them. How do he expect for them to ride. They said Roosevelt is just making a monkey out of them. He didn't know what he was doing. The conversation was so crazy until I wouldn't stand and listen any longer. We had one of our member who had a ford car. And we would raise money to pay for the gas. And we travel from different community trying to get all the poor farmers into the farmers union and started buying the defense bonds and stamps and plant more food to help win the war. Severl night we had meeting on the black river where no union man was allow to be caught. If they would find any union man organizeing the sharecroppers, the planters would organize their mobs immediately and put him in the black river. The planters had put many Negroes in the black river because they had asked for the Government checks are cotton settlment. On this black river you was not allow to ask for anything concern your crop if you was a sharecroppers on one of the black river planters plantation. If you did you would find yourself floating down the black river by day light. So when you was on the black river and if you was a stranger you would have to be careful what you said are who you talked too.

In our state office of the farmers union, we had a young white boy who was a french decent. He was acting state sec'y of the farmers union. He was unexperence of the work of the farmers union and that made it a little hard for me to work by myself to get the most of problem complete.[53] So I would write friend of who I know had union experience, an ask them to write letters out to my leading members. And my friend did so. They would not only write letters for me, their would send out bundle of cloths to my local members. And I will say it was a great encouragement to them. There was severel good friends in Washington D.C. and in the state of New York who would give me great help in organizeing the farmers down in Louisiana.[54] And that was the only way you could get the sharecroppers to organize, when you could get the suport of some real good friend that have great intrested in the poor farmers. The poor farmers the one who have being suffering so long. The F.S.A. was willing to help the poor farmers hold heartely if they would organize themself togather in their community. And we find out that the F.S.A. was our best friend trying to help the poor farmers to get on his feet. In Concordia parish we were getting all the churches to suport our union in helping

53. Clark is describing Kenneth Adams. Gordon McIntire offered a similar description after meeting Adams in the summer of 1941: "I don't think that we can expect much from Adams but it may be possible to hold things together where they would otherwise go bust . . . I think that he does have definite possibilities. Foremost is that he is a native and can handle French" (McIntire to Johnson, July 15, 1941, CJP).

54. On November 2, 1941, Clark wrote from Natchez, Mississippi, asking Brown to send him some good books. "Also I would like for you are Dr. Wilkerson to write these men a real good letter and mention my name in each letter I know they will assissit me if you all will write them a real good letter tell them of the good work. and how importain it is to organize in the south." He then lists the names and addresses of six men: two doctors, two ministers, a blacksmith, and an undertaker (box 10, SAB).

to win the war program. We was doing everthing that was posable to help win the war. The local I had organize across the Misssissippi river was going to cooperative with us to help buy defense bonds and stamps and getting scrap togather for the defense program. The news had spread all over the parish that we was organizeing to help win the war. We were going so strong with our union work until people was coming from long distent to get imformation about our problem and how could they help to build our union strong. One sunday we give a banquate in a cafe. Fourty members attend the banquet. We had a preacher to open and close our banquet. We sang many farmers union songs togather. Many people was standing around looking on to see and to hear about our aim. So the president of our parish union know just how to talk on our aim and what our problem was. So he made the first speach and the group gave him a big hand. After the President was through with his speach, we had each member to talk for five minute. When the talk had been around, I then taking the floor for twenty minute. Peoples was coming from the churches and stop by to hear the speach. From the talk and the new spirit we gave them, we made seven new members after the banquet was over. From that day on, I couldn't rest for the sharecroppers coming to my room asking question about the F.S.A., A.A.A. and many other government matters and on how to build the union. The more they would come to see me, the more friends I would make and the stronger our union would get. I had contact many preacher to help me carry on my work and most of them had offer me their churches to have my meeting and to prove to us they wanted to help. Several of the preacher join our union and give me they suport.

At the first beganning of our meeting, we would have our meeting in different members shacks. But when we contact the preacher and the teachers and the F.S.A. Supervisor, we immediately started our meeting in the churches. When Rev. J.J. Parker of Ferriday La. told us in our meeting in his churches one night that he was 100% for our union and his people getting togather and change they way of living, he said to us that his big book says togather we stand and devided we fall. Many of the sharecroppers would tell me many time how the planters hated Rev. J.J. Parker because he didn't hold back his voice when the planters would do any of his people wrong and steal the sharecroppers Government checks. I will say Rev. Parker was a man with great spirit to fight for the poor farmers. He would speak out no matter where he would be in the rural.

The planters was taking from the sharecroppers so fast and holding them down, until the members wanted to raise the money for one of the sharecroppers and myself to go to Washington D.C. and see if we could get some action done by the offical of the Agriculture Department. So when they had $20 raised, we decited to get the White fellow to come over to the parish and help us to work the problem that we had planed. So on December 25, 1941, the parish union degree to give me exspense to go to New Orleans La. and talk the matters over with the white fellow. His name Kenneth Adams a french decent. So I wire him to let him know that I was on my way to the City. The members had asked me to bring him back with me. That they would pay his exspense back to the City if he would come and spend a couple days in the meeting with them. When I arrived in the City and had a talked to Kenneth on the matter of Concordia parish, he degree to go back to the parish with me. So while being in the City, I thought to spend several days with a few friend there. I spend the New year there and then Kenneth and myself went through Pointe Coupee parish and spend a couple days there with the old farmers union members. And too after Kenneth Adams had degree to go back with me to concordia parish, I immediately wrote cards to the leading members telling them to look for our arrival on Jan 5, 1942. It was several cards that I had wrote to different members about our arrival, so they would have the meeting arrange for us when we would arrivel in Ferriday Jan 5, 1942. So on monday Jan. 5 Kenneth Adams and myself taking the bus from Lettsworth La. on our way to concordia parish. Around one-O.Clock we arrived in Alexandia La. and there we had to change bus. So after we had changed the bus and headed for Ferriday La., when the bus landed in Jonesville La. about half way to Ferriday, the bus stop, and the bus driver said something to the Jonesville sherriff. And the sherriff jump on the bus. All the same time when we were rideing the bus from Alexandria, I was noticeing the bus driver looking suspicous. But I never paid any attention until we arrived in Jonesville. After bus driver had said something to the Jonesville Sherriff, and the sherriff said something back to the bus driver very low, then the sherriff asked the bus driver what time will he come back to Jonesville. The bus driver told the sherriff about five O.Clock. Then the bus driver, his name Jack Adam, winked his eye to the Jonesville sherriff. And the sheriff gotten on the bus. The sherriff sit close behind the bus driver talking to each other. When the bus was getting close to Ferriday La., the sherriff began to look back toward Kenneth and myself in the bus. He continue to look back until the bus land in Ferriday, La. When the bus stop in Ferriday, the sherriff jump down off the bus first. Then Kenneth and myself came down behind the sherriff. Kenneth wanted to go with me to my room. I told him it wouldn't be a good idea. So he said he didn't have enough money to go to the hotel. So I had 85¢ left from bus fare. I gave the 85¢ to him because I thought it wouldn't be a wise idea for a stranger white fellow to go with me to my room in that parish. Because the people are too suspicious. So the Jonesville sherriff never taking his eyes off Kenneth Adam until he went to the hotel. I think the offical was already imform where my room was. I went to my room and put my suit case down and went across the street to see if I could locate one of my friend in the Hayes Cafe where he would always hang out, as he was the Supt. of the Franklin Funeral home for Colored people. Mr. Vaughn was his name.[55] And he was out of Town, so then I went across the street to see one of my member. So my member and I started to talking on the union matters. He began to tell me about the meeting that was carry on sence I had left there. He told me about one of the member, his name was Arron Steward. At one time the parish union members didn't wanted to take him into the union. But some how he had join in one of the local. So while I had been going to New Orleans, Aron Steward gotten into an arguement with the members about the dues. So the members agree to give Aron his money back, what he had paid to join the union. So this member Frank Reed of whom I was talking to, Frank was telling me the story of the agruement the member had while I was out of the parish. The meeting that the member had planed to have in the church, they had planed to change the meeting to some of the members shack. Because some stoolpigon had told some of the planter of the farmers union meeting was going to be held in the church and the planters was organizing they mob gang to break up the meeting and the members didn't wanted to have no trouble with the planters. Before Frank and I could wind up our discussion about the union matters, up pop the Town Marshall. He walk up close to Frank and myself and the town marshall said what one of you all is Clark. So I said to the town

<hr/>

55. In a statement made in New Orleans after his release, Clark identifies this friend as L. D. Vaughn (Kenneth Adams and Clinton Clark, notarized statement, April 18, 1942, box 112, SAB).

marshall, This is him. And at the same time handed him one of my cards. The marshall look the cards over carefully, then said Clark, I want you. I said to the marshall, O.K. Then he said to me, Clark where is your room. I told him over there in front of us. He said lets go in your room. So he taking me to the house, push the door open, went into my room and start looking into my suitcase. Before he could get the suitcase open, I was trying to get the suitcase open for him to show him what I had in the suitcase. The marshall said to me, Watch where you put your hands. The City marshall taken my suitcase and the Jonesville sherriff taking a box of books and letters and papers along with him. And put them in his car. The marshall drove his car near the drug store where the state cop was waiting in his car. The city marshall turn me over to the state cop. The state police told the city marshall to go over to the hotel and get that white fellow. So while the city marshall was going to get Kenneth Adam, the state police left me with the Jonesville sherriff. The state police then went over to the telephone office. Before leaving for the telephone office he wrote my name and Kenneth name on a piece of paper. A few minute later it was brood cast over the police call. So the Jonesville Sherriff was reading one of the farmers union paper and ask me a question about the paper. I asked the Jonesville Sherriff, Whats that. The state police said to me, Look here nigger. You must say Yes sir and no Sir to a White man down here. I will take this pistol and crack over your dam head. Then the state cop said to the Jonesville Sherriff, it not that nigger, it is that white fellow. The cop said Clark, What you fooling with that white fellow for. Cant you see its nothing to him. Look what kind of cloths he wears. Where he get that typewritter from. Dose he have a office in New Orleans. I said why sure the Louisiana farmers union have a office in New Orleans. The state cop said Clark where you all was having your meeting. And why you all was having your meeting in the night. I said to the cop, Because all the farmers was busy in the day working on the farm. The state cop taking us over to the city jail. He wanted to put us in the city jail. But the city marshall said no it be better to take them to the parish jail. Then the state cop and the Jonesville sherriff togather taking us to the parish jail at Vidalia La. So when we arrive at the parish jail, the Jonesville sherriff taking Kenneth Adam along with him in the jail and the state cop held me behine. And the cop said to me, Clark, I am going to file a charge against that white fellow. I never said a word. When the cop was taking me up in the jail, he began showing me they hang Negroes. And when they taking us to our cell, the jailer began to shake us down. They was looking at all the notes we had in our pocket. Then their lock us up into the cell. The next morning the cop came in my cell and ask me, Who hire that white fellow. I told him the membership of the farmers union. He said, Clark, I seen where some body didn't like that white fellow. How come you hire him.

I said the membership hire him. The cop said wasn't that white fellow your Sec'y. I said no he was the sec'y for the Louisiana farmers union. The state cop then went to the window and call me to see a tree. And said to me Clark, You see that tree. Its going to be a nigger and a white man hanging in that tree.

Then the cop left, and the High Sherriff came into our cell and call me close to the bar where he was standind. And said Clark, Wasn't you ashame to fool those poor nigger out of they money like that. I said to the sherriff, I wasn't fooling those poor people. I was trying to help them to help themselves. The sherriff said why you went to those old ignorance nigger for like old Rev. Ben Lewis and Henry Owen. Why didn't you go to those big nigger farmers like Rev. Sam Fox. I said to the sherriff it didn't make no different to me how big he was if he beleave in getting better condition for the poor farmers. I would talk to any of them when they would come out to our meeting are the church.

Then the sherriff said to me, Clark why you was stirring up these niggers while all this war was going on. I said we was doing all we could to help in this war. And let them know that this war was going on. Because many of them didn't even know this war was going on.

Also we was organizeing to buy defense bonds and stamps cooperative. And was getting up scraps for the defense program. The sheriff said Clark, You know it was 20 American Solider killed this morning. I said to the sherriff, I know this is bad that why we was doing all we can to help fight it in any way we could do the job.

So the sherriff said to me, Clark, That is not what I want to hear you say. Wasn't you beating those poor niggers out of they money. I said no I didn't. I was teaching them how to better their condition through organization. The sherriff then left and came back that night with some of the farmers union membership cards. He had been around to some of the sharecroppers shacks and taking they membership cards from them. And tried to show them that the farmers union was just taking their money for the fun of it.[56] While the sherriff was showing the cards to some of the planters in the jail, the jailer came into my cell and said Clark, Did those

56. The sheriff was accusing Clark of collecting money for membership in an organization that doesn't exist.

sharecroppers tell you anything about that killing down there in the swamps. I said to the jailer, Yes some one had beening talking about some killing down in the swamps. But no one said much about the killing to me. I didn't tell the jailers, but I had hear all about the killing. It happen that two widow women, their husband had been killed by one of the planter who was relative to the High sherriff.[57]

And these two widow had join the farmers union. And the sheriff had find it out. And the offical was worrie about it being leak out to much. And the sheriff had went to get them afread so they wouldn't talk any more to any one because this killing had been kept under for some time. So the next morning, the D.A. and the State Cop, Sherriff came into my cell. When they enter the cell, the D.A. said well, This is the Decon. The State Cop said Yes.

The D.A. said to me, Say nigger! You must thank you are as much as a white man, Dont You! Dont you think you ought to be on a farm. I said sure, then he said nigger cant you run! Get going.

When they had came in the jail they had left all the jail doors open. The state Cop told the D.A., No let go down and read some more. The Sherriff ease up to me and gave me a blow with his fist in my mouth and in my face three times.

The blood start running from my mouth. I began to wipe the blood from my mouth. The Sherriff said to me, Its not bleeding like its going too yet. He said after he had pounch me in the mouth, It no one in here but us now. Tell us some thing about this union. When the sherriff had pounch me in the mouth, it made me so angry until when they said tell us something about this union, I said to them in this way, I was organizeing the farmers union, union, union, union.

Then their smile and walk out of the jail and close all the doors. And later on the sherriff came back into my cell. And said, Clark, We are going to let you out tonight so the gang can get you. And he left out. The next day the D.A., the Sherriff, the State Cop came back into my cell. And ask me how many members I had in different local and when the charter was suspended from the Louisiana farmers union. After I had explained the matters to them, they went over to Kenneth Adams cell and question him for a while. The next day the state cop came back

57. An April 11, 1942, *Louisiana Weekly* article covering the release of Clark and Adams identifies these men as Johnny Green and William Barnes; they had been murdered in the fall of 1941 in an area about twenty-five miles south of Vidalia by a relative of a law enforcement official. Clark charged that they had been imprisoned as part of an effort to conceal the killings.

into my cell along with three planters telling me that that the planters would sure hang me befor the next day.

And the cop said, Clark, You thought you was getting by with those Natchitoches hilly billy up in that red river bottom. But when you get down here in this Mississippi bottom you never get away with us like that. You never be a free man again under 26 months. You better ask the sherriff to let you plea guilty and go to the pen for two years, because some body is watching you outside. I bet you couldn't walk across that mississippi bridge over to Natchez Miss. if they let you out. Then he said Clark, You think that is something. A nigger elected in the Government Staff. This is why he said these words, he seen a letter that I had receive from a friend up north saying that a Negro Minster was elected in the Government staff in New York City.[58] Then he said Clark, They sure going to hang you. And they coming get you tonight. And the jailer said, I got the key. And if they come with the rope I ant going to let them kill me. Then the jailer whisper something in the State troopers ears. The trooper said to the jailer No, No, You Ant going to get me in no trouble. Then The trooper left and said Clark, Good by incase I dont see you any more. And too when the D.A. & Trooper and the Sherriff came into my cell, they wanted to know who is that fellow Gordon McIntire. I told them, Mr. McIntire was the State Sec'y of the Louisiana Farmers union. And the trooper said, That is the fellow the F.B.I. had up down in Baton Rouge La. Then the D.A. ask me who was that fellow Jim Patton. I told them Mr. Patton was the National President of the Farmers union.[59] Then the trooper walk around and said that is the fellow the F.B.I. had up down in Baton Rouge La. too. Then they left.

58. This might refer to the election of Adam Clayton Powell Jr. to the New York City Council in 1941.

59. James Patton was president of the National Farmers' Union from 1940 to 1966. He communicated directly with the local district attorney when Clark and Adams were arrested in 1942, explaining their relationship to the union and gently demanding their release. (For a version of Patton's wire, see McIntire, letter to Members and Friends, March 10, 1942, CJP.) Patton was raised in the New Utopia Cooperative Land Association, an experimental community in Colorado, and became involved in the NFU through the Colorado Farmers' Union and its Farmers' Union Mutual Life Association. Michael Flamm writes: "Patton's ideological outlook was a mixture of nineteenth-century populism and twentieth-century liberalism. Family farmers, he believed, were essential to the political and social health of the democracy. At the same time, he harbored an overriding distrust of corporations and a deep faith in abundance, in the idea that America had the potential to meet the material needs of all its citizens" ("The National Farmers' Union," 62).

And the next morning the U.S. Postmaster inspector came in the jail and call Kenny and myself out of the cell to ask us question. The first word the Postmaster said to us, he said, What you boys promas these farmers for them to join the farmers union. I said to the Postmaster, We didn't promas them anything but the farmers union, that they may improve their living condition through cooperative and working togather. Then he said did you boys tell those Negroes you was a Government man. I said No, I would let all my people know that I was a union Organizer. And for them to not get the wrong idea, and would also let them know the different between the farmers union and the work of the farmers union. And that the farmers would urge all its members to cooperative with our Governments Offical in order to help win this war. Then the Postmaster asked Kenny Adams.

Did he wanted to sign a Statement for him to take back with him. Ken said no. Then the Postmaster said if you boys get out of this mess, will you let this union along.

Ken said I don't know, so the Postmaster left, and after that the D.A. and the trooper and Sherriff came into my cell. The trooper said Clark, You know how come you all lost your Charter. It was because the union was fooling with that communist. I said to them, I dont know anything about that, and not anything as I know about the Communist. And my beleave is that the poor farmers ought to organize to better their condition. One day after, the Sherriff came into my cell with a Negro preacher, Rev. Sam Fox. And the Sherriff asked me did I know Rev. Fox. I said I have heard of Rev. Fox, but never have met him. So Rev Fox said to me, What kind of union is that you was organizing.

I told Rev. Fox the farmers union. And Rev. Fox said, what you charge those farmers to join the union. I said to Rev Fox, The dues are $2 a year. Rev Fox asked, What you give to the farmers for the $2. I said the farmers union and Education, so that they may better their condition through cooperation.

Rev. said if that all you would do for me you would never get $2 of mine. Rev Fox then repeated these planters is sure going to get you. Then the Sherriff said 60 planters was in a meeting Sunday and we cant stop them. Then I said to the Rev. Fox pray for me. He said my prayer want do you no good unless you confess your false. Then he said you better pray yourself. I said I am praying. Well, the Rev. said, your prayer wants do no good not unless you confess your false. The Rev then told me a little joke to let me know that the planters was out to kill me. He said if you know one fellow have you to do something and you get caught into the mess and they is going to kill you. And the other fellow is going to kill you. So the best thing for you to do is to confess you false.

Then the sherriff said Clark that is not what I wants to hear you say. Didn't you beat those poor nigger out of their money. I said to the sherriff No! Sir! The members have their money in their tres. I didn't have anything to do with the members money.[60] Then the Rev. wanted to know where was the farmers union Charter and the constitution. I said the union leaders have the constitution and it will be up to them to let you see that.

Rev. Fox said to the Sherriff, That nigger is not crazy, he have plenty sense. And their both left out. The following day the Sherriff taken into our cell a few planters to see me. One of the planters said to me, Say Boy! dont you think you ought to be on a farm. I said to him sure, Can I get on your farm. He said No! I wouldn't have you on my farm with that racket you have. Another planter asked me, Say Boy! what was you telling those farmers. I said I was teaching them how to be reliable and how to cooperate with the food program to help win the war. And the planter said to the other planters, Boy! Those fellow sure have a racket dont they!

One of the planter said to me, Boy! you must see me when you come on my farm, if you dont it will be to bad. The planters talked with each other for a while then left out.

After we was in jail for about three weeks, two lawyer came from New Orleans. The NMU and the TWU together send them there to get us out of this hell jail house.[61] About 6 O-Clock the two lawyer came up in the jail to see Kenny and myself. The jailer then called us out of the cell in to another privat cell. The lawyer said to us, Boys! we have been all over the county to fine a lawyer to represent you two, because we are to far to represent you Boys. So the only lawyer we could fine wants $1000. You Boys cannot raise that much money can you.

The planters have agreed to let you boys go if you two boys will agreed to leave the county.

So we agreed with the lawyers to leave the county.

60. Here Clark defends himself from charges of collecting money under false pretenses and keeping it. Typically, membership dues had gone to the state secretary, where a portion was passed on to the National Farmers' Union and the rest was used to fund state organizing activities.

61. The National Maritime Union and the Transport Workers' Union were both active in New Orleans.

And the two lawyer left on the understanding that we would be turn out the next morning. A few minuite after the lawyers left, the jailer came into our cell, walking up and down the cells alleys. Saying to us, I dont know will we let you boys out or not. We will have to talk this matter over again. So I asked the jailer, What is you holding us for after we have agreed to leave the county. Then the jailer said to me, Aren't your friends going to help you. I said to the jailer, That was my friends that send those two lawyers here. The next following day the State cop came up to our cells and called me and said, Say Clark! These people is going to hang you and when they hang you, they will hang you by your feets. And I will have my picture taken with my hands up beside you in the tree saying, I may be lynch but I am going back south.[62] The sherriff said, Say Clark, we going to give you three years in the Pen. The next day my friend Vaughn came to see me. And the jailer told him to tell me if I could get my friends to raise $200.00 that they would let me go. And that I didn't have to give the money to them all at the same time. I could pay the money on terms. So I said to my friend Mr. Vaughn I cant say nothing about that. My friends knowes what is best to do. So my friend Vaughn understood their tricks and what they was trying to do. And he wink his eyes, while the jailer was standing by looking and listen what answer I would give to my friend. So every time I would receive some money friends, the jailer would say to me, Say Clark! We will soon have enough money after while want we.

I wouldn't give him no answer on these question. The jailer seen that I was slow telling him about the money to get me out of the jail. He then turn and tried Kenny Adams. He told Adams if he could raise $200 or $100 he could get out of this mess. So after the jailer seen that my friend Vaughn wasn't trying to help them get the money out of me, the State cop started threaten Vaughn. The State cop told Vaughn to stay away from the jail.

And the State cop told Vaughn, Dont you know that nigger Clark is worst then a Germany.

A few days later my sister came to see me. The jailer let my sister into the cell to talk with me and told my sister to stay in the cell as long as she wanted to. The jailer was expecting my sister to help get the $200 that he had asked for my released. But the matters work out the other way. The jailer was only giving me a

---

62. He is taunting Clark with the quote from the 1940 rally in Chicago which was published with his picture in the *Chicago Defender.*

better chance to get my mail out to my friends, and let them know what the tricks that the offical was trying to put over on me.

After we was in jail about two months, Dr. Dickinson came to see us. The morning when Dr. Dickinson came, he stop in the court rooms discussion the matters with the offical about our case.[63] The jailer came up to my cell in a hurry and said to me, Clark, a lawyer told me to talk with you. He said did Vaughn gave you that $5 check or not. I said I told Vaughn to spend that money for somethings. Then the jailer said how much money you have. He helded up three fingers. It seem like $15. I never answer. And he left.

About 1 P.M. Dr. Dickinson came up with the Sherriff. Dr. Dickinson said to me, Clark, having you got enough of this yet. At the time he came in the cell I was laying down in the bunk and was slow getting down. The Sherriff said to me, Come on down and talk with the man, because I am in a hurrie.

So Dr. Dickinson said to me, Clark, You know why I am here. It is because Jim Patton send me a telgram to come here. Do you know why these people are holding you fellows. Because the charter was suspended. Who told you to continue with organizing. I said Mr. McIntire. Who told McIntire. I said because he was in contact with Mr. Jim Patton. Then he said Clark, they tell me you are going around here organizing the City workers into the farmers union. Cooks and so on. I said well one girl did cook in town and her father joined the farmers union. And that made his doughter honorary member of the union. Dr. Dickinson said Clark, Did you collect any money from the farmers. I said the members had collect their own money and had their tres holder. He then said have you got bonds yet. I said the Sherriff told me I will have to have help to get bonds.[64]

63. Dickinson was the southern member of the National Board of the National Farmers' Union at the time of Clark and Adams's arrest (McIntire, letter to Members and Friends, March 10, 1942, CJP).

64. The National Farmers' Union had suspended the charter of the LFU in December 1941, after the membership dropped below 1,000. Even though Dickinson implied that Clark shouldn't have still been organizing when he visited him in the jail cell, the NFU's national leadership defended Clark and Adams, stating that the suspension did not mean that they could no longer recruit members and collect dues. The NFU also offered to honor the memberships of anyone who had paid dues to Clark and Adams (McIntire, letter to Members and Friends, March 10, 1942, CJP). These pledges from the NFU probably led to the men's release. Dickinson was also concerned that Clark was organizing into the Farmers' Union people other than farmers, which was true. Clark had always been concerned with the well-being of rural black families and communities; through his connection to the SNYC in the year before this arrest he had been working more and more with women and young people.

Dr. Dickinson then left and said he was going to see the judge to get our bonds.

And later on I receive a letter from Dr. Dickinson telling me that he was imform that I had collected $76, but that I had said $12. And that Mr. Patton, the National President of the farmers union, said he was going to send a man down to contact the members that had made a charge against me and see if they will agreed to drop the charge. And that the union would either give them they money back are issure them they membership cards.

Immediately after I had receive this letter sent words to my members to please write a letter to Dr. Dickinson and let him know that the members had they money in their tres. And the members did write to Dr. Dickinson and told him that they money was in the tres.

And every once in a while the State cop would come up in the jail. Threaten. He asked, Say Clark having they hang you yet. I said to the Cop, You arrested me. Why you ought to release me. He said, I put you in jail. So let the one had you put in jail get you out.

The cop said to me, I want be satify until they hang you are send you to the pen. The State cop was telling the Negroes in Ferriday that Clark was mix up with that C I O. And the State cop wife of who is a School teacher, she said that nigger Clark must be a hudo. He didn't have no money in his pocket when he was arrested.

The State cop and the Sherriff had one of my picture that was taking at the Apm meeting in Chicago and was put in the Chicago defender paper. And they was carring this picture around and showing it to the planters.[65] The planters didn't seem to be worrie about the hold matters as much as the State cop and the sherriff, because they didn't look so mean when they was taking in the jail by the State cop and the sherriff. They would talk with me just as friendly. It would seem to me like the State cop was the only one pushing all the trouble up.

Some night the jailer would come into my cell and ask me question. He would ask me how many minister did I knowed in the county. He would call different minister name to see if I knowed them.

I would tell him of the ones I knowed as he would ask me the names. Just before the court started april the 6, I receive a letter from the I L D telling me that

65. A photograph of Clark speaking at the American Peace Mobilization rally in Chicago was published in the September 14, 1940, *Chicago Defender.*

they was rallying around me. The jailer came into my cell and said, Clark that sound like a good letter didn't it.[66]

I said to the jailer it sure do sound good. So on april the 6, Mr. George M. Brooks Attorney at Law-203 Godchaux Bldg, New Orleans La. came along with one of our friend of New Orleans to investiagate. He came up in our cell and asked me how much money was in the local farmers union tres, and did we collected any money from the members. I told him No we didn't. The members had $36 in their tres. So he went back down in the court and talked the case over with the D A. and the Grand Jurymen. And a few minute later the jailer came up to our cell and told us to get our close ready. Our lawyer would be ready to go in a few minute. And a few more second the lawyer came up in the cell, and said lets go boys. So we gotten into his car headed for new Orleans. Before we left the State cop walked up the car and said, Clark, are coming back here. I said sure. If I dont come back, I will send some one because we cant let the union fall down. So after we had reach New Orleans, I receive a special deliver from Ferriday, saying that the State Cop had told my friend Vaughn to leave town before the sun goes down.

66. The International Labor Defense (ILD) was the legal arm of the Communist Party and had represented the Scottsboro boys in the 1930s.

Afterword

Clinton Clark's autobiography ends with his release from three months of imprisonment in the spring of 1942. He ends his story on a determined note, pledging to return to the area or send another organizer in his place, yet he would never return to rural organizing, and his release from prison would mark the end of the statewide work of the Louisiana Farmers' Union. Though he lived for another three decades, every aspect of his life changed dramatically in the 1940s: his work, his home, his health, his relationship to labor organizing, and his sense of self. World War II redirected the priorities of the organizations and agencies with which he worked, and the anticommunism of the later 1940s destroyed the networks that had supported him. It is also important to note that our sources on his life after 1942 do not consist of his own words. Rather, the events of his life are documented by his FBI file and medical files, records that were covert or confidential, hidden from public scrutiny, and written by hostile—or at best unsympathetic—white observers. From these records we can reconstruct the events of the second half of his life, but, other than a few letters, we do not have Clark's own story of his experiences.

Watched as He Worked, New Orleans, 1942–43

During the year following his release from the Concordia Parish jail, Clark spent his days loading trucks on the New Orleans waterfront and his nights typing his story single-spaced on any paper he could find. Clark had begun writing his memoir before he was arrested in Ferriday, only to have it confiscated with his papers and books by the Ferriday city marshal and later turned over to the FBI. In New Orleans, Clark quickly returned to writing. There is evidence that he sent Harold Preece pages of a draft in June of 1942, and in December 1942 he sent sections of the manuscript to Sterling A. Brown. He wrote Sterling Brown a few short lines about his effort: "You know that I am having a hard time writting this story And working all the same time. And when I get off at night go to work on this story."[1] The return addresses of these letters place Clark as living first on Franklin Street, then on Josephine and Thalia in the African American neighborhood known as Central City. Clark did not write about any union work in his letters to Brown later in the year—just that he was working during the day and writing his memoir at night.

The fullest description of Clinton Clark during his year in New Orleans is an interview recorded in his FBI file. It reports the words of a coworker of Clark's, told to a supervisor, and then told to an FBI agent or informant—possibly three layers of bias and distortion. Nevertheless, the description gives a sense of how Clark carried himself publicly at the time he was writing his autobiography. Clark was an enthusiastic union member and spoke to his fellow workers on the job about organizing for racial equality:

—— of THOMAS TRUCKING AND FREIGHT FORWARDING COMPANY, 1117 Calliope Street, advised that —— worked as a loader for his company, having worked his last day on April 16, 1943. —— advised that CLARK was a union agitator in that he was always ready to report any violation of union rules to the Local. He further stated that he had heard CLARK tell other negroes that he was a Union under-cover man. Mr. —— advised that CLARK was not liked generally by the other negro workers and stated that two of them refused to work with CLARK or to sit beside him because they feared that association with him would get them in trouble. —— said that CLARK always had a supply of Communist Party literature and that he gave it to other members that were interested. —— also said that CLARK was continually preaching race equality. —— advised that CLARK was peaceful in other respects, sober, and either thrifty or had other sources of income in that he was slow to collect his pay and never seemed to be broke. He advised that CLARK was well educated from his talk and that he did not dress as a laborer. He said that he had heard that CLARK had left town but was unable to state where he might be located; however, he advised that it was possible that he could determine CLARK's present whereabouts and activities from some of his employees, and on a later date the writer contacted —— and was advised that he had been unable to do so.[2]

It was perhaps Raymond R. Tillman—an officer in the Transport Workers' Union, Local 206 of New Orleans, who was active in the Southern Negro Youth

Congress and who two years earlier had worked to help draw national attention to Clark's imprisonment—who helped Clark find work at the Thomas Trucking Company and join the Transport Workers' Union.[3] Clark had returned to a much different labor community in New Orleans. It had been two years since Gordon McIntire had been hospitalized with tuberculosis. In 1942, after two years confined to bed, first in Charity Hospital, then in hospitals in New York and Denver, McIntire was just beginning to recover. While Clark and Kenneth Adams, the union's state secretary, were in jail, McIntire had tried to rally union members with a long letter written from bed in a Denver sanatorium. The union had lost its recognition from the National Farmers' Union, and many members of locals were out of touch and no longer paying dues. Adams was probably drafted after he and Clark were released from jail, leaving the Louisiana Farmers' Union without a state secretary.[4] An FBI informer reported that, shortly after his release, Clark had said that the National Farmers' Union would provide him with credentials but not financial support.[5]

During the year Clark lived and worked in New Orleans, the New Orleans CIO was consumed with an internal struggle, as the national leadership of the International Longshoremen's and Warehousemen's Union accused Willie Dorsey of mismanaging the local and its funds. The local's failure to pay dues to the ILWU International had provoked the San Francisco office to send a representative, Harold Goddard, to Louisiana to investigate. Dorsey attacked Goddard as a Communist, while Goddard criticized Dorsey as a black nationalist. The conflict provided an opportunity for anticommunists in the New Orleans labor community to express their views. The internal struggle became increasingly public as a local priest defended Dorsey, and management of the union was ultimately decided in the courts—against Dorsey. David Wells writes that the conflict was a sign of "a developing rift in the ranks of the CIO in New Orleans."[6] With the CIO leadership fighting against itself in New Orleans, and with no structure or support from the LFU to return to the countryside, Clinton Clark used the time to focus on writing his story. He may have been using the last office supplies of the Louisiana Farmers' Union as he typed his story.

Since much of the little we know about Clinton Clark's life during the early 1940s comes from his FBI file, it is important to understand why the FBI was following him. From 1940 to 1945, the FBI tracked where Clark was living and what he was doing, primarily so he could be quickly arrested—in the FBI's lingo, taken into "Custodial Detention." He first came to the attention of the FBI in 1939, when an agent reading the records of the Louisiana Coalition of Patriotic Societies found mention that Clark had joined the Communist Party or Young Communist League in San Francisco in 1932. The FBI claimed that it investigated Clark on an "impersonation complaint" in August and September of 1940. That they recorded his arrest in Natchitoches this way provides an example of the biases and limitations of the information in his file. It has the dates right but records the episode through the falsities of the local sheriff, rather than noting that Clark was arrested to prevent a huge rally of Farmers' Union members. However, it was Clark's speeches at American Peace Mobilization rallies in Chicago and Washington in the fall of 1940 that made the FBI take greater notice.

When its surveillance of Clark began, the FBI was only a few years into investigating organizations that were thought to have Communist connections. President Franklin D. Roosevelt initially had been concerned about Americans with ties to Nazi Germany, but in 1936 FBI director J. Edgar Hoover convinced him that Communist-affiliated organizations should also be monitored. Hoover worried about Communist influence in several major unions key to the daily functioning of the country's economy—the ILWU at the Pacific ports, the United Mine Workers' Union, and the Newspaper Guild. When Roosevelt requested more information on Fascist and Communist activities in the United States, Hoover began an entire program of surveillance of Communists and labor unions.[7] The FBI field offices recruited informants who attended meetings, subscribed to publications, and, in the case of the LFU, fished documents out of garbage cans.

Hoover soon took this surveillance further and developed an elaborate bureaucracy to classify people according to their dangerousness and target them for detention during a war or national emergency. The Custodial Detention Index was literally a file of index cards on people to be monitored and possibly detained. Clark's FBI file shows that in March 1941, Hoover forwarded Clark's dossier to the Special Defense Union for consideration "for custodial detention in the event of a national emergency." Hoover's office must have processed a batch from Louisiana or the LFU all at once, as he also recommended Margery "Peggy" Dallet for custodial detention that same day. Documents in Clark's file imply that Hoover did not wait for a ruling; a month later he sent a letter to all special agents in charge that was titled "Internal Security, Custodial Detention List." Documents in his file make reference to this letter, so Clark's name may have appeared in it or in a list included with the memo. By August 1941 Clark had what was called a Custodial Detention card in the New Orleans Field Office. His name and address are typed at the top, below are some key examples of his work in the Louisiana Farmers' Union and the American Peace Mobilization, and COMMUNIST is typed in the upper righthand corner. A memo in his file suggests that the FBI was not just putting him on a list of people to be detained but actually was about to detain him. A New Orleans special agent sent Hoover a memo with information about Clark on January 13, 1942, just weeks following the attack on Pearl Harbor:

Dear Sir:

There is attached hereto a supplementary Summary Memorandum on the above named individual, who is being considered for Custodial Detention by the New Orleans Office.

Very truly yours,
J.E. CLEGG
Special Agent in Charge[8]

In March 1942, Hoover classified Clark as "Group C": "Individuals believed to be the least dangerous and who need not be restricted in absence of additional information, but should be subjected to general surveillance." Four months later, Hoover reclassified Clark to A-2. Group A included "individuals believed to be the most dangerous and who in all probability should be interned in the event of War." In October 1942, he was moved back down to C-1. By this time the United States was at war, and Japanese, Italian, and German nationals, as well as Japanese Americans, had been detained. Fortunately, Attorney General Francis Biddle did not act on the classifications of the FBI's Custodial Detention Index. Biddle found the classifications useless, and he sent a memo telling Hoover that the FBI should be investigating people who had violated laws rather than deciding who could be dangerous. He further ordered that the statement "This classification is unreliable" be put into each person's file.[9] Undeterred, Hoover simply changed the name of the list. The Custodial Detention Index became the Security Index and was continued as a list of persons with suspected Communist affiliations. Within months the FBI was sending memos to update Clark's Security Index file.[10]

Clark was watched in many ways. FBI informants spoke with LFU members, including the secretary, and informants attended Communist Party meetings where Clark was mentioned. (Almost all names are censored in the declassified file, from informants to people who knowingly or unknowingly provided information to agents and informants.) Agents pulled Clark's records from the New Orleans Retailers' Credit Bureau and the New Orleans Police Department. They checked his draft registration. The agent checking the draft records found that Clark had been misfiled as older than he was, so Clark was given a new draft classification. When Clark later moved to New York, agents would check his mailbox and pull medical records from the clinic where he went for treatment. The case-summary reports filed periodically ended with a page on *"UNDEVELOPED LEADS"*–next steps for the investigating agents. Finding Clark's address was often one of them. For most of the term of his surveillance, agents didn't know where Clark was living–he gave the LFU office in the Godchaux Building on Canal Street in New Orleans as his address. The other "undeveloped lead" was more general: "Will through Confidential Informants attempt to learn more details with reference to the activities of this subject and his connections with or membership in the Communist Party of Louisiana." They didn't seem to have very much information about him.[11]

Interestingly, Clark was not named in the FBI's "Survey of Racial Conditions," Hoover's 1943 compendium of reports on African American activism and civil rights organizing filed by FBI field offices in 1942–43. The FBI had launched a nationwide investigation of civil rights and black community organizations, provoked by some ambivalent, and some outright critical, statements made by black Americans about the war. Hoover suspected pro-Japanese allegiances in the black community and ordered an investigation into "Foreign-Inspired Agitation Among the American Negroes." Not surprisingly, the Louisiana report found that "agitation" among Negroes in New Orleans and Louisiana was not stirred by enemies Japan and Germany but by the black press, the Communist Party, and several civil rights organizations. The report points toward the work of Clinton Clark and the Louisiana Farmers' Union: "Informant has advised that numerous reports have been received in the Communist Party of a growing tendency toward the building of a Negro mass movement among the Negro farmers in Louisiana." The report also carefully counted the city's Communists, finding the most in the leadership and membership of the Transport Workers' Union (four and eleven, respectively). This was the union that Clark joined during his year writing his story in New Orleans.[12]

Most of the information from the first two years the FBI kept a file on Clark describes his work with the LFU, his speeches at the rallies of the Communist-affiliated American Peace Mobilization, and conversations about Clark at Communist meetings. During his year in New Orleans, FBI agents reported that Clark visited the Communist Party office shortly after he arrived in the city, and that he sought assistance and guidance from them. There in April 1942 a woman reportedly offered to help him resume his organizing work through the party. "It seems that the National Farmers Union would give him credentials but no financial help and —— suggested that subject go to New York to rest and that after his return he could go to regular Party classes and get the basic Party education. She said that they would also try to place him in the Trade Union Movement here in New Orleans, 'where you will be able to make great contributions to the movement,' and subject agreed to accept this advice." [13]

In the two years since Gordon McIntire had been hospitalized with tuberculosis, Clark had solicited help from many organizations and individuals in an effort to continue his organizing work. In the same way that he had looked to the structure and support of the Southern Negro Youth Congress in 1940 and 1941, organizing local SNYC youth groups that overlapped with LFU locals, Clark may have seen the Communist Party as a source of financial support and an outside armature through which he could continue his work in rural Louisiana. According to the FBI file, he did some work recruiting for the Communist Party, but it seems his thoughts were still with rural people. In August he asked local Communist leaders if he could return to work organizing in farm areas. He wasn't given an answer. [14] After that month, the agents recorded no substantial evidence that he was continuing to work with the Communist Party.

Clark would spend almost exactly a year in New Orleans, where only a few of his union contacts were helpful. The contents of the LFU office in the Godchaux Building had been packed up and put in storage. He did not have the resources to return to work in the rural areas, but it was not yet apparent that his arrest in Ferriday would prove to be the end of his work organizing in Louisiana. Clark continued to correspond with colleagues around the country; Harold Preece in New York and Sterling Brown in Washington, D.C., may have encouraged him to use the time to write his autobiography. He spent much of the year following a grueling schedule of working on the waterfront all day and writing at night. Still, he wrote the story of his work with enthusiasm and hope, ending it with a pledge to a state cop in Ferriday that the union would return and resume its work in the area. "If I dont come back," he writes, "I will send some one because we cant let the union fall down." He mailed the manuscript off to Harold Preece and Sterling Brown toward the end of 1942, and in the spring of 1943 he prepared to move to New York.

New York City, 1943–49

In April 1943 Clark sent Sterling Brown a last letter from New Orleans. He planned to visit Brown on his way to New York:

> My dear friend Mr. Sterling
>
> Your letter and the money order was receive. My reason for not answering before now. I am waiting for a letter from my friend up in N.Y. Giving me the imformation just when to leave out. So far have not receive no letter. I wanted to let you know when to exspected my date to see you. Just as soon as he write me will send you a air mail. I will stop over for one day. I am just too happy that you have the story completed and the book is on the way, I am just too anxious to get hold of one of those book. It was a friend in D.C. wrote me and said they seen in the. Afro about your book, will write again soon. Good Luck.
>
> Sincerely. Clinton Clark.[15]

It was probably on this trip north that Clark visited Howard University and spoke to one of Sterling Brown's classes. His contact in New York was Harold Preece. When Clark moved, he gave Preece's address as his forwarding address to the Draft Board in New Orleans. (We know this today by matching addresses listed in each man's FBI file.)[16] Preece had many connections with Communist figures and publications, and in the 1940s he was subjected to extreme surveillance by the FBI–they searched his trash, monitored his mail, even searched a storage space he had rented. During these years Preece wrote frequently for black audiences, including a column titled "The Living South," which ran regularly in the *Chicago Defender* and was syndicated to other black newspapers. In his writings he presented himself as an example of "a new white man" in the South, one who saw race differently as the South shifted from an isolated agricultural world to one of industry and trade unions.[17] Preece would return to the South within months of Clark's arrival in New York, moving to Monteagle, Tennessee, with his wife and infant son to work at the radical Highlander School.

Clark arrived in Harlem during a tumultuous year. Historian Cheryl Greenberg characterizes life in Harlem during the early years of the war as having a "mix of improvement and inequity." In 1943, political organizations and labor unions were active and vocal; they had begun to win significant victories against workplace segregation. The threat of a march on Washington had pushed President Roosevelt to sign an executive order in 1941 that banned racial discrimination in defense industries. This empowered many local organizations in their efforts to get employers to hire blacks. But Depression conditions—high unemployment, deep poverty, and terrible housing—persisted in Harlem. Unemployment in New York was actually higher in 1942, the first year of the war; than it had been at the end of the 1930s, and when Clark arrived in 1943, it was just beginning to drop. Most blacks worked as unskilled labor or in service jobs. Clark would have entered an enlarged world of black political organizing, with many events to attend and campaigns to join, but, with the rest of Harlem, he would have had limited opportunities for work. James Baldwin saw Harlem that summer as a community on edge, for the movement of people to southern military bases and defense jobs around the country had increased racial violence and tension. Baldwin describes Harlem families as being so nervous when their sons were stationed in the South that they were relieved when the young men were sent overseas: "Everybody felt a directionless, hopeless bitterness, as well as that panic which can scarcely be suppressed when one knows that a human being one loves is beyond one's reach, and in danger." [18]

In New York, Clark soon became involved in a different world of union work. He was hired as a doorman at the Hotel George Washington and joined the Hotel Front Service Employees Union, Local 144 of the Building Service Employees International Union. Local 144 was just three years old when Clinton Clark arrived. Front service workers were the service employees who worked outside a hotel's kitchens, dining rooms, and cleaning rooms—doormen, baggage porters, elevator operators, checkroom attendants, and hat-check girls. Local 144 was part of the Hotel Trades Council, a group of AFL unions that organized and signed union contracts hotel by hotel, unionizing all the hotel's workers, from electricians to maids.[19] In 1939, the Hotel Trades Council had pushed sixty-two large New York hotels into an agreement that unionized the hotels and increased the wages of twenty thousand hotel workers by an average of 10 percent.[20]

When Clark joined Local 144, the union was growing rapidly and being profoundly shaped by the unfolding war. Its newsletters for these years are filled with talk of members serving abroad and activities that supported the war. Union members put their organization and their experience in the hotel industry to work entertaining and supporting some of the thousands of servicemen who traveled through and out of New York. Hat-check girls organized dances for servicemen, and union members sent packages to soldiers, organized to donate blood, and encouraged one other to buy war bonds.

Soon after Clark arrived in New York, black members of Local 144 formed a Negro Council, and Clark spoke at their initial meeting. The meeting's speakers expressed a civil rights agenda within the overriding issue of the day—World War II. "All emphasized," wrote the reporter for the union newsletter, "that the main job was the winning of the war and that restrictions on one-tenth of our population, the Negro people, hindered our all-out effort." Union officers spoke in support of the war effort and discussed how racial discrimination hindered it. The meeting's main topic was the upcoming Negro Freedom Rally, which would emphasize these twin themes of winning the war and winning equal rights for Negroes. Looking beyond the rally, the group discussed the longer-term goals of fighting discrimination and working in the Anti-Poll Tax Campaign. They elected officers. The union newsletter reported that "Clinton Clark, now a hotel worker and formerly state organizer of the Louisiana Farmers' Union, told of experiences in organizing farm workers in the deep south."[21]

Clark surely would have attended the Negro Freedom Rally held at Madison Square Garden on the evening of June 7, 1943. Over twenty thousand people packed the arena, and another seven thousand listened outside. The crowd included servicemen in uniform and women in nursing and civil defense uniforms. The fight for democracy abroad had given new force to arguments against racism and segregation. The meeting was organized by the Negro Labor Victory Committee, with broad-based support from unions, civil rights groups, and civic organizations. Speakers ranged from labor leaders to Vito Marcantonio, a New York congressman who told of the recent fight to pass a bill ending poll taxes. Speakers emphasized that the war against Hitler couldn't be won if segregation and discrimination limited the contributions of Negro Americans; the rally emphasized the talent and commitment that black Americans could contribute if Jim Crow were dismantled. "Out of this rally must come measures which will utilize the energies, the skills, and the strength of all people, regardless of color, creed or race, who desire to participate in the People's War," Ferdinand Smith, chair of the Negro Labor Victory Committee and an official in the National Maritime Union, told the crowd.[22] The message that organizers wanted to communicate to the country was the strength of a growing, progressive, interracial labor movement allied closely with civil rights organizations. The rally was huge and euphoric. Articles in the *Daily Worker* convey some of the enthusiasm of the evening. One reporter described an "atmosphere of fighting confidence," a crowd certain that they were on "their last lap of the fight for full emancipation."[23] Another *Daily Worker* commentator saw the rally as a sign of the near-end of "the grossest features of the entire jim-crow system" in New York and Chicago. Change in these major cities, he argued, would set an example for change in both the armed forces and the South.[24]

That August, Harlem would be devastated by riots begun when police shot a black serviceman. Looters struck out at white-owned businesses. "I truly had not realized Harlem *had* so many stores until I saw them all smashed open," wrote Baldwin in "Notes of a Native Son."[25] Malcolm X and Ralph Ellison, likewise living there at the time, also wrote about the riots.[26] What might Clark have experienced during this turbulent time? In the days immediately following the riots, members of his union met with other restaurant and hotel workers and issued a response. The riots had political and economic causes, they wrote, beginning with "segregation and discrimination in the Armed Forces." They called upon unions to absolutely oppose racial discrimination against workers and to oppose "any attempt by employers to use the Harlem events as an excuse for firing or refusing to hire Negroes." Recognizing the role that high prices in Harlem stores had played in the riots, they called for more union and Negro representatives on the price panels run by the Office of Price Administration, and they urged unions to set up consumer committees to help members understand the wartime price and rationing programs.[27]

There is little information about Clark's life and work during these years. His name appears sporadically in the pages dedicated to Local 144 in the weekly *Hotel and Club Voice*. He is one of a number of employees of the Hotel George

Washington who contributed to a welfare fund in 1944, and in June 1945 he wrote a letter to the union newsletter thanking the union for help gaining back pay. He pledged to put the $120 he'd gotten into war savings bonds. "This is my effort to help bring V-J Day."[28]

Clark continued to read and educate himself. During his first summer in New York, he attended a workers' school, an education program probably organized by the Communist Party, taking part in a class that was training instructors to teach at other schools around the country.[29] (Clark had attended a workers' school in Sacramento a decade earlier, when he first became involved in organizing through the Unemployed Benefits Council.) After he had been in New York for about a year, Clark began to ask Brown to return his manuscript. "I have a friend who will write my book," he wrote, "and will be able to get me a little piece of money."[30] He told Brown he was doing lots of reading, trying to build his vocabulary and change his southern accent. He was on his way to hear the author Howard Fast speak about his new novel *Freedom Road*. Brown responded (in a letter now lost) and must have told him that he was still at work on his manuscript "A Negro Looks at the South." Clark wrote back with words of support, saying that many people were anxious to read it. Brown, who treasured the different ways of speaking found in black communities across the South, also must have told Clark to be proud of the way he spoke. Clark wrote back: "You are right about not changeing my accent. I will not worry about changeing it since you mention it."[31]

After Clark moved, the New Orleans FBI office forwarded his information to the New York office. A New Orleans agent even went to the Port of New Orleans office to get a copy of a photograph of Clark that had been taken when he had applied to work on the docks as a loader. In New York, Clark registered with the Selective Service, giving a home address and also writing that he could be contacted through the Social Hygiene Clinic at a hospital in Washington Heights. An FBI agent went to the clinic and was allowed to read Clark's medical file; he filed in his report that Clark was receiving treatment for syphilis. New York agents checked the name on his mailbox to confirm where he was living. Later they would question Clark's landlord or someone who lived in Clark's apartment building—the names are censored—about his daily habits, friends, and affiliations. "Nothing of a suspicious nature was ever observed in his room," the agent writes. This same June 13, 1944, FBI report concludes, "A file review reflects that subject has been comparatively inactive in COMMUNIST PARTY affairs since his arrival in

New York." The FBI agents decided that Clark had moved to New York for medical treatment, and they recommended closing his file.[32] About a year later, the FBI canceled his Security Index Card, ending their surveillance.

His family treasures a photo of Clark from these years, one of a few clues that remain of his life in New York. He is wearing a suit and tie, and a beautiful smile. He stands in front of a full bookcase, a typewriter on the table beside him—perhaps the typewriter that banged out his single-spaced, never even a break for a paragraph, manuscript.[33] The photo suggests an intellectual and political life beyond hotel work, and it leads one to wonder how Clark's hard work speaking and organizing full time in the extreme conditions of rural Louisiana would have served him in the unions and civil rights organizations of New York. We have not found evidence that he held an office in Local 144. Even though antidiscrimination and equality were central tenets of Local 144, one has to wonder whether the union leadership would have recognized and made use of Clark's intelligence and organizing talent. The Louisiana Farmers' Union was a bare-bones operation in which Clark had tremendous autonomy, and he was perfectly suited for the job. He was a great speaker, had grown up in a sharecropping family, was determined and clever, could read and write enough, and he had a sense of the larger United States and what was possible beyond the Louisiana plantation. The hierarchical structure of Local 144 would have made it difficult for him to play a leadership role in the union, and the talents and experiences it favored would have been much different. But after independently organizing and leading locals in Louisiana and working with national civil rights organizations, hotel work alone would have been extremely dissatisfying to Clark.

There was a lot going on in Harlem and New York during these years. In the fall of 1943 Clark might have worked in the successful campaign of black Communist Benjamin Davis, who won a seat on the New York City Council. During these years, there were two rival councils of black trade unionists. The Negro Labor Victory Committee sponsored the Freedom Rallies, organized antidiscrimination committees within locals, and used the federal Fair Employment Practices Committee as an instrument for challenging discrimination against Negro workers. It had strong connections with Local 144 and other hotel workers' unions, with representatives from Local 144 serving on the executive board. The older Negro Labor Committee, which had roots in the Socialist Party and garment workers' unions, ran the Harlem Labor Center, providing labor education and job placement help to Harlem residents, and convened a Negro Labor Assembly of representatives from affiliated organizations. Clark's name does not appear in the records of the leadership of either organization. Union records may yet reveal that he had a leadership position in Local 144.[34] His FBI file notes that he gave his employment address as the union office, and his niece remembers that he worked for the government while he lived in New York. It is also possible that, rather than continuing his organizing work, he focused on continuing his education, leading the kind of life that he had lived during his year in New Orleans—working long days and reading and writing in his off hours.

In November 1945, Clark wrote Brown again, and his mood had changed. "I am enthusiasm to see my manuscript cancel or publish. Please give me some immediate, authentic information." At the end of the note he apologizes for his tone, in what seems to be a description of depression, coined in his own words: "Sorry, but I am suffering with the complex, dejection, or negative action."[35] Hereafter in his letters the bright, enthusiastic voice is overtaken by a voice of disappointment and cynicism. The next and final letters from Clark in Brown's papers are from late November and early December 1947, some written on the same day. Each follows a polite etiquette, with a return address and date typed in the upper right corner, each closing with "Cordially, Clinton Clark." Each asks for some kind of word or response, but as they go on they ask, too, for recognition—"Remember My Sacrifice," he writes as he closes. Each letter has a number printed in the upper left corner; one letter suggests an explanation: "I have changed mind about returning South again. because the copperhead is to willing. and that is why; I am forced to write you one thousand notes."[36] If the numbers in the upper left mark his progress toward one thousand, Clark wrote at least 141 letters.

The short letters convey a sense of discouragement and despondency that is directly related to his experiences of racial discrimination.

Dear Professor Brown.

You can do what ever you please with my manuscript. my spirt is dead. Dont see any light to elevate myself—the copperhead both Negro and White—fighting me just like; I am some kind of King—finish-High-School-Complete-Course-in College-or some big University.

I am one of those black man. Who have never had a pleasent opportunity.
without some enemy blocking my process.
Regards to your family.

Cordially.
Clinton Clark.[37]

The short, cryptic letters describe his overall condition and emotional state, without giving the specifics of his current life in New York. "If they do this to a black man in the Capitol of the World. What will they do to a black man in the South."[38] He has lost the hope and belief that had driven his organizing. He flaunts his vocabulary to Brown, almost to show the ultimate worthlessness of his reading and writing. All of his learning–his engagement with books, his accomplishment of writing an autobiography–could not lift him above subjugation:

Dear Professor Brown

Some people are egotistical–Some are gregarious–Some Obsiquious–
Some Pander–Some are Maudlin–Some Asceticism–Some Rationalize–
Some Vicarious–Some are Wanton–Some Effete–Some are Sublimination.
And some are substantial to they desire. But when you are in subjugation.
Your desire is doom.
Remember my Sacrifice.
Regards to your family.

Cordially,
Clinton Clark.[39]

The letters give the sense of a man whose talents, accomplishments, and remarkable self-education were completely unrecognized in the world in which he lived. It is only in the last letter that he gives some specific details on his daily life and economic condition. "I am still not working," he wrote on December 3, 1947. "Dont wont no more hotel work. if can prevent it. After the holidays will look for something different."[40]

Clinton Clark had lost his job at Hotel George Washington earlier in 1947. He may have been fired when he overstayed a vacation,[41] or he may have lost his job when veterans returned at the end of the war. World War II had created the conditions within which Local 144 could prosper as a multiracial union of men and women and continually win better working conditions for its members. The military pulled many hotel workers from their jobs into active duty yet kept the New York hotels operating at capacity housing servicemen. Union leader John Goodman acknowledged that "war conditions had helped us to break down the barriers erected by the employers against the employment of Negro workers in the hotels. Today those workers, together with the many who have followed them in the past two years, are among our most loyal and active members."[42] At the end of the war these forces would reverse, with many veterans returning to their jobs. Halois Moorhead, also of the Hotel Front Service Employees Union, wrote about "the mounting numbers of unemployed" in one of her columns in the union newsletter in 1946.[43] The war's pull of people into the armed forces had created job opportunities for women and African Americans. When it ended, the push of people back into the economy may have cost Clark his job.

It is also possible that Clark lost his job to the intense wave of anticommunism that began in 1947 and swept many Communists and progressive activists from their jobs and homes. In 1947 President Truman established a loyalty program, a system for investigating federal employees suspected of having affiliation with Communist or "subversive" organizations.[44] Unions were put under increasing pressure to eliminate from their leadership people with Communist affiliations. The antiunion Taft-Hartley Act of 1947 included a provision that union leaders regularly sign statements that they were not Communists. Several black Communist and labor leaders were imprisoned or deported; many rank-and-file union members lost their jobs—some because of affiliations with the Communist Party, some because of other activism, and some because they were black. Writing of black civil rights activists in New York City, one historian finds that "virtually every leading activist suffered persecution, investigation, repression, or censorship."[45]

Because of this growing anticommunist feeling, Clark may have lost not just his job but his network of organizations and allies. The organizations with which Clark had worked would be drastically transformed within a few years. The SNYC, which had supported Clark's last two years of organizing in Louisiana, was labeled subversive by the government in the 1947 executive order and could not continue its work, collapsing in 1948.[46] The CIO distanced itself from Communist and Communist-affiliated members like Clark, first removing Communists from union leadership, then kicking out eleven "left-led" unions—unions with Communists in their leadership—in 1949 and 1950. Clark's friends in the movement also were dramatically affected. Raymond Tillman, the SNYC contact who had mobilized national civil rights leaders to protest Clark's imprisonment in Natchitoches in 1940, was removed from his job as the international representative of New Orleans Local 206 after the Transport Workers' Union followed the CIO toward positions that were liberal rather than left, aligned with the Democratic Party rather than the Communist Party.[47] Clyde Johnson, the masterful white organizer who brought outside help to Clark when he was organizing in Louisiana, had to work as a carpenter during the 1950s.[48] Gordon McIntire and Peggy Dallet, who had married in Denver in 1942, became trapped in Italy in the 1950s with their two young children when McIntire was fired from a new job at the United Nations Food and Agriculture Organization and the U.S. government confiscated their passports. It took them years to discover the charge against him—suspicion of being a Communist, arising from his work with the Louisiana Farmers' Union.[49]

Harold Preece, the writer who had been Clark's contact when he first moved to New York, had returned to the city early in 1948 after five years of working at radical and progressive schools in the South and in Boston. Preece spoke out and wrote against racism and anticommunism through the spring of 1948. Then, around 1949, he adopted a completely different lifestyle and subject for his writing. He spent his days at home, working as a freelance writer while his wife taught at a local school. He recreated himself as a western writer, publishing profiles of cowboys and pioneers in magazines such as *Texas Rangers, Thrilling Ranch Stories,* and *Ranch Romances.* In 1951 an FBI agent visited his apartment building and interviewed many of his neighbors. With no evidence of any activism or Communist involvement, the FBI dropped him from its Key Figure List in 1951 and from its Security Index in 1955. For the rest of his life, Preece would present himself as a Texan and a western writer, with no mention of his many years writing about labor, peonage, and civil rights struggles.[50]

During his six years in New York, Clark's outlook had shifted from enthusiastic to despondent. Between 1942 and 1949, he suffered a series of disappointments and losses. The state structure of the LFU had dissolved, leaving the locals that Clark had established without outside support. He had been followed by the FBI from New Orleans to New York. He had worked in a job that must have been crushing to his spirit, and then lost that job and his means of supporting himself in 1947. The manuscript of his autobiography had not been published nor returned to his possession. He seemed to have lost his place in the labor movement, and anticommunism was dismantling organizations that he had helped to build. His mother died in 1949. He was losing his youth and perhaps his health. He had come to a city that had a thriving progressive and black cultural and political life, but he found himself mostly alone, his accomplishments and leadership unrecognized.

Manhattan Island

Clark entered Bellevue Hospital outside of Harlem on November 6, 1949. Harold Preece brought him to the hospital, where Preece went by his first name, Richard, when he spoke with the doctors. He said that Clark had been a porter at the George Washington Hotel until 1947, when he lost his job after overstaying his vacation. In January 1948, Preece had seen a change in Clark, the doctors noted—he had trouble concentrating and showed "mental sluggishness" and a loss of interest in everything, even his family. He had been unable to find a job. When asked how Clark had survived, Preece implied that he had been helping to support him. It was Preece who decided that Clark needed to be hospitalized.[51]

Within days the process to have Clark certified as mentally ill was underway, and Preece was notified of the hearing to send Clark to the state hospital. "IF YOU ARE WILLING TO HAVE PATIENT GO TO A STATE HOSPITAL, YOU NEED NOT APPEAR."[52] The petition to have Clark certified lists Preece as his only contact, with "no known relatives or friends in New York State."[53] On November 15, 1949, Clark was admitted to Manhattan State Hospital, where he would spend the next five and a half years of his life. Though the file does not record any resistance from Clark, it is clear that he was compelled to go. On his admission forms, "legal status (at time of admission)" is given as "certified," while the next, unchosen choice on the form is "voluntary." The details of these years of his life come to us through his medical record, which was released by the Manhattan Psychiatric Center to his nephew Rodney Clark in April 2003. The file contains legal papers, doctors' notes, ward notes, and some correspondence, with notes on diagnoses and treatment blackened out. In other words, what we know of Clark's life during these years comes through the eyes of his doctors, and their frankest assessments—their diagnoses and treatments—are mostly withheld.

Manhattan State Hospital is on Ward's Island, just between the Upper East side of Manhattan and Queens. When he arrived, Clark was given a physical examination, including tests of his blood and spinal fluid. A Dr. Richman—probably a resident—examined him, interviewed him at length in early December, wrote a summary of Clark's case, and then presented it in a staff conference with a Dr. Stein on December 12. In the interview, Clark told the doctor that he hadn't been able to get a job for two years, and that he had lived by borrowing from friends. On some topics, Clark was candid with the doctor. He told the doctor that he had been treated for syphilis. He told him that he had a daughter from a relationship with a woman in Texas. He seems frank with the doctor about an unhappiness rooted in his inability to support himself.

> Are you happy? "I wouldn't say that I am happy."
> Would you say that you are unhappy? "Yes, I would."
> Why is that? "Just because I am not being able to live like I wish."
> How do you wish to live? "Well, I want to have a job and take care of my situation and not have any money troubles at all." [54]

He was guarded and hesitant in answering other questions. The doctor thought that he was especially vague or secretive when asked how he had supported himself for the last two years. He never spoke in detail about the friends who had helped him. Clark hesitated when asked if he thought anyone was trying to harm him.

> Do you think that anyone is trying to persecute you or harm you? In response to this question patient appeared vague and stated: "Well, I wouldn't say yes, and I wouldn't say no, but on the whole I say no."
>
> When the examiner repeated this question and requested the patient to state if anyone had ever tried to persecute him, the patient replied with a flat "No." . . .

Do you think you have any enemies? "I wouldn't know, but I don't think so."[55]

When asked if he had ever been jailed, Clark again hesitated, then told the doctor that he had been jailed twice, once in New York and once "down South." When the doctor asked what the charges were when he was jailed in the South, Clark paused again:

> The patient starts to play with his fingers and does not answer examiner's question. Finally, after repetition the patient states: "I was in jail for 93 days down in Louisiana."
> What was the charge? "I don't know what the charge was."[56]

Clark didn't explain to the doctor that he had been held without charges. The doctor seemed to move on, satisfied, without asking Clark anymore about this experience. Simple questions made up most of the rest of the interview, testing Clark's intellect and memory.

Richman wrote up his summary of the case the day after the interview. He wrote that Clark was vague and evasive on some topics, had some drinking in his past, some depression, no suicidal ideas, no paranoid ideas, was well oriented, had fair to good memory, and was in good physical condition. He was "friendly and pleasant." "He smiles frequently without apparent cause, and his affect appears to be flattened." Richman judged his "insight and judgment partial," though he gave no evidence or explanation why.[57] With these symptoms, Richman deemed Clark psychotic and gave as his main evidence Clark's two-year unemployment. He thought that Clark's past history of syphilis was the most likely cause. Most of Richman's specific diagnosis, treatment, and prognosis are blackened out, but other notes in the record indicate that he ordered Clark to be treated with penicillin–the treatment for syphilis that had become available just a few years earlier.

When Richman presented Clark's case at a staff conference a few days later, Dr. Stein was skeptical of his colleague's conclusions, stating, "Patient appears quite clear and gives a fairly good account of the events leading to his hospitalization. He admits a history of lues, drinking and arrest, but unfortunately we have no anamnesis to check on it properly. Therefore, would suggest that every effort be made to obtain historical data. The present findings are either indicative of CNS lues or an alcoholic psychosis." [58]

CNS lues is syphilis of the central nervous system. Stein asked that Clark's case be reconsidered in six weeks. Six weeks later, a Dr. Stamm was now in charge of Clark's case, and he wrote a new summary. In his interview, he found Clark quiet and cooperative, never inappropriate or irrelevant, but sometimes slow with his responses. Stamm's analysis emphasized hallucinations and visions. "To this interviewer," the doctor wrote, "he definitely admits, after much questioning . . . that he frequently hears voices at night and sees spirits." [59] Stamm's summary and diagnosis are heavily censored. Though it is clear that he emphasizes Clark's history of syphilis and admission of recent drinking, neither alone could explain Clark's condition. When the case was re-presented to Dr. Stein, Stein seems to have agreed: "Patient admits excessive drinking, and to me, his present mental illness could be ascribed to it. There are no gross sensorial defects, and neither are there neurological signs of significance. His complete serology is negative except for a ——. In my judgment, the diagnosis of —— due to Alcohol Deterioration would fit best. It is by no means a clear-cut case, and it would be advisable to repeat the serology in about three weeks." [60] Days later, Clark was transferred to ward "M-11." There is no clear explanation of why he was transferred, though the note indicates that he had been placed in restraints that day, possibly for striking another patient.

At the time of his discharge more than five years later, in an undeleted passage in his medical file, Clark's diagnosis is given as "Psychosis with Syphilis of the Central Nervous System, Meningo-Encephalitic Type." [61] When left untreated or not successfully treated, the spirochetes that cause syphilis can reach the brain many years after the initial illness, and the symptoms can resemble different types of mental illness, from the deterioration of dementia to depression to paranoia and hallucinations that resemble schizophrenia. Clark admitted to the doctors that he had contracted syphilis in the 1930s. Syphilis would have been common in the sharecropping communities where Clark lived and where there was very little access to medical care. The only treatment for syphilis then available was a series of twenty to forty painful injections of arsenic compounds, given over months or years in doses high enough to kill the parasite but not the patient. [62]

When Clark moved to New York in 1943, the FBI had pulled his medical records and concluded that Clark had moved in search of treatment for syphilis. His FBI file provides some details of his diagnoses and treatment. Just after arriving in New York in May, Clark had had a Wasserman test for syphilis and had tested positive. The agent noted that Clark "had received a total of twenty arsenic injections at various places in Louisiana up until 1940"; since arriving in New York he had been given ten more injections. In that same year, 1943, penicillin was found to be a cure for syphilis, but this new treatment did not reach Clark at the Social Hygiene Clinic. The FBI file contains a cryptic, secondhand assessment of Clark's health: "—— advised that the length of time during which subject may find it necessary to continue receiving treatments for full health is problematical but that he is in a non-infectious state at the present time."[63]

At Manhattan State, a spinal fluid test for syphilis was positive, and Clark was treated with penicillin during his first month in the hospital. His declining condition in 1948 and 1949 may have been a new phase of a continuing battle with the disease. But there are also reasons to doubt that it had impaired his mind. The Wasserman test was often inaccurate; patients who were no longer infected could still test positive. Clark didn't have any of the physical symptoms usually associated with the advancement of syphilis into the nervous system and mind—no tremors, no difficulty walking, no problems with his eyes or senses. Dr. Stein pointed this out in his second discussion of Clark's case and thought his symptoms more likely due to alcohol than syphilis. Syphilis is a disease that expresses itself differently in every person; even today neurosyphilis is difficult to diagnose.[64] From the distance of fifty years, it is impossible to know now how much it affected his mind and led to his hospitalization.

What is most interesting about Clinton Clark's medical file is what is not there. The doctors did not seem to suspect, and Clark didn't reveal, the story of his life as an organizer—the experiences and leadership he describes in his narrative. Their incomplete picture of Clark seems as much due to their racial prejudice as it does to Clark's illness. Their questions reveal how much they underestimated his intelligence. They tested his knowledge by asking him simple questions about state capitals; the names of the president, governor, and mayor; and the largest river in the United States and in New York State. He answered all correctly. They even asked him to name five vegetables. Yet when he shared more complex thoughts, the doctors didn't take him seriously. "Many of his statements are vague and pedantic," wrote one. The statement given by the doctor as an example is understandable and genuine: "I'm interested in religion in the manner to make myself to be benefitted and make a better appearance and do better."[65] They didn't allow him to be intelligent. The doctors never asked questions that would have opened up a discussion of his experiences of racism, and they seemed completely blind to the fact that Clark would have had experiences as a black man in a segregated society that would have affected his well-being and mental health.

At some moments, it seems Clark's greatest "symptom" of mental illness was a hesitancy to talk about certain topics: "When questioned regarding how he was able to live without any visible means of support, he states that he borrowed here and there from various friends, but when asked to elaborate further regarding this subject, he becomes vague and evasive and appears relieved when the examiner changes the subject."[66] In a later report, another doctor again used the word *evasive:* "When seen today, patient is quiet and cooperative during the interview. At times his responses are somewhat slow and he is somewhat evasive, especially when questioned about hallucinatory experiences and previous arrests."[67] With years of underground organizing and FBI surveillance behind him, and with anti-communist attacks on left unions and organizations growing, Clinton Clark would have had good reason to not tell about his work and arrests. He would have had reason to believe that people were against him. He seems to have chosen not to talk to the doctors about the core events and beliefs that shaped his life—the exact things that he wrote about in his narrative. Clark probably experienced hospitalization as yet another wrongful imprisonment, and may have handled the doctors' interview as he had the questioning of sheriffs in the Natchitoches and Vidalia jails. Rather than considering that he might have reasons for silence, the doctors saw his evasive answers as paranoia or a psychotic detachment from reality.

The misdiagnosis of black patients by white psychiatrists was a problem noted by a number of researchers in the 1950s and 1960s. A 1950 study in nearby Connecticut found that being admitted to a state hospital was almost the only psychiatric care available to African Americans.[68] One study found that early clinical interviews had much less "depth of self-exploration" when there were differences in race and class between therapists and patients.[69] Another study examining the diagnosis and recommended treatment of white and nonwhite psychiatric patients in emergency rooms observed that white male residents gave more sympathetic diagnoses and optimistic treatment to white female patients. When the sociocultural differences between patient and doctor increased, they suggested, the doctor's diagnosis became less accurate and the recommended treatment more general. This same study describes a scenario in which a resident, bewildered and unable to relate to a nonwhite patient well enough to communicate, would schedule the patient for another interview, only to be puzzled again.[70] Clark had a similar experience of multiple, repetitive superficial interviews; when the doctors could not agree on a diagnosis, they let six weeks pass and repeated the examination. Psychiatrists during these years often did not ask any questions about racial or cultural experience, sometimes not even recording a patient's race.[71] Once a diagnosis was made, black patients—including Clark—received lower-quality, low-intervention treatment, such as drugs and care from nonprofessional staff, rather than psychotherapy.[72]

Two initiatives to develop psychiatric treatment sensitive to the social conditions in which African Americans lived were launched in Harlem during the same years that Clark was hospitalized. At the Northside Center for Child Development, a Harlem clinic that served children, doctors examined the impact of cultural background and awareness of social situation on psychiatric diagnosis and treatment. They published their results in 1953 in an article in the journal of the New York State Department of Mental Hygiene—the same state system that committed, diagnosed, and held Clark. In one example, they described a child who was completely terrified and immobilized in school, showing signs of serious emotional disturbance. An evaluation that was sensitive to his background and social situation found that his family had just moved from the South, from a sharecropping community where all their interactions with white people involved threats and terror. With this knowledge, it was clear that the child was not emotionally disturbed but understandably frightened to be in the unknown situation of interacting with a white teacher. "It has become the custom," the authors wrote to their colleagues throughout the New York system in 1953, "never to make a diagnosis unless some member of the staff is present who is familiar with the particular cultural background."[73]

Ralph Ellison wrote about the Lafargue Psychiatric Clinic in Harlem in 1948, the year before Clark was committed to Manhattan State Hospital. In his essay, Ellison offered a social diagnosis of what he called the "confusion" of Negroes who had made Clark's same journey, from the rural South to Harlem. (In Clark's medical file, doctors used the word *confused* many times to describe him.) Ellison argues that the leap from the rural—he calls it "feudal"—South to modern New York, with the accompanying loss of a known world, family, religion, and folklore, and the exclusion from northern institutions, would reasonably leave someone vulnerable to mental illness. "Not that a Negro is worse off in the North than in the South, but that in the North he surrenders and does not replace certain supports to his personality."[74] Ellison's essay suggests that Clark's experience may have been widely shared. And in describing the Lafargue clinic's badly needed and unique approach, it describes the kind of treatment that Clark should have received. The clinic offered a treatment that tried to take into account all the implications of a patient's being black in America, a treatment that saw "a being who in responding to the complex forces of America has become confused."[75] Ellison describes the clinic as a place where an exceptional, positive effort was made to provide treatment and challenge the protocol of the segregated hospitals. He describes the staff of the clinic as working to reject stereotypes and understand patients within their experience of race, politics and the economy, and modernization. It is exactly this kind of approach that was missing in Clark's treatment.

Understanding Clark as a black man in a time of high unemployment, and as a progressive labor leader in a time when suspected Communists were being thrown out of organizations or even jailed, one finds it reasonable to surmise that the crisis he suffered in the late 1940s was brought on by discouragement, isolation, and destitution. The doctors saw an evasive, paranoid man incapable of holding a job and with a history of arrests. Instead, Clark was a leader who had taken enormous risks to help people in rural Louisiana and who had been jailed, threatened with lynching, and followed by the FBI. He had suffered enormous disappointments and hardships in the 1940s—the dissolution of the Louisiana Farmers' Union, illness and painful treatments, losing the manuscript of his life story, and the death of his mother. He could not find work in New York that made use of his talents, and after several years working as a hotel doorman, he lost his job and could not find work at all. Family members today mention other possible reasons for his hospitalization—he had been hurt in a mugging, or he had a white girlfriend who left him. There is also the possibility that Harold Preece may have had Clark committed to be rid of him. Preece told a doctor that his help had enabled Clark to survive during 1948 and 1949. When asked by a doctor how he had come to be admitted to the hospital, Clark said that he had gone to see a friend. "I told him I couldn't get on relief, I couldn't get no support, and the friend suggested I go to the hospital."[76]

After Clark was transferred to ward M-11, the doctors' notes in his medical file became brief and infrequent. The next note after the day of his transfer is dated eleven months later. The photocopied pages of his medical file are not in a clear chronological order and may be incomplete, so it is hard to determine how often he was seen by doctors. His sister Caroline in Louisiana learned of his commitment by the spring of 1950 and wrote to the hospital. Hospital director Dr. John Travis replied, "His mental condition has improved somewhat, but he is still in need of further hospitalization."[77] There are several carbon copies of letters from Travis to Caroline, all in reply to her inquiries, all giving brief, very general, and similar descriptions of his condition. On admission, the doctors seemed to have genuinely attempted to diagnose him. But once he was transferred to a ward, the doctors seemed satisfied to record behaviors they observed and considered eccentric. One doctor wrote a paragraph describing Clark's bizarre dress, habit of talking to himself, and constant letter writing. But when he actually spoke to Clark, his view changed. "On interview," the doctor wrote, "he surprisingly made a better impression than observed on the ward."[78]

Doctors' notes indicate that Clark spent a lot of his time reading and writing. He read the Bible, but there is no indication whether he had access to other books. "He writes many letters to friends," wrote one doctor, "and recently he wrote one to Joseph Stalin and signed it from 'Our Lord.'" A year later, another doctor commented, "The sentences are poorly constructed and contain such statements as 'The Devils can't win. God is angry' but no clear delusions." In 1952 Clark wrote J. Edgar Hoover with complaints about the hospital. He sometimes dressed in ways the doctors found "bizarre"–wearing a skull cap, glasses with one lens, a button celebrating communism, and leggings. In July 1952 he caused a stir at the hospital with an escape attempt; he was found standing under a bridge in shallow water. When questioned by the doctors, he said that he had just wanted to go for a swim. A few of the documents convey the extreme monotony of his days. His visitor record lists only four visitors, making five visits over five years, and the record of his weight shows him steadily gaining, going from 168 to 219 pounds.

In 1955, his sister Caroline must have decided that it was time to bring Clark home. On April 19, a note in his medical record finds him oriented and in good physical condition, with some improvement. As the doctor also notes that a letter from Clark's niece Beatrice Overton says that there are "plans to come and get him," it seems that his family's concern prompted the reconsideration of his condition. (The last doctor's note on his condition had been two sentences written ten months earlier: "There is no essential change in this patient's condition. He continues as above noted.") The doctor decided to reduce his medication so he would no longer be "excessively drowsy, apathetic and lifeless."[79] Caroline sent Travis a letter on April 26, telling him that she was sending her niece for Clark's release. It's a remarkable letter, handwritten, trying to incite action from across a great geographical and social distance:

Dear Dr. Travis

I am sending my neice for Clinton Clark release
I do hope it will be a aproveval
if his mental condition dont improve after a period of time I will refer him
    to a nearby institution.
I can rest assure he is getting close attention
I cannot find words high enough to express my sincer thanks to you and
    managers.
we are very poor.
Could not visit Clinton in a distance State.
Finance would not allow not one of his relative.
I am asking in earnest desire please release my brother. My God bless
    you all.

Sincerly yours
Caroline C. Cook[80]

Within a few days, Veronica Overton Carey, Clark's grandniece, arrived in
New York and visited him in the hospital. She was chosen for the trip, she explains
today, because she was the "oldest of the youngest," newly married, and had the
education to handle business at the hospital. She also had a strong connection to
Clark, having been a child in the late 1930s when he would visit his family and
entertain her with car rides between Palmetto and Melville. He recognized her in
the hospital, she remembers. He looked healthy to her, though she was startled by
the way he was dressed—in short khaki pants—and the presence of other patients
and the people controlling them.[81]

Over the next few days, a Dr. Davidson and a Dr. Unger would assess Clark
and discuss his readiness for discharge. They found that he had "shown a gradual
and steady improvement" over the previous year. He was oriented, in good physical condition, had "satisfactory" behavior, and "denies having abnormal ideas."
They recommended releasing him into the care of his sister.[82] A week later, Travis
sought approval for Clark's release from the assistant commissioner of the Department of Mental Hygiene, writing that Clark "has recently shown much improvement in his mental condition and his convalescent care has been recommended to

the custody of his sister."[83] Clark's release to convalescent care was approved on May 17. From New York, Veronica would travel to Virginia to rejoin her husband, who served in the army, and Clark would be released and return to Louisiana on his own. The hospital waited until Caroline sent a railroad ticket and eight dollars; then Mr. Healy, a transportation agent, put Clark on a train on June 9, 1955.[84] His nephew Rodney Clark remembers driving with his father to Cross Point, Louisiana, where his uncle stepped off the bus carrying a small bag and wearing "not an exact fitting suit." Rodney had, of course, never met his uncle; he had only heard stories of him. From the way his father and Clark talked, he remembers, he knew that they hadn't seen each other in a while. On June 12, 1955, Caroline wrote Dr. Travis: "This is to inform you Clinton Clark arrive home safe."[85]

Louisiana, 1955–1974

For the next nineteen years, Clark lived within a circle of family, first in Melville and later in New Orleans. In Melville, he acquired a mule and a wagon and made his living hauling wood and junk and plowing gardens. He did manual work for a white man in Melville and sold fruit from trees in the man's yard. In December of 1956, a year and a half after his release, Clark sent Dr. Travis a Christmas card and letter. When he first returned, he writes, "I did nothing but walk to and fro around the town." But in 1956 he got busy, and his letter details his enterprises. He picked and sold blackberries, plums, and figs. He planted a garden and sold the produce. He picked 2,500 pounds of cotton that season. In his letter, he details how much he earned and what wages were paid, just as he had in his autobiography. With his earnings he bought a horse, wagon, and farm equipment. He writes Travis that, with winter coming, he is facing three to four months without work, but he has applied for a federal assistance program for farmers and farm helpers. "I am still living with my sister Caroline Cook. But I taken care of my self."[86]

He first lived with his sister Caroline, then built his own house behind her house. Along with his sister, brother Roger, and white friend and employer, Clark's company in Melville during these years were his nieces, nephews, and two neighborhood boys. In the late 1950s, his nephews Rodney and John and neighbors Richard "Hock" Sterling and Ben Charles "Scott" Sterling, all around ten years old, helped Clark with hauling, planting, and other jobs during the day and watched him retreat into a world of books at night. He was very serious with them as

Clinton Clark in Melville, Louisiana, in the late 1950s. Photographer unknown.
Courtesy Rodney Clark

they worked, instructing them and getting angry with them if they didn't act in-
telligently. Clark liked the boys' company, and they in turn liked his stories and
conversation. "He had an answer for you no matter what you said," remembers
Hock Sterling, "and it really was interesting what he was saying." Scott Sterling
remembers that Clark "always told you the history of the poor man, and how hard
it was for a poor man to make it." Clark told Hock and Scott Sterling that he had
been a policeman in New York. The one story he told from his time organizing
was about his stay in the Natchitoches prison. He told Hock Sterling how he had
been beaten and mistreated. Although Clark didn't talk about his work with the
union, he shared his passion for organizing. He organized his nieces and nephews
into a youth group. For about a year their union met for an hour around four or
five every Saturday afternoon. They paid dues, and they had a secretary and a
treasurer.

Clark's books and writing fascinated the young people. Hock remembers that
Clark "had quite a few books, but he didn't have the books that he wanted," the
books that he had had in New York. Clark's shack had a dirt floor, and Hock
remembers Clark working by lamplight, typing from papers that he had writ-

ten out in longhand. Clark sent letters to Washington, D.C., and received letters back. Hock remembers that Clark wrote the president and received a reply. Clark wouldn't say what the letter said. "It's too much for you to know," Sterling remembers him saying. One time the local post office stopped a letter that Clark had mailed because they thought that he was not in his right mind.

Some letters from this time in Clark's life are duplicated in his FBI file. In May 1962, Clark wrote Robert F. Kennedy, then attorney general of the United States, from Melville. "I am a former member of the United State's Communist Party," Clark wrote, then goes on to explain, "My membership were -Pre- before the United State's had outlawed the U.S. Communist Party." He tells Kennedy that he is now a detective and asks for information on the current activities of the U.S.A. Communist Party. His letter is handwritten, very polite, and succinct. It appears that Clark was trying to learn what had happened to the Communist Party—and perhaps what had happened to people he knew—from the politically distant location of Melville, Louisiana. Kennedy's office forwarded the letter to the FBI; a memo in Clark's file indicates that Kennedy's office answered Clark.[87]

Perhaps in this same search for people in his past, in the early 1960s Clark suddenly left Melville and returned to New York, traveling by boxcars and hitchhiking. Rodney Clark remembers that around 1963 or 1964 Caroline and her niece Beatrice went north to visit Clark in New York, or perhaps bring him back again, while Rodney stayed in Bea's house in New Orleans. Hock and Scott Sterling remember a dramatic return to Melville. Their father, returning from Baton Rouge with Clark's brother Roger, spotted Clinton Clark in a gray beard standing at a fruit stand. Roger Clark didn't recognize his brother. Hock Sterling remembers that Clark went to New York to retrieve his books, but he couldn't find anyone who knew him or knew what had happened to his things. After his return, Hock and Scott Sterling became even closer to him, and he talked with them more. Clark told them he had been a policeman in New York and also that at one point he had worked in an office. During his second stay in New York, he had been hit and robbed. He had been beaten in the head, and his mind had changed, remembers Hock Sterling. "Sometimes he would talk, sometimes not."

In the early 1960s, the home of Clark's niece Beatrice and her husband Willie Overton on Spain Street in New Orleans' eighth ward had become a center for family visiting and moving to New Orleans from the country. Clark moved to New Orleans in 1965. When Hurricane Betsy hit in September, Clark was living in a tool shed behind Beatrice's house. Rodney Clark remembers that his uncle wasn't talking to anyone at the time. As the floodwaters rose, the family, including five or six children, climbed first to the neighboring house, then along a fence to a warehouse that had a second floor and some supplies. As they broke in, Rodney remembers that "Uncle Clinton talked," speaking to them for the first time in months. They were eventually evacuated by boat to a shelter in a school, where they stayed at least a week before returning to a damaged house.

The younger generation's recollections from the late 1950s and 1960s combine details of Clark's eccentric behavior with respect for his intelligence and knowledge. He kept distant from others; he "didn't mix." He sometimes spoke to himself or not at all, and he preached in the school yard. Nieces remembered that he had once dressed like a woman to avoid a white man who was trying to find him. But overall, those who knew him as "Uncle Clinton" describe him as smart and admired him as a person who traveled widely, wrote, and read. From their parents' stories they knew that he had been a leader in the freedom struggle, and the photograph of Clark with a wall of books and a typewriter sat on their television while they were growing up. "He talked sane," his niece Florence Clark Smith remembers. "I always thought he was a very important man, a smart man." Everyone mentions his books. "I don't care where you saw him," Rodney Clark remembers, "he had books."

A month after Hurricane Betsy, Clark wrote FBI director J. Edgar Hoover a series of letters addressed from his niece's Spain Street home. Four are reproduced in his FBI file. They are numbered in the upper righthand corner—for example, "J.E.H. #8"—much like the letters Clark wrote to Sterling Brown in the 1940s. Clark numbered the letter written on October 30, 1965, as "J.E.H. #23," suggesting that he wrote Hoover daily for at least three weeks. The handwriting of these letters is larger and looser than that of his polite note to Kennedy just a few years earlier. The letters do not mark a specific occasion or make demands, but they are hauntingly grounded in codes of morality and justice. In one letter he writes out the Lord's Prayer. In another, Clark writes a history of law that begins with Genesis and ends by alluding to the contemporary courts and legislatures. He seems to be contesting a local court or state legislature, as he writes at the end the instruction that the " lower court is to obey the higher court." Then he writes a call for change that is abstract, not tied to the details of the day: "The law is like the inside of a human body, when it is unclean, we must clean it out, and filth is in everything. The old law must be clean out once and awhile. And be made refresh." In another letter he accuses the FBI of violating federal law, and he writes that he would never plead guilty, even if the FBI tortured him. The last letter to Hoover begins with a threat or warning:

> All old prophecy are being fulfil. The day shall come you shall flee your house and not return to get any thing out of it. You shall be working in the field and not return to get your coat . . .
>
> Every day Every human being are put to a test—
>
> The Bible advise us.
>
> The Judge who Judged are Judged. And those that Judge, does the same thing.[88]

Someone in the FBI office wrote "Appears mental" on the letters. But considering Clark's history, the vague accusations and threats he directs at Hoover suggest a distant, continued, incoherent struggle with his past and the events of the 1940s, and perhaps the events of the 1960s. "I have nothing to do with the local violator," he writes. "I watch only Federal violator." The insistent letters to Hoover and the changing ways he identifies himself indicate that Clark was having some kind of crisis, but the letters also show that he felt deeply injured by the FBI. He knew Hoover's role in his own surveillance and the end of the movement that Clark had helped to build.

Clark later moved with his sister Caroline to a house on Arts Street. During his last years in New Orleans, Clark was still a reader, with a room full of books. He was out of the house all day, walking everywhere, but he didn't have a regular job or pastime. He looked depressed, not keeping up his appearance. Before he died in 1974 he had been sick for about a month, perhaps from a stroke. His niece Florence bought groceries for him; in his last days his nephew Rodney visited daily to help him shave and bathe. He died in the second room of Caroline's shotgun house. For his funeral, Beatrice provided a suit for him, and Caroline brought a tie and a white shirt. His sister Orelia traveled from California to attend the funeral, at which no one mentioned his work with the union. In his circle of family, only his two surviving sisters had known him during the years he had led the Louisiana Farmers' Union.

In an early draft, Clark titled his manuscript "Remember My Sacrifice." The phrase was a personal motto with a biblical echo. He had the phrase printed on a card bearing his address and photograph after he was released from three months in prison in Vidalia. That year Clark wrote his story in a rush of exuberance, exhaustion, and terror resulting from his organizing work and recent imprisonment. His time in jail in the winter and spring of 1942 had been longer and lonelier than the weeks he spent in a Natchitoches prison in 1940. He may have felt in danger of being forgotten by unions and progressive organizations as he waited. He wrote about his work and sacrifices—narrow escapes, nights spent in fields and swamps, imprisonment and near lynching—possibly to rally outside support to restart the union or to try to raise his profile to protect himself. Yet he wrote with hope and optimism, confident that he would return to the rural areas and continue his work.

Sometime during the next six years, while he lived in New York City, Clark lost this optimism and the work that had defined him. His health deteriorated, and in New York he struggled with racial discrimination that expressed itself in familiar and new ways—in the workplace, the health care he received, and perhaps in the union. Clark may have been less able to work as an organizer in New York, but also during these years the movement in which he had worked was transformed. Anticommunism had brought an end to the multiracial union movement that had stretched from the rural unions like the LFU and STFU to industrial and service unions in northern cities. In Clark's life we see an individual's experience of the rise, crest, and fall of a trade union movement that organized hundreds of thousands of black workers in the 1930s and 1940s.[89] Clark experienced the high point of this movement as a member of the Hotel Front Service Employees Union in mid-1940s New York City. Entire hotel staffs had been brought into the union fold, including African American and women service workers. The organizing efforts of the Communist Party and the CIO in the 1930s, the passage of the National Labor Relations Act in 1935, and the labor shortages and dislocations of World War II all contributed to successful organizing of African Americans in workplaces throughout the country. In the late 1940s, particularly with the passage of the Taft-Hartley Act, employers, as well as moderate and segregationist union leaders, used anticommunism against these progressive, multiracial unions and their leaders. When the CIO expelled its left-led unions in 1949 and 1950, it cast out its most multiracial memberships.[90] Similar purges were conducted within unions. After 1950, unions were whiter and less oppositional, and the civil rights movement of the next two decades lacked leaders like Clark, working-class activists who brought the priorities and assets of labor organizing.[91]

In the rural areas where Clark had organized, mechanization and other technologies were bringing an end to sharecropping and dramatically reducing jobs.

The AAA payments to farmers for taking crops out of production–the payments for which Clark had helped sharecroppers fight for their share–had shrunk the amount of land farmed, forcing many evictions. In the longer term, the payments gave plantation owners extra cash for hiring wage workers and buying tractors. As a result, the number of tenant farmers in cotton areas dropped steadily from the beginning of the 1930s into the mid-1950s, when they became a group too small for the census to count.[92] The families that had been tenant farmers were shifted to wage work; many people left the countryside, looking for opportunities in cities, northern states, and on the West Coast.[93] On Louisiana's sugar plantations, union organizing of workers had continued into the 1950s. Strikes of sugarcane workers were stopped by court orders and provoked the legislature to pass a right-to-work law in 1954 which eliminated the requirement that all workers in a unionized workplace join the union–one of the basic components of union organizing. Clark had returned to Louisiana just as the courts and the state legislature had crushed the organizing of farm workers in the state.[94]

World War II, which had played a role in ending the LFU and transforming southern agriculture, provoked a new civil rights movement and launched a new generation of organizers. In rural Louisiana communities, organizing focused on voter registration campaigns, which finally succeeded with the Voting Rights Act of 1965.[95] Greta de Jong, examining records of the Louisiana Farmers' Union and the civil rights organizations active in Pointe Coupee Parish in the 1950s and 1960s, finds that some LFU members stayed active in civil rights organizing.[96] Clark's "odyssey of an organizer," his account of how he carried inspiration and experience between organizations, and from California back to Louisiana, suggests that these kinds of continuities may be more numerous than the written record shows. However, Clark's life after the close of his autobiography gives us several examples of why organizations like the LFU and leaders like Clark didn't have more influence on the subsequent civil rights movements. Illness, racial discrimination, and the impacts of anticommunism, both direct and indirect, took Clark out of the freedom struggle. While World War II was a starting point for the civil rights movement of the 1950s and 1960s, and while wartime experiences started many on a lifetime commitment to civil rights organizing (just as the bleakest years of the early Depression had gotten many started in Communist and labor organizing), these same years disrupted the work of an earlier generation, a generation that had focused on jobs, wages, and the economic bases of equality.

In the years after he wrote and lost his autobiography, the phrase "Remember My Sacrifice" came to represent not just the dangers Clark had faced in rural Louisiana but, more significantly, his life's work and contribution. As his letters to Sterling Brown grew increasingly despondent, Clark began closing them with the phrase. "Remember My Sacrifice" meant not just recognizing his ten years of organizing work and the tremendous effort of writing his life story but also recognizing him as a leader, a thinker, a person. Knowing something of the suffering he endured after 1947, including years alone in a state mental hospital, we see now how great his sacrifice was. Fortunately his family pulled him from the hospital and gave him shelter and company as he worked to support himself again. But because he chose to dedicate his thirties to organizing his people, he had no savings, his health was compromised, and he suffered the emotional toll of surveillance, violence, and loss. During the Depression years he had stepped forward, risked his life, and worked to exhaustion. Looking back at the long sweep of his life and times, we can see now that he took full advantage of the moment in history when he could make the greatest difference for black people in his community and region. The effort he spent in writing his story allows us today to remember this remarkable man, his achievements, and his sacrifice.

Notes

1. Clark, letter to Brown, December 12, 1942, box 112, SAB.

2. "Clinton Clark," July 13, 1943, New Orleans, p. 2, FBI-CC. Most of the documents in the FBI files used here are reports on individuals and organizations made by agents in the local area. There was a standard form used for these reports, and they are identified here by title (the subject of the report, an individual or organization), date, and city of report. They usually summarize and update information in previous reports. In most cases the author's name has been censored from the copy released to the public, along with many of the names within the report.

3. Tillman's August 12, 1940, letter to Louis Burnham, Youth Secretary of the NNC, outlines the details of Clark's imprisonment. He closed, "At present little or nothing is being done. There is an urgent need for steps to be taken to get Clinton released and insure his safe passage to New Orleans. There is also the great need to continue the organizational work of the farmers in that district" (reel 22:0573, part 1, NNC).

4. McIntire mentioned in his letter to the locals that Adams would probably be drafted when he was released.

5. "Clinton Clark," March 4, 1943, New Orleans, p. 3, FBI-CC.

6. Quote from Wells, "The ILWU in New Orleans," 35; for his account of what he terms "the Dorsey issue," see pp. 11–47.

7. Theoharis, "A Brief History," 15; Hill, introduction to *The FBI's RACON*, 668.

8. J. E. Clegg to Director, FBI, January 13, 1942, FBI-CC.

9. Theoharis, *Spying,* 43; Theoharis, "A Brief History," 20–21. Biddle wrote in a July 16, 1943, memo: "There is no statutory authorization or other present justification for keeping a 'custodial detention' list of citizens. The Department fulfills its proper functions by investigating the activities of persons who may have violated the law. It is not aided in this work by classifying people as to dangerousness" (quoted in Theoharis, *Spying,* 43). This emergency detention program lasted many decades, under changing names and criteria, until it was finally ended in post-Watergate reforms. See Theoharis's chapter in *Spying* about the FBI's Emergency Detention Programs. Only the second page of Biddle's statement can be seen today in Clark's released file–further evidence that it was a fairly ineffective attempt to change the ways of the FBI.

10. There was a remarkable bureaucracy involved in maintaining Security Index cards. Hoover grew angry with the New Orleans office when it forward Clark's Security Index card before the New York office knew he had moved there. There is correspondence from the New Orleans office to Hoover which requests a card for Clark with an updated address, which is answered with a card to be attached to the original.

11. "Clinton Clark," New Orleans, August 15, 1941, p. 6, FBI-CC.

12. Hill, introduction to *The FBI's RACON,* 319. Robert A. Hill's introduction and edition of the report give a chilling account of RACON. Hill argues that the FBI didn't monitor civil rights organizations until after Pearl Harbor, when ambivalent statements about the war by African Americans were branded by Hoover as support of Japan and Germany. The resulting investigations were the starting point of three decades of illegal FBI investigations of African Americans, including the bugging of Martin Luther King Jr., COINTELPRO, and investigations of black student groups and the Black Panther Party.

13. "Clinton Clark," New Orleans, March 4, 1943, p. 3, FBI-CC.

14. Ibid.

15. Clark, letter to Brown, April 18, 1943, SAB.

16. An FBI report on Clark includes the address 111 West 88th Street, while Preece's file reports that he and his wife Celia Kraft moved to this address in September 1942 and received mail there as late as January 1944 ("Clinton Clark," New Orleans, July 13, 1943, FBI-CC; Edwin O. Raudsep, "Richard Harold Preece," New York, March 27, 1944, p. 4, FBI-RHP). Even though Preece's name has been deleted from the released copy of Clark's FBI file, the remaining description of Clark's New York contact lines up with details in Preece's file: "It is noted that reference report reflects subject's New York address as of April 22, 1943 to be in the care of —— 111 West 88th Street, New York City. A check of the indices of the New Orleans Field Division reflects one —— in the report of Special Agent —— dated October 8, 1940 at Cincinnati Ohio entitled "Communist Party, Ohio," as at the time of the report Chicago correspondent for the Daily Worker, and an admitted Communist Party member. The file of the New Orleans Field Division further reflected one —— . . . as a writer and a former Communist Party organizer who took applications for enrollment at the 44th Annual Session of the Writer's Work Shop held July 12 to 26, 1942 at Monteagle, Tennessee" ("Clinton Clark," New Orleans, September 13, 1943, p. 2, FBI-CC).

17. "Question of the Week," *People's Voice,* June 3, 1944, cited in E. E. Conroy, letter to Director, FBI, June 26, 1944, p. 2, FBI-RHP.

18. Greenberg, *"Or Does It Explode?"* 199, 218 (the last chapter discusses Harlem during World War II); Baldwin, "Notes," in *Notes of a Native Son,* 84.

19. Monthly rolls of union workers at the Hotel George Washington submitted to the Hotel Trades Council show that Clark was added as a member of Local 144 in July 1943, paying $2.00 in monthly dues and a $1.75 initiation fee (folder 2, box 25, NYHTC). Also, union mailing lists with 1943 materials show his name ("Additions to New York City Mailing List," p. 2 of 9, undated but with 1943 materials, box 36, WSU). For a fascinating list of hotel jobs and wages, see "New York's First Union Hotel Contract," box 43, WSU. Laundry alone had sixteen different positions and wages, including guest bundle washers, wringer men, pullers, shakers, and tumblers.

20. Josephson, 279–83. The campaign and council were led by the Hotel Restaurant Employees Union, Local 6, which gave a small corner of its weekly newsletter to the Hotel Front Service Employees Union. By 1941 there were union shop agreements with 90 large New York hotels (Josephson, *Union House, Union Bar,* 286).

21. "Negro Council of Local 144 Is Launched," *Hotel and Club Voice,* June 5, 1943, 3, box 35, WSU. This group may have later changed its name to the Anti-Discrimination Committee. Negro members of the Hotel and Club Employees Union Local 6 had begun a Hotel Negro Council a year earlier. See "Hotel Negro Council Lesson in Solidarity," *Daily Worker,* May 25, 1943, 5. The next February the Anti-Discrimination Committee of Local 144 and the Negro Council of Hotel and Club Employees, Local 6, cosponsored a Negro Exhibition in celebration of Negro History Week. The opening of the exhibit was marked with a mass meeting, featuring speeches by A. Clayton Powell; Benjamin Davis; Michael Obermeier, the president of Local 6; and Louise McDonald, of both the Teachers' Union and the National Council of Negro Women. "The mass meeting and the exhibition have been planned as an educational feature to help bring about close relations between our Negro and white members in both locals. We feel it would be fitting on our behalf to send a message of greeting to the mass meeting. Under your leadership, the Building Service International has been in the forefront of the fight against discrimination," Local 144 secretary-treasurer John Goodman wrote to BSEIU president William McFetridge (February 7, 1944, box 43, WSU).

22. Ferdinand Smith, "Excerpts of Address by Ferdinand Smith at Rally," *Daily Worker,* June 10, 1943, 4.

23. John Meldon, "The Great Negro Offensive Opens to 'Let My People Go,'" *Daily Worker,* June 9, 1943, 3.

24. Robert Minor, "The Negro Freedom Meeting: A Discovery of Strength," ibid.

25. Baldwin, "Notes," 92.

26. This observation comes from Robert A. Hill, who notes in his introduction to *The FBI's RACON* (69, n. 185) the riot's impact on James Baldwin's "Notes of a Native Son," *The Autobiography of Malcolm X,* and Ralph Ellison's work. For more on the Harlem riots, see Sundquist, *Cultural Contexts.*

27. "Meeting of the Culinary Industry Workers, Local 6, August 6, 1943," enclosed with letter from Michael Obermeier to Negro Labor Victory Committee, August 10, 1943, reel 9:0934, part 4, NNC.

28. "Union Boosters Help Build Welfare Fund," 3d anniv. ed., Local 144, January 1944, p. 5, box 43, WSU; "$120 Back Pay to Doorman: He Says 'Thanks,'" *Hotel and Club Voice,* June 2, 1945, box 51, WSU.

29. "Clinton Clark," New York, June 13, 1944, p. 2, FBI-CC. Although he probably attended the New York Workers' School, there was also a Harlem Workers' School operating at the time. On the New York Workers' School, see "Party Education," *Daily Worker,* May 29, 1943.

30. Clark, letter to Sterling Brown, September 17, 1944, SAB.

31. Clark, letter to Sterling Brown, September 21, 1944, SAB.

32. Name deleted, "Clinton Clark," New York, June 13, 1944, pp. 1, 3, FBI-CC.

33. Some of his relatives remember a picture of him in a police uniform from these years, but his nephew Rodney Clark has made the observation that it may have been a hotel uniform.

34. There are some records of Local 144, including issues of the *Hotel and Club Voice,* the newsletter it shared with the H.E.R.E. Local 6, in the SEIU collections in the Archives of Labor and Urban Affairs at Wayne State University; some materials about Local 144 are also located in the papers of H.E.R.E Local 6 and the Hotel Trades Council in the Tamiment Library/Robert F. Wagner Labor Archives at New York University.

35. Clark, letter to Brown, November 5, 1945, box 10, SAB.

36. Ibid., November 27, 1947, box 112, SAB. The letter is numbered 56 in the upper lefthand corner.

37. Ibid., November 27, 1947, box 112, SAB. This letter is numbered 77 in upper lefthand corner.

38. Ibid., December 1, 1947, box 112, SAB. This letter is numbered 120.

39. Ibid., December 2, 1947, box 112, SAB. This letter is numbered 128.

40. Ibid., December 3, 1947, box 112, SAB. This letter is numbered 141.

41. His medical record indicates that "from 1943 to 1947 he worked as a porter in the George Washington Hotel, 23rd Street and Lexington Avenue, New York City" (John Travis, letter to James A. Brussel, May 10 1955, MHS). Preece told a doctor that Clark had lost his job in 1947 after not returning on time from vacation (Dr. Richman, December 28, 1949, MHS). Doctors' notes in Clark's medical file are cited by doctor's name and date, when available.

42. "Local 144 Officers Tell of Union Gains," *Hotel and Club Voice,* March 23, 1946, 4, box 58, WSU.

43. Halois Moorhead, "Looking Forward," *Hotel and Club Voice,* March 2, 1946, 4, box 58, WSU.

44. His executive order came with a list of seventy-eight subversive organizations; Executive Order 9835, March 27, 1947.

45. Biondi, *To Stand and Fight,* 137; see 147–53 for her account of this period.

46. Hughes, "We Demand Our Rights," 48–49.

47. Fairclough, *Race and Democracy,* 142; Freeman, *In Transit,* 321.

48. Kelley, "A Lifelong Radical," 257.

49. "Peg's Family's Reflections"; Peg McIntire, interview.

50. SAC-New York, letter to director, FBI, March 8, 1951, FBI-RHP; J. Robinson Field, "Richard Harold Preece," New York, March 8, 1951, FBI-RHP; SAC-New York, letter to director, FBI, July 29, 1955, FBI-RHP.

51. Dr. Richman, December 28, 1949, MHS.

52. State of New York, Department of Mental Hygiene, "Service of Notice upon the Alleged Mentally Ill Person and/or Others," November 10, 1949, MHS.

53. State of New York, Department of Mental Hygiene, "Form for the Court Certification of the Mentally Ill," November 10, 1949, MHS.

54. Dr. Richman, "Auto Anamnesis," December 6, 1949, p. 2, MHS.

55. Ibid.

Afterword | 155

56. Ibid., p. 3, MHS.

57. Dr. Richman, "Summary Note," December 7, 1949, MHS.

58. "Staff Conference Notes," December 12, 1949, MHS.

59. Dr. Stamm, January 30, 1950, MHS.

60. "Staff Conference Notes," February 6, 1950, MHS. This statement is reconstructed from several copies of the same page from which different statements were blackened out.

61. Director, Manhattan State Hospital, report to Department of Mental Hygiene, October 4, 1955, MHS.

62. The infamous Tuskegee Syphilis Study, which withheld treatment from African American men in Tuskegee, Alabama, was begun during the same years that Clark was first treated.

63. "Clinton Clark," November 5, 1943, New York City, p. 1, FBI-CC. Clark's Wasserman test was a 2 plus positive reaction.

64. Dr. Alan Ramsey, personal communication, June 11, 2003.

65. Dr. Hurewitz, January 6, 1951, MHS.

66. Dr. Richman, January 7, 1949, MHS.

67. Dr. Stamm, January 30, 1950, MHS. The initial doctors' reports in Clark's file are written in a format that resembles an FBI report. They begin by summarizing information from the previous report, then add the new finding. With this format, subsequent writers pick up the language, as well as the suspicions, of writers of the earlier reports.

68. Mollica, Blum, and Redlich, "Equity," 281.

69. Carkhuff and Pierce, "Differential Effects of Therapist Race and Social Class," 634.

70. Gross, Herbert, Knatterud, and Doner, "Effect of Sex and Race," 641–42.

71. Thomas and Sillen, *Racism and Psychiatry,* 63.

72. Mollica, Blum, and Redlich, "Equity," 283; Thomas and Sillen, *Racism and Psychiatry,* 136–37.

73. Chess, Clark, and Thomas, "The Importance of Cultural Evaluation," 108–9.

74. Ellison, "Harlem Is Nowhere," in *Shadow and Act,* 298. Ellison's dismissal of two northern institutions that do not make up for the lost support of southern communities may give some insight into Clark's situation; "the religious ones being inadequate," Ellison writes, "and those offered by political and labor leaders obviously incomplete and opportunistic" (300).

75. Ellison, "Harlem Is Nowhere," 295.

76. Dr. Richman, "Auto Anamnesis," December 6, 1949, p. 4, MHS. For a fictional parallel, see Shelly Eversley's reading of Ralph Ellison's story "The King of Bingo": "Well, I ain't crazy, I'm just broke" ("The Lunatic's Fancy," 453–54).

77. Travis, letter to Caroline Clark, April 26, 1950, MHS.

78. Dr. Kesselbrenner, May 8, 1952, MHS.

79. Doctor's notes from June 22, 1944, and April 19, 1955, MHS.

80. Caroline C. Cook, letter to John Travis, April 26, 1955, MHS.

81. Veronica Carey, interview.

82. Dr. Davidson, "Discharge Note," May 3, 1955, MHS.

83. Travis, letter to James A. Brussel, May 10, 1955, MHS.

84. Dr. Davidson, June 9, 1955, MHS.

85. Caroline Cook, letter to John Travis, June 12, 1955, MHS.

86. Clark, letter to John Travis, December 10, 1956, MHS.

87. J. Walter Yeagley, memo to director, FBI, July 18, 1962, FBI-CC.

88. Clark to J. Edgar Hoover, October 19, 1965, p. 2; October 30, 1965, FBI-CC.

89. Korstad and Lichtenstein, "Opportunities Found and Lost," 787, put the number of black members of the CIO in the 1940s at half a million.

90. In several instances memberships were substantially nonwhite. The ILWU and the National Union of Marine Cooks and Stewards, both kicked out of the CIO in 1950, were around 50 percent nonwhite (Rosswurm, *The CIO's Left-led Unions*, 3–4).

91. See Rosswurm, *The CIO's Left-led Unions*, 13, and Korstad and Lichtenstein, "Opportunities Found and Lost," 811.

92. Kirby, "Transformations of Southern Plantations," 271. Rural Louisianans would labor in the cotton fields well into the 1950s. Clark describes picking 2,500 pounds of cotton at a rate of $2 to $3 per hundred pounds in a December 10, 1956, letter to the Manhattan State Hospital director, John Travis; his nephew Rodney remembers picking cotton in the 1950s near Melville.

93. De Jong has some remarkable estimates and specific figures for the outmigration from rural areas in the 1940s. She writes that "approximately 60,000 rural people, representing more than one-quarter of Louisiana's farm population, left the land between 1940 and 1945" (*A Different Day*, 250, n. 92). See also her parish-by-parish table of black migration in the 1940s, pp. 120–21.

94. Many years earlier H. L. Mitchell had worked with LFU organizers Clyde Johnson, Gordon McIntire, and Peggy Dallet but had balked at merging his Southern Tenant Farmers' Union with their organization. Mitchell came to Louisiana to organize small farmers and agricultural workers in Louisiana in the early 1950s. The STFU had just affiliated with the AFL and changed its name to the National Farm Labor Union; it became the National Agricultural Workers' Union in 1951. They organized their first sugarcane workers in Reserve, Louisiana, early in 1952, and by harvest time in the fall of 1953 had 2,000 members. They launched a strike when the planters refused to bargain with the union. This strike had long-term repercussions for labor organizing and agricultural workers in Louisiana. Nine days into the strike, a local judge banned any strike organizing, arguing that the harvest-time strike had created an emergency for the sugar industry. The following year the Louisiana legislature passed a "right-to-work" law. When the law was repealed the next year, it was left standing for agricultural workers, delivering a second blow to organizing sugarcane workers. In the late 1960s, Mitchell launched several initiatives to help tractor drivers on sugarcane plantations. (Like cotton production, the sugar industry had become increasingly mechanized.) Centered in Edgard and Reserve, Louisiana, some of these programs resembled the LFU's 1930s work. The union secured federal funds for adult education programs, built better housing for workers who were still living in old slave quarters, and testified annually at the National Sugar Act hearings, which set minimum wages. A nonprofit organization, the Southern Mutual Help Association, was set up around 1970 to continue this work. See Mitchell, *Mean Things*, 314–24; Cook and Watson, *Louisiana Labor*, 267–84.

95. See Scott, *Witness to the Truth*, for an account of one community's long struggle for the right to vote. Both de Jong, *A Different Day*, and Fairclough, *Race and Democracy*, follow civil rights organizing in Louisiana from the beginning of the twentieth century through the 1970s.

96. De Jong, *A Different Day*, 258, n. 28.

Selected Bibliography

Andrews, William L. *To Tell a Free Story: The First Century of Afro-American Autobiography, 1760–1865.* Urbana: University of Illinois Press, 1986.

Baldwin, James. *Notes of a Native Son.* 1955. Reprint, New York: Bantam, 1964.

Barry, John M. *Rising Tide: The Great Mississippi Flood of 1927 and How It Changed America.* New York: Simon and Schuster, 1997. (Touchstone 1998 paperback ed.)

Beadling, Tom, Pat Cooper, Grace Palladino, and Peter Pieragostini. *A Need for Valor: The Roots of the Service Employees International Union, 1902–1992.* Washington, DC: Service Employees International Union, 1992.

Biles, Roger. *The South and the New Deal.* Lexington: University Press of Kentucky, 1994.

Biondi, Martha. *To Stand and Fight: The Struggle for Civil Rights in Postwar New York City.* Cambridge, Mass.: Harvard University Press, 2003.

Brown, Robert. "The Mississippi River Flood of 1912." *Bulletin of the American Geographical Society* 44, no. 9 (1912): 645–57.

Brown, Sterling A. "Count Us In." In *What the Negro Wants,* edited by Rayford Logan. Chapel Hill: University of North Carolina Press, 1944.

———. "The Muted South." *Phylon* 6 (Winter 1945): 22–34.

Carey, Veronica. Interview by Elizabeth Davey and Rodney Clark. New Orleans, Louisiana. May 1, 2002.

Carkhuff, Robert R., and Richard Pierce. "Differential Effects of Therapist Race and Social Class upon Patient Depth of Self-Exploration in the Initial Clinical Interview." *Journal of Consulting Psychology* 31, no. 6 (1967): 632–34.

Chess, Stella, Kenneth B. Clark, and Alexander Thomas. "The Importance of Cultural Evaluation in Psychiatric Diagnosis and Treatment." *Psychiatric Quarterly: Official Scientific Organ of the New York State Department of Mental Hygiene* 27, no. 1 (1953): 102–14.

Clark, Clinton. "Louisiana Rural Youth." *Cavalcade* 1, no. 1 (April 1941).

Clark, Clinton, and Kenneth Adams. Affidavit. April 18, 1942. Box 112, SAB.

Cohen, Robert. "Student Movements, 1930s." In *Encyclopedia of the American Left,* edited by Mari Jo Buhle, Paul Buhle, and Dan Georgakas. 2nd ed. New York: Oxford University Press, 1998.

Cook, Bernard A., and James R. Watson. *Louisiana Labor: From Slavery to "Right-to-Work."* Lanham, MD: University Press of America, 1985.

Costello, Brian. *A History of Pointe Coupee Parish*. New Roads, LA: B. J. Costello, 1999.

Dallet, Margery. "Eviction of 100 Families Is Prevented by Action of Farm Union in Louisiana." Attributed to *Southern News Almanac*, January 25, 1940. CJP.

Davey, Elizabeth. "The Souths of Sterling A. Brown." *Southern Cultures* 5 (Summer 1999): 20–45.

Davis, Benjamin J. *Communist Councilman from Harlem: Autobiographical Notes Written in a Federal Penitentiary*. New York: International Publishers, 1969.

De Jong, Greta. *A Different Day: African American Struggles for Justice in Rural Louisiana, 1900–1970*. Chapel Hill: University of North Carolina Press, 2002.

———. "'With the Aid of God and the F.S.A.': The Louisiana Farmers' Union and the African American Freedom Struggle in the New Deal Era." *Journal of Social History* 34, no. 1 (2000): 105–39.

Egerton, John. *Speak Now Against the Day: The Generation Before the Civil Rights Movement in the South*. 1994. Reprint, Chapel Hill: University of North Carolina Press, 1995.

Ellison, Ralph. *Invisible Man*. 1952. Reprint, New York: Vintage, 1995.

———. *Shadow and Act*. 1964. Reprint, New York: Vintage, 1995.

Eversley, Shelly. "The Lunatic's Fancy and the Work of Art." *American Literary History* 13, no. 3 (2001): 445–68.

Fairclough, Adam. *Race and Democracy: The Civil Rights Struggle in Louisiana, 1915–1972*. Athens: University of Georgia Press, 1995.

Fariello, Griffin. *Red Scare: Memories of the American Inquisition, An Oral History*. New York: W. W. Norton, 1995.

Fisher, Robert. *Let the People Decide: Neighborhood Organizing in America*. Boston: G. K. Hall, 1984.

Flamm, Michael W. "The National Farmers Union and the Evolution of Agrarian Liberalism, 1937–1946." *Agricultural History* 68, no. 3 (Summer 1994): 54–80.

Freeman, Joshua. *In Transit: The Transport Workers Union in New York City, 1933–1966*. New York: Oxford University Press, 1989.

Georgakas, Dan. "Mooney-Billings Case." *Encyclopedia of the American Left*. Edited by Mari Jo Buhle, Paul Buhle, and Dan Georgakas. New York: Oxford University Press, 1998.

Goodman, Ethel Lee. "Rural S.N.Y.C. Councils." *Cavalcade* 1, no. 1 (April 1941).

Goodman, James. *Stories of Scottsboro*. New York: Pantheon, 1994.

Greenberg, Cheryl Lynn. *"Or Does It Explode?" Black Harlem in the Great Depression*. New York: Oxford University Press, 1991.

Griffiths, Frederick T. "Ralph Ellison, Richard Wright and the Case of Angelo Herndon." *African American Review* 35, no. 4 (Winter 2001): 615–36.

Gross, Herbert S., Myra Herbert, Genell L. Knatterud, and Lawrence Donner. "The Effect of

Race and Sex on the Variation of Diagnosis and Disposition in a Psychiatric Emergency Room." *Journal of Nervous and Mental Disease* 148, no. 6 (1969): 638–39.

Halpern, Rick. "The CIO and the Limits of Labor-based Civil Rights Activism: The Case of Louisiana's Sugar Workers, 1947–1966." In *Southern Labor in Transition, 1940–1995*, edited by Robert H. Zieger. Knoxville: University of Tennessee Press, 1997.

Haywood, Harry. *Black Bolshevik: Autobiography of an Afro-American Communist.* Chicago: Liberator Press, 1978.

Herndon, Angelo. *Let Me Live.* New York: Random House, 1937.

———. "Negroes Here Oppose Conscription Bill as Threat to Entire Race; They Remember the 1918 Jim Crow." *Daily Worker*, August 5, 1940.

Hill, Robert A. Introduction to *The FBI's RACON: Racial Conditions in the United States During World War II.* Compiled and edited by Robert A. Hill. Boston: Northeastern University Press, 1995.

Hoskins, Samuel. "Clinton Clark Free." *Louisiana Weekly,* August 24, 1940.

Hudson, Hosea. *Black Worker in the Deep South: A Personal Record.* New York: International Publishers, 1972.

Hughes, C. Alvin. "We Demand Our Rights: The Southern Negro Youth Congress, 1937–1949." *Phylon* 48, no.1 (1987): 38–50.

Johnson, C. L. "How to Organize." *Southern Farm Leader,* July 1936, 2. CJP.

Jones, James H. *Bad Blood: The Tuskegee Syphilis Experiment.* New York: Free Press, 1993.

Josephson, Matthew. *Union House, Union Bar: The History of the Hotel and Restaurant Employees and Bartenders International Union, AFL-CIO.* New York: Random House, 1956.

Kamanda-Kosseh, Helen C. Interview by Rodney Clark. Atlanta, Georgia. August 31, 2002.

Kelley, Robin D. G. *Hammer and Hoe: Alabama Communists During the Great Depression.* Chapel Hill: University of North Carolina Press, 1990.

———. "A Lifelong Radical: Clyde L. Johnson, 1908–1994." *Radical History Review* 62 (1995): 254–58.

———. "Southern Negro Youth Congress." In *Encyclopedia of the American Left,* edited by Mari Jo Buhle, Paul Buhle, and Dan Georgakas. New York: Oxford University Press, 1998.

Kemper, J. P. *Rebellious River.* 1949. Reprint, New York: Arno, 1972.

Kester, Howard. *Revolt Among the Sharecroppers.* 1936. Reprint, with an introduction by Alex Lichtenstein, Knoxville: University of Tennessee Press, 1997.

Kirby, Jack Temple. "The Transformation of Southern Plantations, ca.1920–1960." *Agricultural History* 57 (July 1983): 257–76.

Klingler, Thomas A. *If I Could Turn My Tongue Like That: The Creole Language of Pointe Coupee Parish, Louisiana.* Baton Rouge: Louisiana State University Press, 2003.

Korstad, Robert, and Nelson Lichtenstein. "Opportunities Found and Lost: Labor, Radicals, and the Early Civil Rights Movement." *Journal of American History* 75 (1988): 788–93, 801–6.

"Louisiana Farmers Hold Anniversary Meeting." *Cavalcade* 3, no. 1 (1941): n.p.

McIntire, Peg, with Jo McIntire. Interview by Elizabeth Davey. St. Augustine, Florida. June 8 and 9, 2002.

McManus, Robert Cruise. "Communist Beachhead in Agriculture." *Farm Journal* 68 (October 1944): 23, 84–85.

Medley, Keith Weldon. "Ernest Wright: 'People's Champion.'" *Southern Exposure,* May/June 1984, 52–55.

Meier, August, and Elliot Rudwick. "Communist Unions and the Black Community: The Case of the Transport Workers Union, 1934–1944." *Labor History* 23, no. 2 (1982): 165–97.

Mitchell, H. L. *Mean Things Happening in This Land: The Life and Times of H. L. Mitchell, Co-Founder of the Southern Tenant Farmers Union.* Montclair, NJ: Allanheld, Osmun, 1979.

Mollica, Richard F., Jeffrey D. Blum, and Fritz Redlich. "Equity and Psychiatric Care of the Black Patient, 1950 to 1975." *Journal of Nervous and Mental Disease* 168, no. 5 (1980): 279–86.

Mooney, Kevin. "Texas Centennial 1936: African American Texans and the Third National Folk Festival." *Journal of Texas Music History* 1, no. 1 (2001): 36–43.

Naison, Mark. "The Southern Tenants' Farmers' Union and the CIO." *Radical America* 2, no. 5 (1968): 36–56.

"Negro Council of Local 144 Is Launched." *Hotel and Club Voice,* June 5, 1943. WSU.

Nelson, Bruce. "Class and Race in the Crescent City: The ILWU, from San Francisco to New Orleans." In *The CIO's Left-led Unions,* edited by Steve Rosswurm.

"Officers SNYC for 42–43." *Cavalcade* 2, no. 1 (May 1942).

O'Reilly, Kenneth. *Hoover and the Un-Americans: The FBI, HUAC, and the Red Menace.* Philadelphia: Temple University Press, 1983.

Painter, Nell Irvin. *The Narrative of Hosea Hudson: His Life as a Negro Communist in the South.* Cambridge: Harvard University Press, 1979.

"Peg's Family's Reflections." *Florida Coalition for Peace & Justice Honors Peg McIntire.* 2000.

Perkins, Margo V. *Autobiography as Activism: Three Black Women of the Sixties.* Jackson: University Press of Mississippi, 2000.

Preece, Harold. "Epic of the Black Belt." *Crisis* 43, no. 3 (March 1936): 75, 92.

———. *Peonage: 1940s Style Slavery.* Chicago: Abolish Peonage Committee and International Labor Defense, [1940].

———. "The South Stirs." *Crisis* 48 (October 1941): 317–18, 322.

Richards, Johnetta Gladys. "The Southern Negro Youth Congress: A History." PhD diss., University of Cincinnati, 1987.

Rosengarten, Theodore. *All God's Dangers: The Life of Nate Shaw.* New York: Alfred A. Knopf, 1974.

Rosenzweig, Roy. "Organizing the Unemployed: The Early Years of the Great Depression, 1929–1933." *Radical America* 10 (July–August 1976): 37–60.

Rosswurm, Steve, ed. *The CIO's Left-led Unions.* New Brunswick, NJ: Rutgers University Press, 1992.

Scott, John Henry, with Cleo Scott Brown. *Witness to the Truth: My Struggle for Human Rights in Louisiana.* Columbia: University of South Carolina Press, 2003.

Smith, Florence J. Interview by Rodney Clark. Atlanta, Georgia. August 31, 2002.

Solomon, Mark. *The Cry Was Unity: Communists and African Americans, 1917–36.* Jackson: University Press of Mississippi, 1998.

Sterling, Ben Charles, Jr., and Richard Sterling. Interview by Rodney Clark. Melville, Louisiana. Spring 2002.

Stimpson, Eddie, Jr. *My Remembers: A Black Sharecropper's Recollection of the Depression.* Denton: University of North Texas Press, 1996.

Strong, Augusta. "Southern Youth's Proud Heritage." *Freedomways* 4, no. 1 (1964): 35–50.

Sundquist, Eric J., ed. *Cultural Contexts for Ralph Ellison's "Invisible Man."* Boston: Bedford/St. Martin's, 1995.

Theoharis, Athan. "A Brief History of the FBI's Role and Powers." In *The FBI: A Comprehensive Reference Guide,* edited by Athan G. Theoharis with Tony G. Poveda, Susan Rosenfeld, and Richard Gid Powers. Phoenix, AZ: Oryx Press, 1999.

———. *Spying on Americans: Political Surveillance from Hoover to the Huston Plan.* Philadelphia: Temple University Press, 1978.

———. ed. *Beyond the Hiss Case: The FBI, Congress, and the Cold War.* Philadelphia: Temple University Press, 1982.

Thomas, Alexander, and Samuel Sillen. *Racism and Psychiatry.* New York: Brunner/Mazel, 1972.

Thomas, Richard H. "Persecuted La. Farmers' Organizer Freed." *Chicago Defender,* August 31, 1940.

Walker, Samuel. "Communists and Isolationism: The American Peace Mobilization." *Maryland Historian* 4, no. 1 (1973): 1–12.

Ward, Tom. "Class Conflict in Black New Orleans: Dr. Rivers Frederick, Ernest Wright and the Insurance Strike of 1940." *Gulf South Historical Review* 15, no. 1 (1999): 35–48.

Wells, David Lee. "The ILWU in New Orleans: CIO Radicalism in the Crescent City, 1937–1957." Master's thesis, University of New Orleans, 1979.

Index